THE REBIRTH OF THE MORAL SELF

The Rebirth of the Moral Self

The Second Generation of Modern Confucians
and their Modernization Discourses

Jana S. Rošker

The Chinese University Press

University of Hawai'i Press

The Rebirth of the Moral Self: The Second Generation of Modern Confucians and their Modernization Discourses
By Jana S. Rošker

© The Chinese University of Hong Kong 2016

All rights reserved. No part of this book may be used or reproduced in any manner whatsoever without written permission. No part of this book may be stored in a retrieval system or transmitted in any form or by any means including electronic, electrostatic, magnetic tape, mechanical, photocopying, recording, or otherwise without the prior permission in writing of the publisher.

ISBN: University of Hawai'i Press 978-0-8248-5982-4
ISBN: The Chinese University Press 978-962-996-688-1

Published for North America by:
  University of Hawai'i Press
  2840 Kolowalu Street
  Honolulu, HI 96822 USA
  www.uhpress.hawaii.edu

Published for the rest of the world by:
  The Chinese University Press
  The Chinese University of Hong Kong
  Sha Tin, N.T. Hong Kong
  Fax: +852 2603 7355
  E-mail: cup@cuhk.edu.hk
  Website: www.chineseupress.com

Library of Congress Cataloging-in-Publication Data
Names: Rošker, Jana, author.
Title: The rebirth of the moral self : the second generation of modern
  Confucians and their modernization discourses / Jana S. Rošker.
Description: Honolulu, Hawai'i : Published in North America by University of
  Hawai'i Press, [2016] | ©2016 | "First published by The Chinese University
  Press, The Chinese University of Hong Kong"—Title page verso. | Includes
  bibliographical references and index.
Identifiers: LCCN 2015038916 | ISBN 9780824859824 hardcover : alk. paper
Subjects: LCSH: Philosophy, Confucian. | Philosophy, Chinese—20th century. |
  Philosophy, Modern—20th century. | Confucianism—China—History—20th
  century.
Classification: LCC B5233.C6 R67 2016 | DDC 181/.112–dc23 LC record
available at http://lccn.loc.gov/2015038916

10 9 8 7 6 5 4 3 2 1

Printed in Hong Kong

Dedicated to my parents

Contents

Acknowledgments   xi

1. Introduction   1

2. China's Confrontation with the West and Processes of Modernization: From the Liberalization of the Subject to a Free Market

2.1 The Confucian Revival and the Multiple Images of Modernity   9

2.2 Modernity with Chinese Characteristics   14

2.3 Daring Reforms, Ambitious Innovations and Passionately Naïve Movements   18

2.4 Gradual Westernization: The Case of Taiwan   24

3. Modern Confucianism

3.1 The "Three Generations"   29

3.2 The Rehabilitation of Tradition and the Challenges of Modernization   32

3.3 Theoretical and Conceptual Platforms   39

3.4	Critique	44
3.5	The Problem of "Asian Values"	49

4. The "Second Generation"

4.1	The Teachers: A Short Introduction of the First Generation	59
4.2	The New Moral Metaphysics: Mou Zongsan	65
4.3	Fang Dongmei and the Philosophy of Creative Creativity	74
4.4	Xu Fuguan: A Philosopher of Culture, Philology and Politics	82
4.5	The Voice from Hong Kong: Tang Junyi	92

5. Science and Democracy

5.1	The Old Holism in a New Disguise	101
5.2	People as the Foundation of the State and Man as a Basis of Science	103
5.3	The Heavenly Mandate and the Analysis of the Basis of Integration	110
5.4	Two Truths, Two Subjects	116

6. The Midwives of Modern Cultures: Reason, Subjectivity and their Philosophical Connotations

6.1	Some Fundamental Distinctions: The Problem of Immanent Transcendence	131
6.2	Transcendental Subject and Empirical Self: The Problem of the Individual and their Subjectivity	137
6.3	From the Self-Negation of the Subject to the Modern Form of the Confucian Moral Self	150
6.4	Reason and Intuition	162
6.5	The Unemployed God	178

7.	**The Modern Confucian Legacy and the New Confucian Ideologies in the People's Republic of China: The Case of Harmony**	
7.1	Confucianism in the People's Republic of China—A Brief Historical Overview	194
7.2	A Harmony of Peace and Order	196
7.3	Classical Harmony	198
7.4	Modern Confucian Harmony as Balance and Equilibrium	202

8.	**Conclusion—Modern Confucianism Between Past and Future**	211

Appendix 1: A Chronology of China's History of Dynasties and Republics	219
Appendix 2: A Chronology of the Developmental Phases of Confucianism	223
Notes	225
Bibliography	259
Index	287

Acknowledgments

I would like to express my sincere gratitude to the Taiwanese Chiang Ching-Kuo Foundation for International Scholarly Exchange, the National Slovene Research Agency (ARRS) and Chun-chieh Huang, Chair Professor and Dean of the Institute for Advanced Studies in Humanities and Social Sciences at the National Taiwan University, for their generous support during the research on this book.

I owe a profound debt of gratitude to Prof. Lee Ming-huei for his many valuable suggestions and advice on the manuscript. I am likewise very grateful to the many specialists, colleagues and friends whose contributions were essential to the completion of this study, including Roger T. Ames, Karyn Lai, Bart Dessein, Geir Sigurðsson, Raoul David Findeisen, Nataša Vampelj Suhadolnik, Kwon Jong Yoo, Paul D'Ambrosio and John H. Berthrong.

The present volume also owes much to Erik Holmes Schneider, who took the time to proofread it and who helped me to iron out many errors, both technical and grammatical. He also provided very helpful feedback on the contents of the manuscript.

A special thanks also goes to my colleagues and friends in the Department of Asian Studies, Faculty of Art, at the University of Ljubljana, whose insights, expertise and understanding proved to be of great assistance in my work.

And last but not least, I would like to thank my family, Téa, Janko and Nils for their love and patience.

Jana S. Rošker

1. Introduction

The present study provides a systematic and coherent examination of the contents, axiological innovations and social significance of Modern Confucianism introducing to a wider academic audience in the West its most important contributions to contemporary global theory.

In international sinology, this line of thought is translated with various names, ranging from *Neo-Confucianism* or *Contemporary* or *Modern Neo-Confucianism*, to *New Confucianism* and *Modern* or *Contemporary Confucianism*. The first series, which includes the term Neo-Confucianism, is impractical because it is often confused with Neo-Confucianism, a term which in Western sinology denotes the reformed Confucian philosophies of the Song and Ming periods (*li xue* or *xingli xue*). I therefore generally prefer the term *Modern Confucianism*, given that we are dealing with philosophical discourses that belong to Chinese modernity. A similar confusion can be found in Chinese discourses, which generally denote this line of thought with one of the following expressions: *Xin ruxue, Xiandai xin ruxue, Xiandai ruxue, Dangdai xin ruxue* etc.[1] In the case of Chinese, I find the expression *Xiandai xin ruxue* to be the most appropriate, the reason being that in China, as opposed to European sinological discourses, the Neo-Confucianism of the Song and Ming dynasties has never been associated with the concept of new Confucianism (*Xin ruxue*) and therefore the character which denotes "new" in this phrase is not problematic.

The current is defined as the search for a synthesis between Western and traditional East Asian thought, in order to elaborate a system of ideas and values capable of resolving the social and political problems of the modern, globalized world. The philosophers belonging to this stream of thought, have namely attempted to reconcile "Western" and "traditional Chinese" values, in order to create a theoretical model of modernization that would not be confused or equated with "Westernization". In this study, I mainly analyze the most important works written by the leading theoreticians of the so-called second generation of new Modern Confucians, who were most active in the second half of the twentieth century. The most influential philosophers belonging to this generation were Mou Zongsan, Xu Fuguan, Tang Junyi and Fang Dongmei. The present study focuses on the interpolation of their thought into the methodological and theoretical framework of contemporary theories of modernization.

While most of the philosophers of the second generation of Modern Confucianism were active in the first two thirds of the twentieth century and primarily lived in Taiwan and Hong Kong, this current also began to emerge in the P. R. China (People's Republic of China) during the last two decades of the century. It is generally agreed that Modern Confucianism offered theoreticians in mainland China certain basic elements for the formulation of new ideologies, which combine neo-liberal elements in the economic sphere with authoritarian elements in the political one. As the present study clearly shows, the Modern Confucians generally followed the more egalitarian and democratic Mencian current of Confucian thought, while in their efforts to construct a "harmonic society", the ideologists of the P. R. China mostly rely on the more autocratic and legalistic interpretations of the original Confucian teachings, first formulated by Xunzi. The same holds true for the leading contemporary populist Confucian scholars, as for instance, for Jiang Qing (2003) who developed the well-known political theory which is based upon the notion of Constitutional or Political Confucianism (*zhengzhi ruxue*).

This distinction is of the utmost importance, and indicates the sort of differentiations that must be made in order acquire a proper understanding of Modern Confucianism and its theories, while refuting the idea that it represents some monolithic theoretical formation. On the contrary, it includes a wide range of theoretical discourses based on a tradition that is already very complex and heterogeneous.

In order to provide a broader picture of the current, the present study not only examines the main Modern Confucian philosophical approaches, ideas and methods, but also explores the political, social and ideological backgrounds of the so-called Confucian revival and its connections with the ideological foundations of East Asian modernity. Thus, after the introduction in which I tried to sketch the global significance and the intercultural framework of the subject matter, the book opens (Chapter 2) with the general characterization of modernity, revealing the historical and political conditions in which the Chinese modernization process was embedded. It proceeds with a general introduction of the Modern Confucian movement (Chapter 3), focusing on their central concerns and intellectual approaches and, at the same time, drawing attention to some problematic issues they might imply.

John Makeham (2003, 33) points out that while the works of the Modern Confucian theorists certainly have important implications in the area of cultural philosophy (*wenhua zhexue*), it is quite evident that their primary focus is on a number of underlying metaphysical issues. Despite the ambivalence of some writers, most of the Modern Confucian scholarship during the 1990s focused on the identity of the movement as a philosophical school (Makeham 2003, 33).

Hence, after determining this sociological and cultural framework of Chinese modernization discourses in which the second generation of the Modern Confucian theoreticians, who represent the main subject matter of the present study, were living and working, the book focuses upon the introduction of the main philosophical contributions of this intellectual current. This part begins (Chapter 5) with a debate on their respective political philosophies and then (Chapter 6) proceeds to investigations in the deeper levels of their theories, introducing the main innovations in their ontological, metaphysical, and epistemological studies. In the conclusion, the book offers a short summary of the most important research results and delineates some possible future prospects of Modern Confucianism.

For European researchers, the effort to understand non-European cultures is inevitably linked to the issue of differences in language, tradition, history and socialization processes. A fundamental premise of the present study is that Western epistemology represents only one of many different models of human comprehension. The proposed research thus follows the main methodological principles of intercultural research, taking into account the incommensurability of diversely (culturally) conditioned paradigms, or theoretical frameworks deriving from diversely formed discourses of different cultural and linguistic environments. The methods applied seek to synthesize general perspectives, knowledge, skills, interconnections and epistemologies, in order to facilitate the study of a topic which, while intrinsically coherent, cannot be adequately understood from a single perspective. Within the broader scope of intercultural humanities, the book is thus structured in an interdisciplinary fashion, and comprises methods and forms of investigation pertaining to the following research areas:

- Socio-cultural perspective: different patterns of modernization;
- Epistemology: the cultural and linguistic conditionality of comprehension;
- Chinese intellectual history: the political and ideal background of Modern Confucianism;
- Comparative philosophy (the impact of German Idealism upon modern Confucian philosophers, their elaboration of traditional paradigms and the creation of syntheses between Chinese and Western philosophies);
- Conceptual analysis (the elaboration and cultural renewal of crucial modernization concepts—especially *subject* and *reason*—in Asian philosophies);
- Axiology: the creation of new "Asian Values" and the contribution of Modern Confucian ethics to the new values of the contemporary world;
- Ideology studies: the impact of Modern Confucianism on new theoretical streams in East Asia and the theoretical background of the new prevailing ideology in the P. R. China, which is based upon the concept of harmony.

Regarding the general methodological framework of the present book, it is important to bear in mind that the understanding of so-called "foreign cultures" is inextricably interwoven with the issue of the diversity of languages, traditions, histories and socialization processes. The interpretation of the various aspects and elements of "non-European" cultures are likewise influenced by the geographic, political and economic positions of both the interpreter and the element being interpreted. Intercultural research always includes translation issues, but this is clearly not limited to merely rendering one language into another, but also involves the "translation" or transposition of different discourses. This form of translation involves interpretations of individual textual and speech structures, categories, concepts and values that differ depending on their socio-cultural contexts. For this reason, we often encounter a discrepancy between the etymological and the functional understanding of a given expression. In some cases, the same expression may even be understood completely differently, depending on the general social context of the two different societies in which it appears.

The proper methodology for studying Chinese philosophy—which is still interpreted based primarily on premises deriving from the traditional Western social sciences and humanities—is found not only in the recognition of a "different theoretical model", but in the relativization of the values systems[2] and perception structures. In order for this relativization to take place, we need to gain insights into the conceptual structures and connections among the concrete historical, economic, political and cultural (philosophical) systems that underlie Chinese social reality. The awareness of these underlying fundamentals—which also inevitably influence the basic theoretical approaches, methods and conceptual framework—constitute a platform which permits an understanding of Chinese philosophy at its most profound levels.

Intercultural research in the field of Chinese philosophy should approach the Chinese cultural and linguistic area through its own language and texts. This approach is of key importance, for it is the only way (at least within the frame created by the very essence of Western methodologies) to overcome an absolute dichotomy between the active subject and passive object in cultural research. In the Chinese language, the use of primary sources provides insights into the structure of issues and interpretations that are characteristic of the socialization process, as well as the contents and methodological approaches that form the research subjects.

Another difficulty in researching classical philosophy is understanding and mediating traditional contents, both oral and textual, that are structured in accordance with different grammatical and semantic systems. The essential postulates of modern academic discourses (as well as the methodologies deriving from them) continue to be part of the "indisputable" discourses of the Western (especially European) tradition. Trying to squeeze different aspects of various "non-European" realities into such formal templates and procedures can lead the researcher to an interpretative dead end or, even worse, result in a total misconstruing of the subject matter. At the same time, if we wish to communicate the results of our researches in a way that can be understood by the general academic community, we must adhere to these procedures and templates.

With respect to Chinese proper names, I have applied the official *pinyin* transcription. In so doing, I have also followed the prevailing usage and placed Chinese family names before the given names. For those Chinese scholars (especially of the third generation of the Modern Confucian movement) who have published widely in English, I have kept their names in the form already familiar to Western readers.

Intercultural research necessarily involves translation, but this translation cannot be limited to a linguistic transfer, but must include the interpretation of specific textual/speech structures, categories, concepts and values existing in diverse socio-cultural contexts. In recent years, there has been a growing demand to revive the classic categories and concepts of traditional Chinese philosophy. This approach, however, requires the intercultural relativization of the contents based on methodologies that correspond to the specific requirements of research in the Chinese philosophical tradition, and comparative philosophy or cultural studies in general. The priority in this approach is preserving traditional Chinese philosophical characteristics and maintaining autochthonous and traditional methodological principles. However, this does not mean denying or excluding an intellectual confrontation with Western (and global) philosophical systems. Global (especially European and Indian) philosophy includes numerous elements that cannot be found in the Chinese tradition. The investigation and application of these elements is not only a valuable means for fertilizing new idea systems, but also offers an important comparative tool for better understanding one's own tradition. At the same time, as the modern Chinese theorist Zhang Dainian cautioned, we must avoid the use of incompatible or incommensurable methods that attempt to study Chinese history through the lens of Western concepts and categories:

> Different philosophical theories use different concepts and categories. Concepts and categories used in philosophical theories can differ greatly from one nation to another. (Zhang Dainian 2003, 118)

Chinese philosophy differs from European or Indian philosophy in many aspects. If we wish to establish a new Chinese philosophical tradition, we need to be familiar with its basic premises. If we attempt to systematize it through the use of European or Indian methodological approaches, its subtle essence will elude our understanding.

However, the methodological problems connected with understanding Chinese modernization, its ideologies and underlying ideas are not limited to philosophical and conceptual issues. The geopolitical aspect is equally important and when analyzing a socially relevant idea we must also take into account the economic and historical context within which it evolved. Modern Confucianism is no exception here, and in examining this philosophical current we must begin by recognizing the fact that the transnationalization of capital has also led to the universalization of capitalist production, which has thus become separated from its specifically European historical origins.

Given that Modern Confucians viewed modernization primarily as a rationalization of the world, they explored their own tradition for authentic concepts comparable to the two Western paradigms essential for modernization, i.e. the concepts of subjectivity, and of reason and rationality. Taking this as its point of departure, the book analyzes the central values of Confucianism, and interprets them in different Chinese and Taiwanese sociopolitical contexts in order to evaluate their impact upon prevailing contemporary ideologies. Among other issues, the book also examines the axiological differences within modern East Asian societies, and focuses on Modern Confucian treatments of epistemological and ethical concepts that can serve as a foundation for a "Chinese" modernization theory. Of particular importance in this regard are the notions of moral self (*daode benxin, daode ziwo*), unlimited heart-mind (*wuxiande zhixin*) and intellectual intuition (*zhide zhijue*).

The notion that a so-called "vacuum of values" is responsible for the alienation of modern post-capitalist societies in the global world raises the question of whether this East Asian model is really capable of generating a non-individualistic version of modernity. In verifying this hypothesis, I tried to show that the purported relation between modernity and individualism, which international modernization theories have always viewed as "inevitable" or "intrinsic" is little more than an outcome of Western historical paradigms.

Despite its importance, this stream of thought is still little known in wider academic circles. Although many books and articles on this topic are available in Chinese, academic studies in Western languages are namely still few and far between. Because Modern Confucian efforts to revitalize and reconstruct traditional Confucian thought can be seen as an attempt to counter the dominant ideological trends and preserve Chinese cultural identity, the present study will also hopefully contribute to the development of theoretical dialogues between "China" and "Europe".

I firmly believe that investigations in this stream of thought can tell us a great deal both about the times we live in and about the contemporary and future destiny of one of the most important philosophical legacies in the world. At the same time, I hope that the present book can also reveal the important role of the so-called "Non-Western" intellectual traditions in contemporary philosophical and cultural discourses.

2. China's Confrontation with the West and Processes of Modernization: From the Liberalization of the Subject to a Free Market

2.1 The Confucian Revival and the Multiple Images of Modernity

When evaluating the modern Confucian attempts of establishing a "typical Chinese" philosophical basis for modernization we need to evaluate them within the context of the questions linked to "invented traditions" (Hobsbawm and Ranger 1995). We need to consider to what extent are the "past" philosophical "traditions" based on historic assumptions, and to what extent are they merely a product of the (ideological and political) demands of the current period. The so-called Confucian revival that manifests itself in the philosophical stream of Modern Confucianism is one of the most significant elements within the new Asian ideologies of modernization. An important consequence of the current transnationalization of capital is that, perhaps for the first time in the modern history, the global mode of production appears as an authentically universal abstraction that is no longer limited to its specific historical origins in Europe. Hence, the narrative of modernization is no longer an exclusively European narrative, and for the first time non-European societies are also making their own claims on the history of modernization. Thus, we also need to examine the main elements that enable the amalgamation of traditional Chinese values into the framework of the dominant global ideologies and axiological contexts.

The new value systems developed by the Modern Confucian movement are designed to ensure economic efficiency while also preserving political stability. The social order was historically dominated by state doctrines which focused on hierarchical and formalistic social structures. The current demand for the coexistence of social stability (assumed to be possible only within a capitalist mode of production) with the "democratization" of society, is inherently paradoxical. In the present study, this ambivalence is contextualized within a set of issues related to the economic and cultural transition, which are determined by diverse social phenomena emerging from the (mostly artificially constructed) gap between "tradition" and "modernity".

While Maoist historiography relegated Confucianism to the past, most Western modernization theories also implied that Confucianism would have to be abandoned if Asia wanted to develop a dynamic modern society. Marx and other classical theorists of modernity assumed that traditional Chinese culture was impervious or even inimical to modernization. Max Weber's famous thesis that the Protestant ethic was an essential factor in the rise and spread of modernization contrasts with a notion that has gradually emerged in the last two decades in East Asia, which argues that societies based upon the Confucian ethic may, in many ways, be superior to the West in achieving industrialization, affluence and modernization. Weber also wrote extensively on Asia, especially China and India, concluding that Asian cultural and philosophical or religious traditions were ill-suited to modernization. In order to determine whether such a Eurocentric view of modernity is still valid, the author examines these competing theses and concludes that modernization represents a complex process of social transitions which includes both universal and culturally conditioned elements.

In the present era, cultural fragmentation, which is often disguised under the—much more "positive"—label of "multi-culturalism" might be seen as a consequence of the new global economic conditions. Numerous theoreticians are of the opinion that the domination of "multiculturalism" leads to the end of Eurocentrism. However, the term multi-culturalism is misleading, for it does not cover merely cultural fragmentation, but also undermines the traditional forms of production and social networks. Thus, some theoreticians warn that the end of Eurocentrism might be an illusion, for its internal structure remains a predominant part in the constellation of post-modern, global societies.[1] Arif Dirlik points out that in reality, we might even not be dealing with the fragmentation of cultures, but rather with the fragmentation of space. According to him, such fragmentation offers new possibilities for global capitalism to solve old problems linked to maximizing profits, controlling the market and freeing the production and marketing from the pressures of social interventions (e.g. integrative labour strikes) or political control (state measures). In this context, the Modern Confucian search for new awareness and new values could prove themselves to be of great importance. The awareness and the values they seek to consolidate are namely based upon traditional Chinese axiological presumptions, which manifest themselves in an inseparable unity of self and the others and, for instance, in the cultivation of inner self as opposed to the unlimited free will of the individual (that can be seen, for instance, in groundless unreflected desire to maximize the profit). These presumptions can also be seen in the traditional Chinese spirit of humanness (*ren*) which can, among others, serve as a normative, but context bounded and situational measure to counter the mechanistic laws of the free and otherwise ethically unbounded liberal market economy. In this context, it is also important to see that, in their political philosophy, the first and the second generation of Modern Confucians have always been following the Mencian interpretations, i.e. the more egalitarian and democratic stream of Confucian teachings. Concerning the contemporary streams of Confucian thought in mainland China, however, we cannot ignore ideas like Jiang Qing's Political Confucianism, which mainly follows Xunzi's interpretation, rooted in more rigid and disciplinary discourses.[2]

And this is not all: the fragmentation of space also implies the shattered social status of the individual, a reality which, as the modern Confucians have stressed, manifests itself in the alienation of the modern subject. The excessive focus on Eurocentrism, and its ideas and political connotations, may deflect our attention away from this fragmentation of the world in a different and significant way. The manifold, complex consequences of modernization are everywhere apparent, and the object of the present study has not been chosen at random. A one-dimensional criticism of Eurocentrism, and its version of history and world structure is no longer sufficient. In a wider sense, i.e. in terms of everyday life, Eurocentrism is no longer limited to

Europe, but represents a contemporary, global phenomenon. As a result, the challenges of Eurocentrism also concern and influence those non-European societies that, for many years now, have chosen modernization as their main goal. In this sense, the theories of the second generation of Modern Confucians are part of the "Chinese historical revival", which failed to affirm itself during the period of intensional, "enforced" modernization. All of which fits in nicely with the current "reincarnation" of modernity theories (Dirlik 1994, 20), that are looking for ways to integrate multicultural, alternative modernization models. This departure from a Eurocentrism which underpinned the classic modernization theories that appeared during (and before) colonialism, is only a virtual one, for it is being enacted on the common basis of global economic and political structures.

According to Dirlik it is self-evident and even necessary in this phase of global development for these modernization discourses to absorb and integrate in themselves all of the previously belittled "cultural versions" of modernization, which were previously seen as their "obstacles". The incorporation and internalization of the various "modernization repertoires" (including their specific values and mechanisms of production and consumption) into the economic practices of the contemporary global system thus serves as a driving force for the universalization of institutionalized structures that are necessary for its functioning. All of this coincides with the new postmodern concepts, which include the concept of "multiple modernities" as described by Shmuel Noah Eistenstadt. Even though the establishment of this concept is based on the thesis, according to which modernization of non-European societies is not to be equated with their Westernization (Eistenstadt 2000, 2–3), his theory is in essence conservative, for it places the interpretations of various forms of modernization and modernity into the context of affirming existing global power relations, at which it positions various models within the frames of various states, nations and "cultures" that are seen as their distinguishing characteristics:

> What an idea of multiple modernities ignores is that the resurgence of history is internal to nations and civilizations as well. The question of modernity is subject to debate within the cultural, civilizational, national or ethnic spaces it takes as its

units of analysis; this may be justifiable when viewed from a global perspective, but appears quite differently when viewed from the inside. The problems of Eurocentrism, its foundation in capitalism as a dynamic force and attendant problems of modernity are not simply problems between nations and civilizations, but problems that are internal to their constitution. (Dirlik 2001, 26)

Dirlik's suppositions are obviously grounded in the belief that these universally prevailing economic structures then shape the array of institutions—political, social, etc.—that dominate the individual societies in each category. In contrast to this purely materialist supposition, Modern Confucian theories are not exclusively based upon idealistic positions that preclude taking into account the impact of material forces on human societies. While some of the representatives of the second generation[3] do tend to overlook (or simply ignore) this aspect of social reality, for the most part they remain coherent with traditional Confucian thought, and thus adhere to the holistic worldview of mutual complementarity between material (technological and economic) and ideal (the spiritual quest for meaning, community, and beauty) forces. For these thinkers, both aspects are equally influential in determining the flow of human history (Woods 2010, 287). However, while consequently they may be less attuned to the threats posed by these new global trends, which are moving towards a new universalization of power relations, they cannot be made to fit completely into Eisenstadt's vision of multiple modernities, nor into Dirlik's thread of the new universal despotic empire of neo-liberal powers. The models being elaborated by these theorists are less concerned with examining the surface of the existing modes of production (and the corresponding financial, political and military structures of power), than with revealing their underlying ideologies. In this sense, they can be seen as a radical challenge to the contemporary global system.

Thus, the differences between past and present are not to be sought in the challenges of Eurocentrism from various cultural perspectives, but in recognizing the fact that the classic modernization model, applied at the global level, has created a situation in which the problems it generates are no longer limited to so-called "non-European" cultures, but also affect Euro-American societies. The need to learn about "alternative modernities" (Woods 2010, 287) thus also represents a challenge for Euro-American modernization cultures, for they define the limits or borders of the latter's specific localized modernities.

The present study examines those Modern Confucians who have tried to reveal a part of a special reservoir of values and knowledge in order to contribute in this way to the modernization debate, in the hope that this will enrich our understanding of the differences between tradition and modernity. We must not forget, however, that we live in a period that is not only defined by the attempts to revive various traditions, but also by efforts to harmonize or reconcile them with the demands of the dominant economic, political and axiological structures of a globalized world. Since affirmation of modernity as a palette of living styles and clashing values forms an unquestionable assumption of almost all Modern Confucian discourses, they doubtless represent an important contribution to the future research in this direction.

2.2 Modernity with Chinese Characteristics

One of the main reasons for the loss of the normative authority of the Chinese Communist Party (which it exercised unconditionally until the 1990s) is that the values it asserts within its core ideology no longer correspond to the current social reality. In fact, none of its leading ideologists can show how the values of "collectivism" or "serving the people" (both of which were key elements of so-called socialist morality) can be reconciled with a market economy and the harsh competition it entails. This is even more so the case with respect to the protection of labor rights and the welfare state, both dominant socialist values, but which no longer figure among the priorities of the CCP. Even some Party members who yearn for the ideological certainties of the Maoist era believe "this sort of things shows that the Communist Party lacks a clear sense of direction, principle and backbone" (Davies 2012, 131).[4]

These discrepancies have resulted in a "vacuum of values" that is not only reflected in blind consumerism and the lack of a critical reflection on political measures and social mechanisms, but also in the loss of traditional identities. For Jürgen Habermas, this situation is always the result of a "crisis of rationality" (Habermas 1973, 87), and occurs in every society that finds itself at a crossroads between past and present practices, and the ideological assumptions that underpinned the previous ones.

China had already found itself in a similar situation at the turn of the nineteenth century, when the two thousand year rule of Confucianism[5] began to gradually lose its predominant role in Chinese society. After the Opium wars (1842–44), it became clear that the Confucian ideology was outdated and could no longer meet the demands of the new era, which were defined by the economic and political superiority of the Western colonial powers, and the encounter with Western philosophical and scientific thought. As a result of this confrontation with Western thought, in the mid nineteenth century Chinese intellectuals began to debate modernization as a vehicle of transformation and separation from the traditional political, economic and axiological paradigms that until then had defined and sustained the social reality of the so-called Middle Kingdom.

If we wish to analyze this process based on the "general" theoretical premises of modernity[6] and thus on the central paradigms of Euro-American sociological, philosophical and cultural discourses, we must begin with the classic definition first formulated by Hegel, and then developed in the theoretical works of Marx, Weber and the early Lukács, and by other representatives of the Frankfurt school. These discourses were based on an absolutist critique of reason and ultimately led into a self-referential *cul-de-sac*. As reaction to this situation, in the twentieth century we find various alternative theories that proposed a self-critical foundation of modernity based on a linguistically determined understanding of the term "reason". This linguistic shift led to two different approaches in order to explain modernity. The first manifested itself in the post-modern "surpassing" of the normative understanding of this notion, while the second involved the intersubjective transformation of its classic definition (Habermas 1998, 195). The prevailing Western understanding did not continue to focus its analyses on a specific social situation (which usually manifested itself as a critique of reason), but shifted its emphasis onto the terminological scope of modernity, which includes the connotations of the "conscious discontinuity of the new from the old" or the "modern" from the "traditional".

In examining modernization processes in China, we should also bear in mind that we are dealing with a series of consecutive phases, each of which lasted for a few decades and was connected in its own way either to the specific features of the Chinese tradition, or to the problems of accepting and transforming "non-Chinese" forms of production, reproduction and lifestyles. Hence, in attempting transfer the aforementioned theoretical starting points onto the "modern" period and Chinese "modernization" axioms, we must take into account the following characteristics:

1. In China, modernization in the sense of an all-encompassing political, economic and cultural process and its theoretical discourses was always influenced by the invasion of Western military and technological supremacy; as a logical outcome of this situation, Western technology, political systems and culture became a referential frame for the modernization of China (Geist 1996, 13).

2. Any theoretical discourse has thus always equated tradition with Chinese and modernization with Western culture.

3. Historically, the debate on modernization in China took place within the framework of the classical Chinese discursive methodology, which is defined by traditional binary categories. With respect to modernization, nineteenth and early twentieth century Chinese intellectuals tried to clarify the relation between modernity (the West) and tradition (China) through the binary category of "substance (*ti*)" and "function (*yong*)". In the nineteenth century, Zhang Zhidong's slogan advocating "the preservation of the Chinese Substance (*ti*) and the application of Western Function (*yong*)" was widely shared by Chinese intellectuals (Rošker 2008, 96). This approach sought to preserve the Chinese tradition in the face of modernization which, however, was understood as being limited to assimilating Western technology and administration. In the twentieth century, Li Zehou inverted this binary opposition (Li Zehou

1996, 179) by defining modernization as the transformation of essence, in the sense of a general social consciousness, production and lifestyles.

4. The inner logic of traditional Chinese society was intrasystemic (Moritz 1993, 60), in the sense that guaranteeing stability through a centralized and cohesive society was the chief aim. The past was not only the main reference for reflecting on the present, but also served as a signpost for the future (Moritz 1993, 61).

5. Enlightenment in the sense of spreading the ideological domination of reason, seen as essential to modernization, did not find its dynamic and potential for change in the indigenous (Chinese) philosophical tradition, but rather in the adaptation of Western currents of rationality.

Defined in these terms, Chinese modernization was neither a "natural" process (Luo Rongqu 2008, 1), nor a process that could be limited to the internal dynamics of the autochthonous development of Chinese society. In the mid-nineteenth century, radical changes in the existing political and economic systems appeared as unavoidable, given the inability of those systems to meet the demands of that period. We must also bear in mind that modernization processes in China were determined by the confrontation with foreign powers; hence, these processes were largely defined by European colonialism. However, the China of the eighteenth and nineteenth centuries also had to deal with a profound internal crisis. This crisis was much greater and reached far deeper into the traditional structures of society and the state than the recurrent periods of turmoil and upheaval brought about by the rise and fall of dynasties. A radical reform of social values, the means of production and the political and economic system in general would have been inevitable even without the traumatic encounter with the European powers.[7] Clearly, such a reform would not have resembled the "Western"[8] model of modernization and we can only speculate what China would look like today if it had undertaken this reform "on its own", i.e. drawing only on its own economic, political and philosophical resources and capacities.

What is significant for our argument, is the fact that these indigenous (re)sources have survived until the present day, even if they are no longer the dominant ideologies. Over the last hundred years we have witnessed a number of Chinese historical revivals, despite the fact that these historical "relicts" were supposed to have been destroyed by modernity and thrown onto the rubbish heap of outmoded ideologies. Such revivals were not a denial of modernity, for they all marched under its banner. Modern Confucians have never expressed the desire for a return to the pre-modern period.[9] Contemporary Modern Confucians do not consider globalization as a victory of Eurocentric modernity, but rather as a challenge for its historicization (Dirlik 2001, 17), in the sense that they believe tradition should be reconciled with the present.

2.3 Daring Reforms, Ambitious Innovations and Passionately Naïve Movements

The first modernization movement was the so-called *Hundred days reform* (Rošker 2008, 97), also known as the *Wuxu reform*, which fell victim to the backlash of the conservative ruling class of the gradually disintegrating empire.

> The first transformation can be dated from the start of the 100 days reform, led by Kang Youwei and Liang Qichao, to the outbreak of the first civil war in 1927. In the half century following the 1840 Opium War, until 1898, the Chinese ruling elite had made no attempt at serious social reform. The so-called "Chinese studies as substance, Western studies for practical use" or *Zhongxue wei ti Xixue wei yong*, effectively prevented any significant social change. The 100-Days Reform was a product of the failure of this policy, which wanted to introduce Western technology, but without fundamental social reforms. The efforts to reform China's political system failed with the collapse of the Qing Dynasty in 1911 and the inability of the ruling elites to establish a viable republic in the following years. (Hua Shiping 2001, 3)

The turning point in Chinese modernization, both politically and ideologically, was the May Fourth Movement (Wu si yundong), that began in 1919 with the student demonstrations against what China considered to be the unjust resolutions of the Versailles peace treaty. Over the next few years, these protests grew into a nationwide movement of the so-called "new intellectuals",[10] who agitated for the radical cultural and ideological reform of Chinese society (Hua Shiping 2001, 3). Known historically as the New Culture Movement (*Xin wenhua yundong*) and generally considered to be the origin of the Chinese enlightenment, the movement included patriotic and nationalist elements, while also strongly criticizing or even completely rejecting the Chinese tradition, especially its Confucian state doctrine. According to Li Zehou (1996, 568), despite their apparently conflicting agendas, the two components were actually complementary at the start. Li concludes that the enlightenment tradition of the May Fourth Movement gradually disintegrated in the turmoil of this period, which required the mobilization of all physical, economic and intellectual resources in order to resist foreign aggression and preserve the sovereignty of China, while at the same time laying the groundwork for an internal revolution (Li Zehou 1996, 568). "Socialist centralism, in which minorities submitted to the majority and the lower strata of society were led by their superiors" (Li Zehou 1996, 568) prevailed. According to Li, this principle represented:

> a revolutionary heritage, which was founded, promoted and mediated at great length, until it gained a general social status and became part of the general social awareness... In my view, the enlightenment suffocated under the weight of saving the nation. This is a historical fact that cannot be changed. (Li Zehou 1996, 568)

Although Li Zehou's analysis is widely accepted among contemporary scholars, some historians have queried whether the reason for the failure of the enlightenment is to be attributed solely to the political situation of that time.

Liu Huiru, for example, argues that the failure of the movement's modernization potential, also in philosophical terms, cannot be attributed chiefly to external factors, given that the May Fourth

Movement was never an enlightenment movement to begin with. In his view (Liu Huiru 1993, 48), the "incongruence between 'what is said' and 'what is actually meant'" that was consciously applied by the intellectuals of the May Fourth Movement, originated in Confucian pragmatism and was thus a tried-and-true strategy in the Chinese tradition. Their public proclamations repudiating this tradition which had ostensibly been sentenced to death were thus actually intended to hinder its transformation.

In order to formulate a true critical negation of these acquired ideas and practises, these intellectuals would have had to free themselves from the unconscious, unreflected tradition which formed an integral part of their own thought and consciousness. While challenging a previously unquestionable sacred authority was, in itself, a form of enlightenment, the May Fourth activists did not make a sufficient effort to establish a generally binding "instance of reason" that could go beyond the declarative level in order to create a truly new discourse. Not surprisingly, this much lauded cultural reformation movement, which sought primarily to create an awareness concerning modernity, was considered by many thinkers as incapable of producing a new philosophical approach or system (Liu Huiru 1993, 49). Such an approach would not be merely methodological, in the sense of offering new ways of analyzing the past or considering the future, but would offer a new and creative reflection on reality.

This superficial understanding of the tradition, which was therefore insufficient to actually move beyond it, was linked to an equally superficial and idealized image of "science", seen as the embodiment and vehicle of an omnipotent and unquestionable reason. Science thus appeared as the surrogate that could resolve the "transcendental homelessness" and loss of cultural identity which inevitably followed upon the wholesale negation of one's tradition. Wang Fuwu explains the naiveté of the "modern" intellectuals of that time as follows:

> Science is founded on the principles of causality and identity. In terms of human existence, neither belief nor attitude can resist the magical force of these two principles. This leads one to believe that science can solve any problem life can throw at us. (Hu Shi 1990, 127)

The various slogans, norms and ideas of the May Fourth Movement, which were widely acknowledged on the declarative level, were never truly legitimized by the sort of discursive argument that is the precondition for any form of enlightenment. In this sense, we can agree with Liu Huiru's definition of the Movement as an "unenlightened enlightenment" (Liu Huiru 1993, 55).

The idea of reason as the core of modernization and progress is, of course, closely related to the notions of the subject and individualism. The May Fourth Movement focused its efforts on freeing the individual from the domination of the traditional system, in which the state institutions and bureaucracy, on the one hand, and the great landowners with their clan connections, on the other, were closely interconnected. These institutions controlled both the external (socio-political areas, institutionalized nepotism and corruption, political and economic clan connections and strategies) and internal spheres (formal and concrete relations between clan members). Most of the intellectuals who were active within the May Fourth Movement, believed that the Confucian ideology was based on the notion that society has priority over the individual. Thus, they tried their utmost to turn this relation around. This can be clearly seen in their stance for the freedom of the individual, equal opportunities for all and especially free love, which of course did not mean a sexual revolution, but merely the questioning of arranged marriages and a striving for a free choice of partners regardless of the needs and interests of the clans to which they belonged.

Since its establishment in 1949, the People's Republic of China has developed and implemented a series of modernization concepts. Initially, China's rulers mostly imitated the Soviet model, which put socialist industrialisation in the forefront of national priorities. After 1956, the Chinese government tried to create its own modernization model, which was focused primarily on agriculture. In terms of political and cultural renewal, this was the period of the "Great Proletarian Cultural Revolution". Following the death of Mao Zedong (1976) and the introduction of economic liberalization, the Party attempted to bridge the abyss between capitalist reality and socialist values with the ideologies of "Socialism with Chinese characteristics" and concepts such as a "socialist market economy".

These "modernization" models were rooted in the traditional indivisibility of society and state. This was a holistic system in which politics and the economy were not considered as separate, independent spheres.[11] A state-run economy was thus already one of the basic features of traditional society. In this system, the concept of private property was essentially irrelevant, for the possibility of fulfilling the inherent potential of the private ownership of land or the means of production was minimal. Throughout Chinese history, all attempts to concentrate arable land, as well as all efforts to wrest property from state control, had failed. Property thus generally belonged to a clan which, in addition to certain ideological and moral factors, made it more difficult to transfer or sell. According to Moritz (1963, 65), the nationalization of the productive capacities of the P. R. China had a completely different cultural and historical background and a totally different cultural significance, as compared to the very similar processes that took place in Eastern Europe after WWII. Any attempt to divide Chinese history into distinct, chronologically consecutive periods based only on property (or production) criteria, and thus without taking into account the essential characteristics of a traditional social reality, will inevitably lead to very contradictory and illogical conclusions. The continuity created by state interventions will always remain concealed if one follows this methodology. The holistic effect of the state in spatial terms (in the sense of *imperium mundi*) runs parallel with its holistic effects in temporal terms (Moritz 1963, 66).

As opposed to previous phases, this new market economy reform did not result in a lasting mass movement that could at least offer the illusion that it was based on Enlightenment ideas, i.e. that it met certain theoretical assumptions concerning modernization. This is hardly surprising if we consider that the economic liberalization led by Deng Xiaoping in the last two decades of the twentieth century (after the death of Mao Zedong) was enacted primarily by government decree, which meant that it already differed considerably from the "classic" (i.e. Western) modernization model. However, a spontaneous, albeit short-lived mass movement demanding a parallel political "democratization" did occur during the gradual economic liberalization. This movement, which was primarily led by and composed of students, was as naive as the May Fourth Movement and ended with the infamous massacre on Tiananmen Square, on 4 June 1989. On the other hand, this period of economic reform was reflected at many different levels throughout Chinese society and political criticism often manifested itself in the search for new forms of cultural expression.[12]

Modern Chinese thinkers certainly engaged in a theoretical renewal which came to be known as the New Enlightenment. Although this renewal constituted the main theoretical reflection on contemporary Chinese social reality;[13] the reason that this reflection never became a part of mass movements can be found in the fact that government institutions managed to discharge the intellectuals' critical potential not only through repressive measures, but also—and especially—through the professionalization of the theory. In the post 1989 period the Chinese intellectuals were forced to rethink their historic experiences.

In fact, the majority of intellectuals in the humanities and social sciences renounced the New Enlightenment style which had defined them in the 1980s, due to external pressure or, in some cases, as an autonomous choice. Following a re-evaluation of their role, many intellectuals began to focus on more specialized research and "professionalize" their role. Initially, this change in direction was based on Weber's theories on the professionalization of research, and can be seen as a form of self-justification during the difficult period following 1989. After 1992, the process of economic transformation began to accelerate the phenomenon of social stratification, a trend which clearly accorded with the professionalization of research. This institutionalization of intellectual life gradually led to a fundamentally changed role for intellectuals. In fact, from the 1980s onwards, most intellectuals were gradually transformed into experts, scholars and professionals (Wang Hui 2000, 4).

Besides these tendencies, the digital age has brought new complexity to the one-party rule. As Gloria Davies points out, while "dissidents continue to be summarily arrested and charged with serious crimes, official rhetoric and vox populi now jostle for attention on the Internet" (Davies 2012, 121).

This situation resulted not only in the alienation of intellectuals from the state and its decision-making structures, but also in their dispersion. In fact, in today's China, intellectuals no longer constitute a homogenous social group (Davies 2012, 121). In the last fifteen years of the twentieth century, Chinese intellectuals reacted to this new situation in different ways. While a minority continued to try to produce critical theory, in the belief that informing the public was still a traditional task for intellectuals, the majority turned towards a narrower but more "useful" scientific specialization, or applied themselves to the search for a theory or a method that could fill the "vacuum of values" which most intellectuals believed prevailed in society at the time. In a historical perspective, the theoretical production of the New Enlightenment clearly served as the fundamental ideology for economic reform (Wang Hui 2000, 16).

At the beginning of the third millenium, P. R. China's government has striven to portray itself as having successfully delivered "individual freedom" to Chinese people. But, if so in any measure, it has done so by encouraging them to consume the growing abundance of now available products, commodities and services. But, at the same time, it continued to ban public criticism of state directives and practises. It has, for instance, thoroughly "sought to suppress criticism of its human rights record by dissidents within China" (Davies 2010, 79).

The appearance of the "vacuum of values", its problematization and connection with the transformation of the structure, role and function of social knowledge—determined in part by violence, and in part by the modernization processes themselves—exemplifies the consequences of explosive social transformation. The presentation of this phenomenon and its discussion in both academic circles and among the general public was carried out following a tried-and-true methodology well known to the ruling elites of all latently autocratic societies: that of shifting contents and problems from the political to the private sphere. This method also accorded with the official ideology of the Chinese modernization model, which demanded that intellectuals serve the new market economy either as technocrats or as neoconservative intellectuals (Davies 2010, 79).

2.4 Gradual Westernization: The Case of Taiwan

In this situation, the latter began to gather under the banner of so-called Modern Confucianism (*Xiandai xin ruxue*). At the same time that this philosophical current was being silenced (at least formally) during the first twenty five years of the People's Republic, its theoretical foundations were being laid by thinkers in Taiwan and, to a lesser degree, Hong Kong. As opposed to the P. R. China, where Confucianism was stigmatized as the "ideology of outdated feudalism" until the 1980s,[14] in Hong Kong and Taiwan, both of which were defined by post-colonial social discourses, some intellectuals had begun opposing the growing Westernization already in the 1950s.

These thinkers and critics pointed out that the island's dependency on Western colonial forces was not only cultural. Following the victory of the Chinese Communist Party and the founding of the P. R. China, Taiwan became the headquarters of the government in exile under the aegis of the ruling National Party (Guomin dang). Of course, this small country needed external support in order to survive politically and economically. For the Taiwanese government, which maintained a "soft" autocratic rule in the early post-war years, American aid (which became a standard feature of its "anti-communist" strategy after the Korean War) was essential to preserving economic and political stability. This dependency on American capital investments, technology and an enormous consumer base did not cease even after aid was officially terminated in 1965 (Lai Ming-Yan 1995, 103). America was soon joined by Japan, which had regained[15] a position of economic dominance in the post-war years, in providing aid and investments, and the two countries eventually controlled Taiwanese industrial development and its overseas trade. In 1970, American and Japanese capital represented 85% of all Taiwanese investments (Lai Ming-Yan 1995, 103).

The domination of American and Japanese capital meant that disputes between labor and capital were, in effect, disputes between the native Chinese and foreigners. Hence, it was not so much "class consciousness" as "national identity",[16] defined by the striving for national autonomy and independence that began to spread rapidly among the people of Taiwan. Any analysis of Taiwanese modernization therefore must also use a post-colonial approach.

Taiwanese identity has always been very uncertain. Populated originally by various Pacific tribes, between 1683 and the end of WWII the island was almost always under the control of different colonial powers (Day 1999, 9). The first Han Chinese immigrants settled in parts of Taiwan in the seventeenth century, when Taiwan was still a Dutch colony. Following the defeat and expulsion of the Dutch in

1683, the island came under the control of the Manchurian government of mainland China.[17] When the Japanese conquered Manchuria in 1859, they occupied Taiwan. The highest number of Han Chinese immigrants (about 1 million people) arrived after the end of the civil war between the Communist and Nationalist forces, and the founding of the P. R. China under communist rule. This massive influx of mainland Chinese led to the strengthening of the "Taiwanese" ethnic and cultural identity among the indigenous population. In the final decades of the twentieth century, the differences between the Taiwanese and Han Chinese (continental) identities played an important role in the political and philosophical developments of the island, which, thanks to foreign investments, had undergone an intensive modernization process. The GMD, which until 2000 was the sole governing party, had always promoted Chinese unity and the Han Chinese cultural and national identity, while the second leading party, which finally won the general elections in 2000 (the Democratic Progressive Party, Minjin dang) instead emphasized a unique, "Taiwanese" identity.

> Mainlanders remained in control of the Kuomintang and Taiwan's central government until recently. However, the Taiwanization of politics in this society has rapidly accelerated with the passing of the older generations of Mainland refugees. By the start of 2000, 84% of the population was Taiwanese by birth, whereas only 14% were Mainland Chinese and less than 2% were aborigine. Without exception, those born on the Mainland who have survived politically like Ma Ying-Jeou (Mayor of Taipei) and James Soong (former Governor of Taiwan and head of the People First party) have sought to become "new Taiwanese", identifying themselves with the predominately Taiwanese electorate. Lee Teng-Hui, the first Taiwanese President, often showed his desire to be identified with Taiwan, not the Mainland, and frequently referred to his educational background in Japan. (Scalapino 2002, 33–34)

This complex historical situation helps explain why Modern Confucianism found a fertile ground in Taiwan. Chinese philosophers who were active in Taiwan after 1949[18] were forced to confront the problems of modernization and capitalism much earlier than their counterparts on the mainland, and therefore had little interest in issues such as the sinization of Marxism. These approaches formed part of a continuous philosophical current which had originated in China at the end of the nineteenth century and had been interrupted by the upheavals of civil war and the Japanese occupation (Scalapino 2002, 33–34). The works of these philosophers reflected the desire to address a series of urgent political, social, economic and cultural problems that were essentially practical in nature. Due to the "generous support" of Western countries (led by the USA) who wanted to preserve the Taiwanese "democratic alternative" and the semi-colonial status of Hong Kong as a counterweight to Chinese communism, the explosive Westernization of both societies was already well underway in the 1950s. Ideologically, the integration of these societies into the world of modern capitalism was accompanied by work ethics (based on the hierarchical system of obedience) which, in the case of Japan, had already shown itself to be compatible with the demands and often inhuman conditions of early capitalism. Although this ideology is often regarded as being rooted in Confucian ethics, this view stems from an ignorance and various prejudices concerning the original Confucian ethics. The abovementioned "absolute obedience", for example, was never part of the Confucian hierarchic model, which was instead founded upon the concept of social responsibility.[19]

> This philosophical trend was supported by the experience in Japan and the four so-called "Asian tigers" (Korea, Singapore, Taiwan and Hong Kong), in which successful modernization was considered to be the "victory of Confucian capitalism". (Wang Hui 2000, 19)

Modern Confucians have therefore, from the very outset, based their research on the belief that Confucian philosophy is compatible with capitalist development. Many factors contributed to this unlikely pairing. Most Chinese theorists see this presumed compatibility as stemming from the cooperation principle and the so-called "communicative method" (Trauzettel in Moritz 1993, 65) that is supposedly characteristic of Confucianism. However, apart from the aforementioned hierarchic social structure (which also forms the basis of the traditional Confucian view of interpersonal relations in society), we can also cite the intimate identification with one's clan that forms the basic unit of an individual's social context. In capitalist production this identification is transferred from the clan to the company, which thus enables the efficient integration of employees. Given the absolute and unquestioning obedience to authorities, which is commonly viewed as being rooted in the Confucian view of the autonomous self (although it actually originated in the legalistic reform of the original teachings during the Han period), shifting this identification onto the company can result in significant increases in production and profits.

In *Four Essays on Liberty,* which appeared in 1969, Isaiah Berlin made the distinction between "positive" and "negative" freedom.[20] But Zhang Foquan had already examined this concept in his study, *Freedom and human rights* (*Ziyou yu renquan*), published in 1954. Taking their departure from this opposition of terms, Taiwanese liberals concluded that a democratic order can only be established on the basis of "negative freedom", while "positive freedom" inevitably led to totalitarianism. Modern Confucians not only advocated negative freedom, but argued that Chinese culture lacked freedom in general. At the same time, they stressed that, on the theoretical level, negative freedom must be conditioned by the positive and that "negative freedom" does not automatically prevent totalitarianism.[21]

For many thinkers, negative freedom was, in any case, conditioned by the positive form (Taylor 1985, 221–9). The liberal insistence on the exclusive meaning of negative freedom implied an "individualistic" view of the subject as somehow separated from community, the so-called "unencumbered self" (Sandel 1984, 81). Some theorists therefore concluded that, in this sense, Modern Confucians were much closer to communitarian views than appeared at first glance (Lee Ming-huei 2001a, 78; 2005, 14).[22] They were searching for a "Confucian liberalism", i.e. a liberalism that would develop "naturally" within the context of the Confucian tradition.

3. Modern Confucianism

Modern Confucianism is grounded in the conviction that traditional Confucianism, understood as a specifically Chinese social, political and moral system of thought can, if renewed and adapted to meet the conditions of the modern era, serve as the foundation for an ethically meaningful modern life, while also providing a spiritual antidote to the alienation which these same Modern Confucian philosophers see as a collateral effect of the capitalistic glorification of competition and the single minded pursuit of profit.

3.1 The "Three Generations"

Modern Confucianism as a major philosophical discourse in contemporary China did not emerge only due to the desire for a modern synthesis of the Confucian and Euro-American traditions, but also as a consequence of the crisis in both traditions. The crisis of Confucianism as a leading state doctrine of pre-modern China was part of the much more general crisis of the Chinese state on the threshold of modernity, a crisis due to Chinese technological backwardness, widespread poverty and the failure of the political system to adapt to the actual conditions of society. The specific circumstances of the nineteenth and twentieth centuries demonstrated unconfutable that Confucianism, which had functioned as the central state doctrine and ideological basis of traditional Chinese society for two millennia, could no longer serve as an ideal basis for "modern" society. The most significant critique of Confucianism appeared on threshold of the twentieth century in the form of the May Fourth Movement, which combined a patriotic reaction against the Japanese and Western imperial powers with a sweeping criticism of the ossification and destructive social consequences of the traditional state doctrine. However, the "new intellectuals" who initially identified the cure for the crisis of this outdated system in the assimilation and adaptation of certain aspects of Western thought, were forced to radically rethink their acritical idealization of the European "way" after the catastrophe of WWI and the widespread economic crisis which followed. These intellectuals, who had already witnessed the bankruptcy of European political theories, would also be influenced by the crisis of modern European philosophy (whose role in the specific philosophical tendencies of Chinese modernization will be discussed later). All these factors dampened considerably the Chinese enthusiasm for "progressive" European thought, and many who had once considered it the highest stage of human development were profoundly shaken in their innermost convictions.

Modern Confucianism, as the discourse which most clearly expressed the rehabilitation of traditionalism, was developed by some of the most prominent Chinese philosophers of the twentieth century. In addition to the acknowledged precursors of this current, Xiong Shili and Feng Youlan, we should also mention Liang Shuming, (Carsun Chang) Zhang Junmai and He Lin. These thinkers belong to the so-called first generation of this stream of thought. The categorization into "generations" follows a long tradition in Confucian scholarship, which is ultimately rooted in classical Confucianism. Although slightly different categorizations exist in presentday China, I have (for reasons which will be explained below) chosen to apply the following one:

- First generation: Feng Youlan (1895–1990), Xiong Shili (1885–1968), (Carsun Chang) Zhang Junmai (1886–1969), Liang Shuming (1893–1988) and He Lin (1902–92).

- Second generation: Fang Dongmei (1899–1977), Xu Fuguan (1903–82), Tang Junyi (1909–78) and Mou Zongsan (1909–95).

- Third generation: Yu Ying-shih (Yu Yingshi, 1930), Liu Shu-hsien (Liu Shuxian, 1934), Cheng Chung-ying (Cheng Zhongying, 1935) and Tu Wei-ming (Du Weiming, 1940).

The present study focuses upon the work of the second generation. According to some contemporary interpreters, the prominent Taiwanese scholar Qian Mu (1895–1990) can also be included in this generation of Modern Confucianism. However, given his role as a historian, I have chosen not to include him in a book dedicated primarily to modern Confucian philosophy. On the other hand, I have included Fang Dongmei (1899–1977) in the second generation, even though he is sometimes associated with the first generation. As the teacher of some of the members of the third generation, it seemed more appropriate to include him among the generation of thinkers immediately preceding this group.

I regard his contribution as important, though he never explicitly adhered to the Modern Confucian movement and considered himself, in his innermost convictions, to be not only a Confucian, but also a Daoist and a Buddhist. In fact, he not only taught many of the main figures of the third generation of Modern Confucians, but also many leading contemporary Daoists. We should also bear in mind that the term Confucianism (*ru xue*) often denotes early Chinese thought in general;[1] even though the Neo-Confucians of the Song and Ming Dynasties, who created the theoretical framework that underpins Modern Confucianism, formally distanced themselves from Daoism, Buddhism and similar, more mystical, less rational traditions, even going so far as to view the proponents of these systems as their philosophical "enemies". At the same time, however, one of the greatest theoretical shifts in Neo-Confucian philosophy was due precisely to the integration of many important Daoist and Buddhist concepts and methods into the framework of classical Confucianism.[2] It was the assimilation of those very ideas that orthodox classical Confucian doctrine deemed dangerous, improper (*fei zheng*) and even "heretical", which to a great extent defined the reform of classical Confucian thought which, already at that time, had ossified and become far too formalized. These Buddhist and Daoist impulses saved Confucianism from collapse in the period from the tenth to the fourteenth centuries, and succeeded in transforming the classical state-building doctrine into a system of thought that deserved once again to be called "philosophy".[3] In their attempts to synthesize Euro-American and Chinese philosophies and modernize the Chinese philosophical tradition, many other Modern Confucian thinkers also focused on various traditional discourses which do not belong to the framework of Confucianism in a narrow sense.[4] As a final point, we must also take into account the differences between the original Chinese notions and their semantic connotations that originate in the translations of these notions into Indo-European languages. The expression *ru xue* is translated as "Confucianism" (also in the term "Modern Confucianism"), and thus automatically connotes Confucius (Kong fuzi) and the various historical phases of the Confucian teachings. But *ru xue* actually signifies "the teachings of the scholars",[5] which means that this expression does not exclude *a priori* any of the major influences on the history of Chinese thought. In fact, what Confucian and Daoist philosophy, as well as sinized Buddhism all share is this idea of traditional Chinese philosophy as the "teachings of the scholars".[6]

3.2 The Rehabilitation of Tradition and the Challenges of Modernization

As we have seen, the revitalization of the complex traditions of Chinese philosophical thought during the twentieth century has assumed increasing relevance and significance in recent decades. In the first half of the twentieth century, this tendency could be observed in the works of many of the leading modern Chinese philosophers who were searching for ways to renew the methodological and theoretical aspects of the Chinese tradition, and especially of the pre-modern philosophy which followed the Neo-Confucian revival.

The trend towards revitalizing Confucianism was already evident at the start of the famous debate on science and metaphysics (*kexue yu xuanxue*) in 1923, in which a group of young theoreticians led by Carsun Chang (Zhang Junmai) challenged the naïve and superficial May Fourth enthusiasm for Euro-American models of modernity with a series of closely-reasoned counter-arguments and objections (Bunnin

2002, 27). A scholarly revival involving new interpretations of ancient Confucian, Daoist, Mohist, Legalist, and Buddhist texts was of vital importance, but the main inspiration from traditional Chinese thought derived from the great Neo-Confucian syntheses of the Song and Ming dynasties, especially those found in the writings of Zhu Xi (1130–1200) and Wang Yangming (1472–1529). The subtlety and scope of their philosophical intelligence and the tension between Zhu Xi's realism and and Wang Yangming's focus on Mind offered considerable margins for modern reflective interpretations of their work (Bunnin 2002, 27).

Modern Confucianism as an independent and specific stream of thought was officially announced on the first day of 1958, when a group of Taiwanese and Hong Kong intellectuals published the celebrated *Declaration of Chinese Culture to the Scholars of the World* (*Wei Zhongguo wenhua jinggao shijie renshi xuanyan*). The Declaration, which joined an anti-communist glorification of Western style democracy with a vibrant call to patriotism and the preservation of traditional values, is the fundamental manifesto that defined the goals and contents of the Modern Confucian current. According to Bresciani (2001, 22), this document became the Magna Charta of the whole New Confucian Movement, expressing in a very concentrated form their beliefs, ideals and plans. While this claim might appear exaggerated (see Makeham 2003, 28–29), some of its contents are still widely seen as implying certain central ideas of the Modern Confucian movement.

The Declaration was drawn up by the philosophers Carsun Chang (Zhang Junmai, 1887–1969), Mou Zongsan (1909–95), Tang Junyi (1909–78) and Xu Fuguan (1903–82). These scholars are still regarded as the founders of Modern Confucianism as a system that aimed at a more systematic re-interpretation of traditional Chinese philosophy and culture, based on a deeper and more comprehensive understanding of Western philosophy, especially the thought of Plato, Kant and Hegel (Bunnin 2002, 11). As opposed to the members of the so-called "First generation" of Modern Confucianism, who even after 1949 continued to be active primarily on the mainland, this group of scholars lived and worked primarily in Taiwan and Hong Kong; they became known in modern Sinology as the "Second generation" of Modern Confucianism.[7]

These thinkers thus proceeded with a dual approach: on the one hand, reformulating certain key approaches of traditional (Confucian) thought which they believed were capable of transcending the prevailing ideological trends, thereby preserving Chinese cultural identity, while at the same making their own original contributions to the development of a philosophical and theoretical dialogue between Euro-American and Chinese cultures. This current, which after 1949 to a great extent defined the spirit of Taiwanese, but also (though at first only partially, and latently) mainland modernization, engaged in a wide-ranging effort to revitalize traditional (primarily Confucian and even more so, Neo-Confucian) thought by means of new input and stimulation from Western philosophical systems. In its general tension towards syntheses, the spirit of German idealism was especially important, while among its more theoretical components considerable attention was also given to the contents and approaches of the Viennese circle. However, in their search for antidotes and alternatives to social alienation (in Asian modernization, as well) and the "vacuum of values", these theorists instead looked primarily to the framework of classical Confucian thought.

> Lingering in a state of self-affirmation and self-transformation, it faced a series of powerful, unprecedented challenges throughout the century. At the end of the century, even though Confucianism had already been relegated to the "ash pit of history" as a political institution,[8] it ultimately found peace and its own place in the world as a philosophy. (Cheng Chung-Ying 2003, 160)

With the explosive development of the policy of economic openness and the liberalization that accompanied it, this current has also been gradually revitalized in P. R. China over the last two decades.

The question of cultural renewal created considerable turmoil in Chinese intellectual circles when it first appeared during the Qing dynasty. In a period marked by a constant state of crisis, many Chinese intellectuals were attracted by the gloss of modern material cultures and wanted China to enter into this Brave New World as soon as possible. In their view, traditional Chinese culture was backwards and old fashioned and had to be eliminated. The voices of the Modern Confucians were thus completely silenced by this barrage of new ideas. That China had pursued a form of modernization in which the negative aspects of its own culture predominated, and in which it also risked being expropriated by "external forces" was something that only became evident in recent years. In short, cultural renewal had gone in a completely wrong direction and now found itself at a dead end. The return to its own tradition thus once again became a topic of debate, leading to the "rediscovery" of Modern Confucianism and its intrinsic value by Chinese intellectuals.

The revitalizaton of the Chinese tradition remains one of the most important theoretical currents in contemporary Chinese theory. Due to its potentially stabilizing social function and its harmonious compatibility with capitalism, many scholars see it as the Asian equivalent of Max Weber's "protestant ethic". In modern Sinology, this view is known as the "post-Confucian hypothesis":

> Indeed, many scholars have invoked Confucianism as an important cultural cause of East Asia's economic success. In particular, scholars such as Berger and Tu have gone so far as to propose what is called the post-Confucian thesis, i.e.: that Confucianism has not only facilitated economic development in East Asian countries, but also has enabled these countries to create a different kind of capitalism and take a different path to modernity than the West. (Kwon 2007, 55)

Lee Hong-jung describes the potential of the Confucian tradition in terms of its constitutive role within the concept of so-called "Asian values" (which will be discussed more in detail later):

> Characteristic Asian values were transmuted into state-led economic models, playing a significant role in the economic development of Asian countries. Familism promoted strong cooperation among blood relatives, and created small- and mid-size family businesses based on Confucian familism and family ethics. These family businesses gradually developed to become the framework of Asian capitalism. Community spirit is also a key Asian value. By maintaining strong ties based on community spirit and solidarity, Asian populations have contributed to the economic development of the region. Promoting education, the

most important Asian value, also stems from Confucianism which teaches that it is better to educate one's children than to give them wealth. This tenet has helped pave the way to economic development. The emphasis on education has also raised management capabilities and technological expertise, and has facilitated economic development through improved productivity. (Lee Hong-jung 2003, 32)

The representatives of the contemporary Modern Confucianism are generally convinced that the successful development of modern East Asian societies was due primarily to a specific modernization model, known as "Confucian capitalism" (e.g. Kahn 1979; Vogel 1979). This model is characterized by a strong state leadership with a well-developed administrative structure, a hierarchical social structure and a well-developed network of social relations, and an emphasis on education. It also stresses virtues such as diligence, reliability and persistence, together with cooperation, loyalty and a strong sense of affiliation to one's own community or organisation (Vogel 1979).

Tu Weiming is a third generation scholar who has published a number of important studies on Chinese modernization and its links with the Modern Confucians. As Heiner Roetż points out, Tu's analysis of modernization is not based on a negative critique of the ethics of the Enlightenment:

> A constant point of reference in Tu's writings is the European Enlightenment and its model of "modernity". However, he concedes that any ethics that wishes to build on something other than its exploitability by authoritarian regimes must come to terms with the standards of the Enlightenment. There is no possibility of a "radically different ethics". (Roetz 2008, 367)

What Tu (2000, 207) instead criticizes in Western Enlightenment models is their excessive reliance on individualism and instrumental rationality. In his view, these two "fundamental pillars" of modernization are responsible for the estrangement from Nature and the human alienation which prevails in modern societies. He sees a possibility for influencing a renewed conceptualization of the modern era in the Chinese and, especially, the Confucian traditions. He supports his argument with the concept of "multiple modernities":

> In both the Western and non-Western worlds, the projected transition from tradition to modernity never occurred. As a norm, traditions continue in modernity. Indeed, the modernizing process itself is constantly shaped by a variety of cultural forms rooted in distinct traditions. (Tu 2000, 198)

This concept also confirms his belief that East-Asian or Chinese modernization should not be equated with Westernization. In fact, "modernity" is no longer antithetical to "tradition"; on the contrary, traditions constitute the essential meaning of current modernities. The Confucian tradition, which Tu sees as a form of religion, is definitely capable of creating a model of modernity that would not lead to the alienation and determination which the Western model of modernization has produced in its societies. In its "broad humanistic spirit", Tu sees the possibility for an economic development that can co-exist with state-building (institutionalization), social stability and cultural identity (Tu 2000, 212). The arrogance of Western culture which conceives of "its own" present as the future for all other cultures is not only in bad taste, but also completely misplaced. Like most other Modern Confucians, Tu denies that Confucian ethics hinders modernization; on the contrary, they can accelerate this process. The fact that the Chinese tradition never succeeded in developing the conditions for industrialization and a modern economic system does not preclude it from doing so in a different historical context.

Heiner Roetz points out the problematic nature of these suppositions (Roetz 2008, 371). Bearing in mind that original Confucianism had a negative view of the concept of pure benefit or profit (*li*), the East Asian "economic miracle" acclaimed by most Modern Confucians is best exemplified in the explosive development of the P. R. China. However, it is impossible to ignore the fact that China's rapid rise as a global superpower was also due to certain factors, such as a ruthless capitalism governed by an autocratic political system and development policies which ignore any legal or ethical standards, and which have resulted in a series of ecological disasters. All this hardly resembles the Confucian ideal of "moral rule" based on "self-cultivation" and the harmonious unification of "inner sage and external ruler". On the contrary, the dominant ideologies in the contemporary Chinese state are founded on a pure, unconditioned neo-liberalism, which is rooted in turn in the very concepts that have always been criticized by the Modern Confucians, Tu Weiming included. In fact, these elements are viewed as typical products of the Western modernization model, which is based on excessive individualism and instrumental rationality.[9]

> Even without considering the PRC, it is difficult to see any country in East Asia that could serve as paradigm for a politics of "moral leadership" ... There is also that reserve army of millions of migrant workers, whose exploitation rather than any Confucian work ethic is the backbone of the economic boom. (Roetz 2008, 372)

In their nostalgic exaltation of the bond with Nature and the holistic, organic unity of man and the natural order, Roetz finds certain parallels between Modern Confucian discourses on modernization and the European romantic reaction to the Enlightenment. These European intellectual currents were an attempt to return to the original bond between the individual and their natural and social environment and a form of resistance against the new domination of technology, which implied an atomizing, mechanistic view of life. If we consider these parallels, what we are dealing with are not Western versus Asian or Chinese cultural alternatives, but rather a culturally non-specific dialectic of the same global modernization process. The agonies of China in the course of more than a century of ongoing modernization (*nachholende Modernisierung*) repeat the agonies of the West, and her responses repeat the Western ones, not only with respect to Romanticism, but also in terms of the philosophy of life (*Lebensphilosophie*) or, in our day, communitarianism (Roetz 2008, 372).

3.3 Theoretical and Conceptual Platforms

In order to understand the contributions of the Modern Confucian movement to solving the global crisis of values we must first clarify the nature of its impact on the complex framework of Chinese social and individual entities. To do this, we must begin by examining the concept of traditional Confucian identity, given that a precise definition of Confucianism (both as an ethically permeated onto-epistemology, as well as the fundamental state ideology which dominated the Chinese tradition for nearly two millennia and also functioned as the basic template for the regulation of individual and political relations) not only provides a discursive framework for understanding Chinese history, but also a context which is sufficiently grounded to enable a comprehensive examination of the social reality, both past and present. In particular, we must focus on the ways in which the transformation of tradition, as defined by the Modern Confucians, reset the parameters that had exercised such a powerful influence on pre-modern definitions of Confucian identity. While the dilemmas faced by Modern Confucians in their attempts to redefine the past and constitute new identities, manifested themselves on various conceptual platforms, what united these diverse platforms was the search for possible ways to re-constitute a Confucian identity that was suited to the demands and conditions of modern societies. According to Yao Xinzhong (2001, 313–14), Modern Confucian discourses were formulated and/or actuated primarily within the context of three social categories:

- The rationalistic theoreticians who developed and elaborated Confucianism as a philosophical or metaphysical discourse, in the conviction that mastering this discourse represented the chief criterion for defining the Confucian identity of each individual.
- The philosophers who instead focused on the "religious"[10] elements or aspects of the Confucian teachings and who saw in the veneration of its founders the basic element of Confucian identity.
- Individuals and groups who reproduced classical Confucian

values and the Confucian moral code in the behaviours of their daily lives. Here, we are dealing with the implicit dimensions of Confucian identity.

However, understanding and interpreting the main Confucian principles means first establishing clear and unambiguous definitions. This problem is not specific to the modern era, for the "proper" interpretation and implementation of Confucian teachings have been at the center of philosophical disputes throughout the entire history of Chinese thought. Already at the end of the period of the Warring states (475–221 B.C.), various currents had formed advocating different interpretations of the notion *ru xue* ("Confucian teaching"), with time, space, cultural background, philosophical methodology and religious beliefs constituting the central elements of each current's doctrine. This heterogeneity of Confucian doctrines and their interpretations impacted profoundly on the fundamental problematic of the conceptual designs of Modern Confucianism, as well as on its efforts to establish a unified Confucian identity. One of the main difficulties confronting the Modern Confucians was the loss of the classical criteria by which the Confucian identity (*ru*) had been defined over the course of Chinese history, as these traditional criteria could no longer function in complex, modern, industrial societies. According to Yao Xinzhong (2001, 316), three parameters had been especially important for defining Confucian identity in pre-modern and traditional China:

1. The different genealogical lines that transmitted the "Confucian way" (*daotong*);
2. The linkage between Confucian knowledge and the state bureaucracy, manifested in the official state examinations;
3. The specific code of behaviour (*si wen*) and a specific ideal of personality (*junzi*).

At the beginning of the twentieth century, as Confucianism lost its leading role in social, political and economic life, these three parameters were either significantly redimensioned or, at the least, lost their primary social relevance. The abolition of the Confucian ideology as the central state doctrine resulted not only in its declining political importance, but also in the decomposition of the Confucian system of social classes. Due to the separation between the new state educational system and the Confucian teachings, traditional scholars were no longer needed to underpin the state administrative apparatus. Hence, the traditional parameters could no longer serve as criteria for defining Confucian identity (Yao 2001, 316) which, having lost its normatively binding essential nucleus, had become more or less arbitrary, and a question of subjective self-definition. However, for many in Western Sinology, as well as for many scholars in the East Asian area, considerable confusion still exists as to what Modern Confucianism actually is and who can be considered a representative of this stream of thought.

Despite this arbitrariness, the second generation of Modern Confucians generally identified with the principles of the Declaration, though with at times significant distinctions. These principles thus represent a common thread that ties the exponents of this movement within successively modernized East Asian societies to this apparently outdated tradition, and also explains why the issue of "Confucian modernization" was such a fundamental question for these theorists.

For the Modern Confucians, modernization was essentially a rationalization of the world. In their search for its philosophical foundations, they mainly focused on questions related to ontology, which had been introduced by Western systems of thought. It was their belief that questions related to the ultimate reality of the cosmos, the substance of being and the Absolute determined the meaning of life and were essential for the creation of a new values system compatible with both contemporary social conditions and the preservation of an integral cultural and personal identity.

This "obsession" with ontology can actually be dated to 1923–4, when much of the Chinese intelligentsia was involved in the noted controversy on *Science and Metaphysics (Kexue yu xuanxue lunzhan)*. The advocates of metaphysics argued that theirs was the only discourse that could solve the fundamental problems of life and the world. They believed in a division of tasks between themselves and the supporters of Science (Bresciani 2001, 337), and felt a pressing need to elaborate an ontology that could serve as the basis for restoring the Confucian tradition.

They looked to ontology as the philosophical discipline that would provide clear solutions to the problems they faced, and *in primis* that of Western modernization, in the conviction that only through a genuine and clear comprehension of the cosmic substance would modern man be able to find his spiritual home again. The crucial task, therefore, was to find the "proper" orientation, meaning a series of new, clearly marked "signposts" which pointed the way towards modern culture, while also providing the basic criteria for solving practical problems in the political and economic spheres. Without such a framework of orientations, society would slip into a general spiritual malaise in which individuals and their actions would be determined by the purely mechanistic laws of technocratic utility. If this were to occur, the comprehension of Western thought for the purposes of finding spiritual guidelines for the modernization in course would necessarily remain fragmentary, incoherent and superficial, and would therefore not only be incapable of enriching the Chinese spiritual world, but would actually accelerate the processes of spiritual disorder and alienation (Bresciani 2001, 337).

In order to illustrate the ethical-political approaches of the Modern Confucians, we can refer to the traditional ideal of the "inner sage and external ruler (*neisheng waiwang*)". For the Modern Confucians, the exemplary "Confucian nobleman" (*junzi*) who embodied the union of personal morality with a more general social ethics and a successful life, offered a possible paradigm for mastering the impenetrable complexity of the modern world. Based on their different understandings of this classical ideal, Feng Yaoming distinguishes among the three generations of Modern Confucianism:

> The traditional Confucians took the concept of the so-called "external ruler" from the Daoist classic *Zhuangzi,* where he was defined as the personality that, thanks to his union with the "inner sage", was able to establish the ideal human way.[11] In Confucian discourses, this concerned the ideal of moral rulership. The first generation of Modern Confucians had a similar view of this traditional ideal of the "external ruler", while also stressing the importance of scientific knowledge. The members of the second generation instead concluded that in their social reality, such an ideal moral rulership was unattainable. Their "new external

ruler" was thus, to a great extent, already predicated by Western science and democracy. However, the third generation of Modern Confucians[12] seems to be convinced that modernization can be realized not only through science and democracy but, even more importantly, via a rational adaptation of the development and achievements of capitalism. (Feng Yaoming 1992, 228)

As noted, the Modern Confucian current arose from various attempts to synthesize Western and traditional Chinese thought, in what was a period of crisis for both systems. The Modern Confucian efforts were thus not limited to revitalizing or rehabilitating their own cultural or traditional ideals, as it was evident to them that Confucian modernization could only be realized based on ideas "imported" from those very cultures which had given rise to modernity. They were thus not only intent upon rescuing their own tradition, but also on resolving the problems of a foreign intellectual tradition which had clearly become entangled in its own philosophical knots. In this situation, they tended to view Confucianism as a sort of "philosophy of salvation":

> The scholars who signed the Manifesto were profoundly convinced that the Confucian tradition was the most open, inclusive, and creative of the world's many traditions and was therefore best suited for leading mankind into the future. (Liu Shu-hsien 1996, 103)

For the Modern Confucians, the solution to the modern world crisis lay in placing morality at the center of human concerns. While specific methods for resolving the main problems of human existence would be found, these methods could not be solely technical, organizational or contractual in nature, but had to derive from a deep awareness of the importance of the ethical conditionality of human life. As Heiner Roetz (2008, 379) points out, as a moral being (ens morale) every individual has a potential for maintaining and constantly re-formulating this moral priority, thereby laying the foundation for a modernity of solidarity. This priority was clearly expressed by Lee Ming Huei in his attempts to restore Confucian ethics (Lee Ming-huei 1990, 2001) through his concept of a "creative transformation" to "modern consciousness (*xiandai yishi*)" (Lee Minghuei 1991, 1994). An important methodological step had already been taken previously by Mou Zongsan, with his concept of the self-negation of the moral Self (*daode ziwode kanxian*), which will be discussed below.

> This dialectical thought-figure creates a close link between Confucian ethics and the reformulated "principle of subjectivity", without reducing it in terms of its functions or relativizing it in the name of culture. Like Tu's schema for Confucian personhood, it offers the possibility of an intellectual joint venture of the great philosophical conceptions of mankind—which does not exclude the spiritual conceptions embodied in religions —in the search for a common global ethics that both East and West are in dire need of. (Roetz 2008, 379)

3.4 Critique

Despite their increasingly important role in the modern ideologies of balance, moderation, patience and harmony that underpin China's new social harmony, Modern Confucians have often been the target of harsh criticism, originating primarily from Taiwan and Hong Kong, but also from mainland China and elsewhere. These criticisms are multilayered, and based on both essential and methodological approaches, while also questioning the socio-political functions of these discourses. They can be characterized very schematically as follows:

- The post-colonial critique (the critique of the function of the central ideology of the transnational capital in eastern Asia);
- The world-view critique (the critique of idealism);
- The critique of the inner autocracy (the critique of dogmatism);
- The critique of the lack of innovations (the critique of the function of knowledge and value reproduction); and

- The critique of methodological and logical inconsistency (the critique of teological mysticism).

The potentially negative consequences of Modern Confucian discourses for the socio-political development of the Chinese state and society has been voiced mainly by Western theoreticians, especially those attempting to define the role and function of Modern Confucianism in the light of post-colonial studies. For scholars such as Joseph Levenson, Myron Cohen and Margery Wolf, Confucianism is an outdated patriarchal ideology the gradual disappearance of which is highly desirable, as this would open up areas for the consolidation of a new and much-needed cultural transformation. Instead, for other scholars, Confucianism is a *sine qua non* for any "Chineseness", and thus has to be maintained and further developed in the contemporary world (Ames 2001, 71).

One of the best known post-colonial critics of Modern Confucianism, Arif Dirlik, warns of a possible linkage of this neo-conservative current with the new all-China nationalism. In examining the new intellectual and social movements arising in contemporary China that are in the forefront of this new tendency, he also mentions Modern Confucianism:

> Their re-evocation of a pre-modern past, however anti-hegemonic in terms of their relationship to the West, barely disguises a new form of national chauvinism. For example, the Confucian revival is not unrelated to arguments for a "Greater Chinese" economic region.[13] (Dirlik 1994, 109–10)

Dirlik blames the members of this movement for their failure to conform to the broader historical context, which presumably also includes the concept of revolution. He also accuses them indirectly of contributing to creating the situation which prompted Samuel Huntington to formulate his controversial concept of the "clash of civilisations", as the core of an ideology that aims at the "elimination of socialisms" (Dirlik 2001, 22), and questions their actual relation to the concept of "Asian values", which will be discussed in the next chapter.

As noted, the post-colonial critics are not the only ones to respond negatively to Modern Confucianism, the fundamental ontological and spiritual approaches of which have also been challenged by other theorists. Heiner Roetz (2008, 371–2), among others, queries the supposed religious dimension of original Confucianism, a view which he considers insufficiently grounded. For Roetz, this issue is superfluous and moot, for it is the non-religious reading[14] of these ancient texts that, if properly interpreted and adapted, could make a unitary conceptualization of such a modernity possible, a modernity which would not be limited to an instrumental rationality, but would not negate social progress as a consequence of the Enlightenment.

In their critiques of Modern Confucian discourses, the theorists of the P. R. China generally assume the same style of argumentation (though perhaps "rebukes" would be a better word) that had always been directed against the idealistic suppositions of Confucianism as such. These scholars represent the world-view critique, as directed specifically against Modern Confucianism. A typical example of such criticisms can be found in the following passage from an article by Zou Liufang, in which he first introduced this current to the mainland public:

> First, it should be noted that the modernization models being proposed by Modern Confucians are not realizable. Modern Confucians follow traditional Confucian thought, which means they can never entirely disown feudalism. Confucian thought was unable to show China the path to modernization in the past, and it will be unable to do so now or in the future. The reason for this lies in the basic fact that in modern history, traditional Chinese culture based upon Confucianism was never able to develop either modern science, or modern democracy. And as we all know, science and democracy are the basic, indispensable elements of Chinese modernization. (Zou Liufang 2012, 3)

The critiques of various scholars from Taiwan and Hong Kong mainly originate among the Modern Daoists, especially Chen Guying, and from currents linked to proponents of Western analytical philosophy (e.g. Feng Yaoming).

The arguments advanced by Modern Daoists against the Modern Confucians are quite similar to those advanced against classical Confucians many centuries ago by the exponents of classical Daoism.

This approach, which can be epitomized as the "critique of the inner autocracy (or dogmatism)", takes the Modern Confucians to task for their overly rigid and formalized academic culture which, being based on the absolute authority of the teacher, discourages critical dialogue and the development of critical thought (Chen Guying 1998, 95). As a true Daoist, Chen Guying also lambasts the Modern Confucians for their "obsession with moral issues and ethics" (Chen Guying 1998, 95), and accuses them of seeking a monopolistic position as the only proper doctrine.[15] He points out that the Chinese tradition can hardly be limited to the Confucians, for the Daoists, Mohists and even Legalists also had very important roles in this tradition. He therefore accuses the Modern Confucians of intolerance and absolutism, a mindset which has led them to view most other philosophical schools almost as forms of heresy. Modern Confucians were incapable of achieving openness, which is the pre-condition of any philosophy worthy of the name, effectively ignoring the ancient Chinese exhortation to establish a "free dialogue between the hundred philosophical schools". Given this anti-democratic approach, their declared search for a synthesis between classical Chinese thought and Western democracy and science was a dead letter; and would remain so until they stopped trying to monopolize the philosophical dialogue and showed themselves to be genuinely tolerant and democratic (Chen Guying 1998, 97). In short, their methods were in blatant contradiction with academic freedom and the autonomy of philosophical thought:

> Of course, modern market society needs ethical grounds; in this sense I agree with Mou's[16] current and support its views. But what I positively detest is this putative self-evidence in their writings with which they give absolute priority to what has already been said. Everything must be as the teacher says and there is, at most, a slight supplement of their previous viewpoints. This is in sharp contrast with the basic principles of academic research. (Chen Guying 1998, 97)

Chen also accused Modern Confucians of monopolising the field of Confucianism by claiming to be its followers, but then being unable to create anything new (the critique of the lack of innovation). This movement was originally supposed to elaborate and transmit the

Confucian classics of the Song and Ming Dynasties, but had proved itself incapable of doing so:

> Zhu Xi was an extraordinary scholar with an unmatched capacity for logically ordered thought and the rational perception of reality. Wang Yangming also had extraordinary cognitive abilities. But if you want to continue their tradition of Mind and Nature (*xinxing*), then you should not discuss these (concepts) in a way that is much less systematic and profound than the thought of the Neo-Confucian classics from the Ming and Song Dynasties. The teachings of Mind and Nature reached the peak of their development in the Song and Ming Dynasties! But now you are living in the twentieth century, and you are still mucking about with these concepts from the twelfth century! And besides, you are not even as good as they were; it is much better for us to study firsthand the original philosophy from the Song and Ming Dynasties! These so-called Modern Confucian "philosophers" are nothing but a miserable and false reflection of this old current. (Chen Guying 1998, 96)

Feng Yaoming instead criticizes their almost exclusive concentration upon moral philosophy, noting that the Neo-Confucian concept of innate knowledge (*liang zhi*) was revised by the Modern Confucians to represent not only the moral but also the ontological foundation of being, whereas an immanent metaphysical subject can, at most, become the object of theological, but not of critical (i.e. objective) theory. (Feng Yaoming 2000, 147)

His interpretative approaches can be summarized by the phrase "the critique of methodological and logical inconsistency". He also rebukes Modern Confucians for their inaccuracy of expression, which they justify with the excuse of the "ineffability" of certain concepts. According to Feng, their use of certain notions, such as "all-embracing", "infinity" or "values" clearly indicates their lack of understanding of these notions, both as such, and in terms of their mutual relations.[17]

> Certain concepts of "infinity" can be expressed by manifest hermeneutics, such as the concept of infinity in mathematics. Others can be defined by recursive procedures. The method of

latent hermeneutics, however, can only express what is not the object of discussion. Even if we investigate that object to the ultimate, possible degree, we will still not be able to affirmatively and directly explain what it actually is. In addition, there are very many "timeless" things and things "transcending birth and extinction", which do not necessarily imply an axiological meaning (*re* categories or forms). And with respect to things which do imply values, it cannot be said that their original form does not mean anything in reality (e.g. God, or the soul). Conversely, not every "infinite" necessarily implies "values". (Feng Yaoming 2000, 151)

For Feng, such ideas ultimately lead to logical confusion and contradictions. This inconclusiveness is, in fact, typical of mysticism (Feng Yaoming 2000, 152), which has nothing to do with science.[18]

3.5 The Problem of "Asian Values"

In dealing with Modern Confucianism and Asian modernization, we have often encountered the fashionable catch-phrase of so-called "Asian values". Even though it has often been closely identified with the Confucian tradition (see for example, Fetzer and Soper 2007; Yu, 2000; de Bary 1998; Lee Hong-jung 2003), this expression has almost nothing to do with the Modern Confucians or their philosophy. However, precisely because of this false identification, and in order to clarify any misunderstandings as to the supposed Confucian roots of this idea, it must be examined in greater detail, and placed in its historical, ideological and sociological context.

Hence, the present chapter is essential to understanding the difference between Modern Confucian philosophy—especially as developed by the representatives of the second generation—and the discourse on Asian values, which is often mistakenly understood as forming part of Modern Confucianism. Given the prevalence of this confusion, it is important to explain why and in what ways Modern Confucians are, instead, generally critical of the concept of "Asian values". Thus, it is also important to illuminate how and why they are mainly criticizing it.

In recent years, the term "Asian values" has represented the key concept of an authoritarian ideology that, in order to contain the presumed threat and risks of "Western" individualism within in their own societies, promoted the "virtues" of Asian communitarism and rigorous government.

> "Asian values" as a doctrine of developmentalism can be understood as the claim that, until prosperity is achieved, democracy remains an unaffordable luxury. This "Protestant ethic" form of "Asian values" attributes high growth rates to certain cultural traits. These characteristics include hard work, frugality, discipline, and teamwork. Western democracy hinders rapid development, authoritarian rulers in the Asia Pacific claim, and thus must be delayed until substantial development has been achieved. (Thompson 2001, 155–6)

It is hardly a coincidence that the concept of Asian values emerged amidst the panorama of new Asian ideologies (especially in Singapore and Malaysia) in the early 1980s, precisely in the period when the (semi-westernized) governments of both countries were confronted for the first time with the phenomena of wider democratic movements and growing individualism among their citizens. This ideology warns against heedlessly embracing "Western" democracy and a free press, watching foreign TV programmes and listening to pop music, in short, all those elements that could lead their countries down the slippery slope of degeneration. In this way, Asian values became the antipodes to everything that was wrong with the West.

> Rising crime and divorce rates—as well as new tastes in music, television, and film—were linked to an electoral swing away from the ruling People's Action Party (whose vote share fell nearly twenty percent between 1980 and 1991). The importance of maintaining "Asian values" could thus justify both draconian laws regarding personal behavior and the crackdown on political opposition in 1987. In short, the Singaporean state had created an ideology to combat democratic tendencies and individualism despite the country's advanced stage of economic development. (Thompson 2001, 157)

After the successful elimination of political opposition by the Malaysian government in the 1980s, Asian values gained importance in that country as well. The then Malaysian Prime Minister Mahathir bin Mohamed argued that these values provided the best foundation for official rule, and criticized Western countries for trying to impose an arbitrary version of "democracy" on that country.[19] He also attacked the West for its growing decadence and used that argument in order to promote Asian values as the best alternative to the risks of "Westernization".

A similar view was taken by government of the P. R. China. In 1995, Jiang Zemin declared at the United Nations general assembly:

> The sacred nature of state sovereignty is inviolable. No state has the right to interfere in the internal affairs of another or force its own will on others. Some large countries frequently use the pretext of "freedom", "democracy" or "human rights" to encroach upon the sovereignty of other states, interfering in their internal affairs, damaging the unity of other countries or the solidarity of their nationalities. This is a major factor behind the lack of peace in the world today. (Jiang Zemin in Moody 1996, 166)

While he did not explicitly refer to the concept of Asian values in this address, his views were supported by the majority of Asian countries and the connection between such highly problematic approaches as "cultural relativism" and Asian cultures as a conceptual unity acquired some institutional corroboration. In fact, even before Jiang's speech, in 1993 a meeting of Asian countries in Bangkok had issued a joint declaration stating that human rights were contingent upon the real culture, history, level of economic development and other similar factors (Moody 1996, 166). Western countries, therefore, had no right to impose their views and consider their own concepts and opinions superior to those of other cultures. This view was expressed most vehemently by the P. R. China and was accepted by the majority of Asian countries, with the exception of Japan and the Philippines.

In order to better understand the historical and social functions of Asian values, Mark R. Thompson (2001, 158) drew a series of historical comparisons between modern Singapore and Malaysia, and imperial Germany of the late nineteenth and early twentieth centuries. He observed many historical parallels and claimed that these similarities were not accidental, for imperial Germany had had a considerable impact on Japanese ideologies in the Meiji era and, through Japan, upon other countries of East and Southeast Asia. Like imperial Germany, Singapore and to a lesser extent Malaysia were also equipped with strong bureaucratic apparatuses that regulated industrial development. But while imperial Germany had had a parliament, parliamentary institutions were purely formal in Singapore and Malaysia and had no significant role in government decision-making.

This concept appeared in the forefront of a wider international exchange thanks to the Prime Minister of Singapore, Lee Kuan Yew, who was reproached by Lee Ming-huei for behaving like "the press secretary for Confucian culture" (2001a, 85). This is quite problematic, of course, and hardly favorable for achieving a broader understanding of the Confucian tradition given that the concept of Asian values is to a great extent rooted in the ideas of the despotic (i.e. legalist) line of Confucianism. This line is grounded in the interpretations of Xunzi, the ancient philosopher who represented a sort of bridge between Confucianism and Legalism. His philosophy served the ideologists of the Han Dynasty as a solid basis for the consolidation of a Confucian ideology that was suited to the needs of the new Han Empire, which had succeeded to the huge centralized Qin Empire and needed an ideology that would justify and support a centralized control over the entire state. This ideology therefore comprised numerous despotic elements (e.g., the principle of collective responsibility or the principle of denunciation). As we noted in the chapter on harmony, this line of Confucianism has also been advocated by the majority of the new Confucian ideologues in the P. R. China. Not surprisingly, Lee Kuan Yew's idea of "Asian values" was very warmly received in mainland China and, in 1994, he was appointed honorary president of the International Confucian Association, in Peking.

We can doubtless agree with Lee Ming-huei (2001a, 85), who claimed that Confucian culture as understood by Lee Kuan Yew is an anti-liberal, despotic culture in which the community is much more important than the individual. In his opinion, while Lee Kuan Yew's critique of Western societies is reasonable, his image of Confucian society is still too one-sided, even if it is not completely in contradiction with the historical facts. The fact that the Confucian cultural tradition has, over the course of Chinese history, often been linked to monarchic despotism, in no way means that despotism was a Confucian ideal.[20] When reading the ancient Confucian classics by Lunyu, Mencius or Xunzi, it becomes very clear that original Confucianism implied a tendency to consider the will of the people. This tendency, of course, is not comparable to democracy in the modern sense, but it nevertheless contains ideal foundations that are suitable for the establishment of a democratic order:

> Not surprisingly, most Modern Confucians advocate the idea and values of democracy, and Lee Kuan Yew's views on the Confucian tradition did not find all Asian leaders in agreement. For example, the South Korean president Kim Dae Jung and the former president of the Republic of China (Taiwan) both confirmed the connection between the Confucian tradition and democracy. (Lee Ming-huei 2001a, 85)

Lee Ming-huei has also criticized the thesis of "Asian values", calling its contents "unclear" (2001a, 85). In his view, the evaluation of Confucianism needs to consider its democratic tendencies, as this is the only way its intellectual heritage, which has preserved its vital force to the present day, can also maintain its significance in future.

In their empirical study on the influence of Confucian values on the views of Taiwanese citizens, S. Fetzer and Christopher J. Soper (2007, 153) found that Confucian values—which they consider to be the core of Asian values—were not in substantial contradiction with the principles of liberal democracy, and that none of its three central values (i.e. loyalty or filial piety, social hierarchy and the idea of social harmony) could be regarded as reducing the support for democracy. They also concluded that many Confucian values could reduce certain "phenomena" associated with Western style democracy and its glorification of individualism. In particular, the Confucian communitarian ethics, which are defined by principles of mediation and the concept of the extended family, could offer new ways of joining people in communities, while the principle of social harmony which repudiates the one-dimensional glorification of individual rights regardless of their social and cultural context, also appears as a positive factor for coexistence. In this framework, they even found certain positive aspects in the ethic of filial piety, as a way for individuals to transcend their narrow egoistical interests and recognize their responsibilities towards previous generations (Fetzer and Soper 2007, 154). In their view, democracy is by no means incompatible with Confucian values, such that linking or creating a synthesis of the two discourses is unnecessary. They concluded their study with the declared hope that a growing percentage within the overall Asian population will become the driving force in reviving those traditional elements which are favourable to democratic development and social progress.

However, in his critique of de Bary's book, *Asian Values and Human Rights: A Confucian Communitarian Perspective*, Anthony C. Yu offers a decisive rebuttal of such views:

> Against this line of argument, the following points may be made: First, among contemporary sinologists outside China, Confucian revivalists such as Wang Gungwu, Tu Wei-ming, Julia Ching, Irene Bloom, and de Bary himself, have repeatedly emphasized the reciprocity of obligations expected of differentiated human relations (*renlun*) as a less stridently individualistic and more desirable (because more communitarian) precursor of the notion of rights. What they consistently fail to acknowledge is the asymmetry of these "principles of relations (*lunli*, the literal Chinese translation of 'ethics')" and the resulting inequality of obligations presumed in the hierarchical conception of relations and obligations. (Yu 2000, 300)

Here, we need to point out that hierarchy, which is doubtless paramount in the Confucian concept of social structure, is clearly based on inequality. However, parliamentary democracy is also based upon a hierarchical decision-making process and system, while the basic premise of the Confucian model of hierarchy can instead be identified in the principle of a representation which is reciprocal, correlative and complementary. There is thus a mutual conditioning and co-dependence of both levels within the hierarchic structure, which requires that the superior entity always recognize its responsibility to represent the interests of its subordinates, i.e. of the hierarchically inferior entity. This responsibility towards subordinates is clearly manifested in the canonical Confucian virtue of justice (*yi*), which represents the elementary principle of governance in original Confucianism:

> If the relations between old and young may not be neglected, why should the duties that should be observed between sovereign and minister be neglected? If one wishes to maintain personal purity, how can he permit human relations to come to confusion? A nobleman takes office, and performs the righteous duties belonging to that office. (Confucius 2012a, Wei zi 7)

Of the classical Confucians, Mencius was the one who always stressed the responsibility of the rulers towards their people:

> When the importance of human relations is clear to superiors, kindly feelings will prevail among the people below. (Mencius 2012, Teng Wen gong I/3) ... There should be closeness and affection between father and son, justice and righteousness between sovereign and minister, separate functions between husband and wife, proper order between old and young and sincere fidelity between friends ... People should be encouraged and led; they should be rectified and made straight; they should be guided, so they can grow wings and become possessors of themselves. On such a basis they can become virtuous. (Mencius 2012, Teng Wen gong I/4)

In traditional Confucianism, the concept of the "Heavenly Mandate" (*tian ming*) represents the highest criteria for the measurement or evaluation of a ruler's suitability:[21] "A nobleman is in awe of three phenomena. These are the Heavenly Mandate, great personalities and the teachings of the sages" (Confucius 2012a, Ji shi 8).

Even Xunzi, whose works provided the basis for a new Confucian state doctrine that implied despotic-legalist elements during the Han Dynasty, stressed that a good government should always consider the needs and interests of the people. If a ruler did not show a proper responsibility towards his subjects, they had a legitimate right to take his power from him.

> A ruler is like a boat and common people are like water. The boat can be carried by the water, but water can also overturn it. If a ruler wants to rule in peace, the best thing he can do is love his people. (Xunzi 2011, Wang zhi 5)

Claiming Confucian roots for the concept of Asian values, as its proponents continue to do, thus appears as both groundless and one dimensional. Indeed, the very foundation of this concept is problematic, for even in the context of its allegedly indigenous culture it appears as a completely artificial construct. As Peter R. Moody Jr. (1996, 166) pointed out, the term Asia denotes a superficial and insufficiently defined geographic notion, given that in the pan-Asian area there exist many different cultures with prevailing values that differ from one another in the same way that specific prevailing values differ within Western axiological systems. "Traditional" values which purportedly prevailed before the invasion of Western culture, functions as the single point of reference which is meant to link these values to one another. Of course, this does not reduce the generalization on which this apparently post-colonial ideal construct rests, for the "Confucian tradition"[22] which is meant to symbolically connect all these different values, is likewise an artificial construct; it is, fact, a hybrid model of a "homogeneous" Confucianism that in reality does not exist. Thus, one of the basic characteristics of the concept of Asian values is this function of reproducing the methods of so-called "reversed Orientalism" (Hill 2000, 177).

The general orientation of the concept of Asian values has also been criticized by Yu Ying-shih in his *Confucianism and China's Encounter with the West in Historical Perspective* (2005). In this essay, he tries to differentiate between the values proposed by advocates of Asian values and those advanced by the Modern Confucians, concluding that the authors of the Declaration advocated an interpretation of the Chinese cultural heritage that implied certain modern Western values, such as science and democracy (Yu Ying-shih 2005, 214). In this context, he also criticizes Huntington's thesis on the "clash of civilizations" (Huntington 1993):[23]

> It is rather unfortunate that Huntington speculates a great deal about the prospect of a clash between Chinese and Western

civilizations without a basic historical grasp of the developments of Confucianism in modern and contemporary China. He seems to rely heavily on Lee Kuan Yew of Singapore, as the sole authoritative interpreter of Confucianism who, as Havel says, takes great interest in the Confucian tradition only to use it to condemn Western democracy. I do not deny that a deep-seated antagonism does seem to exist between the regime in Peking and the West. However, the source of this antagonism clearly lies elsewhere. It is only fair that Confucian culture be absolved of all blame. (Yu Ying-shih 2005, 215)

4. The "Second Generation"

Most of the second generation of Modern Confucians whose philosophical discourses played an important role in the "developing years"[1] of the Confucian reform, lived and worked in Taiwan and/or Hong Kong. Their philosophy was thus defined to a great extent by the cultural and political characteristics of these societies between 1950 and 1980. The most important members of this "generation" are Tang Junyi, Xu Fuguan, Mou Zongsan and Fang Dongmei.

Most of the members of the second generation tried even harder to revitalize their cultural identity, in what they termed "replanting the old roots" of their tradition. Due to the challenge posed by Western cultures, they saw this as the only way for their own cultural tradition to survive. However, if this revitalization of the "roots" is carried out properly, it should not only guarantee the survival of this culture but ensure an active and innovative role for Modern Confucianism and modern Chinese philosophy in the international "polylogue" among modern societies (Yu Ying-shih 2005, 215).

4.1 The Teachers: A Short Introduction of the First Generation

The four above-mentioned pioneers of the modern Confucian current have not only laid the foundation of the Confucian revival, but have also had a strong impact upon its further future development. Here, the most influential figure was doubtless Xiong Shili, who many consider to be the greatest pioneer of modern

Confucian reform (cf. Yu Jiuyuan 2002, 127). However, before introducing his main contributions to the Confucian revival more in detail, let us first take a look upon the most significant work of the other four representatives of the first generation.

Feng Youlan (1859–1990) was one of the greatest officially acknowledged philosophical authorities of twentieth century China. He was born in Henan province, where he also completed his schooling. In 1915, he began to study Chinese philosophy at Peking University and upon graduating in 1919, he moved to the United States where, as a student of John Dewey's, he obtained his PhD from Columbia University.[2] Even though he studied with the same tutor as his predecessor, Hu Shi, and although he was greatly influenced by Western pragmatism and neo-realism,[3] especially in his early work, Feng's philosophy differs greatly from Hu Shi's. While Hu pursued his liberal, moderate progressive worldview and tried to Westernize and establish the analytical foundations for Chinese systems through a correct scientific methodology, Feng's intellectual development tended increasingly towards the original values inherent in the Chinese, and particularly Neo-Confucian tradition of thought. It seems somehow paradoxical, therefore, that the more progressive Hu gave up all his academic positions in the PRC and immigrated to Taiwan after the Communist party took power, while the much more conservative Feng readily accepted the new ideological directives of the PRC in order to preserve his position as a renowned academic authority. However, this paradox is only apparent for, in adapting to the new government, Feng by no means abandoned his Confucian outlook. While the new regime criticized classical Confucians, this criticism was essentially formal and superficial, given that, to a certain degree—the new system also functioned within the framework of Confucian values, though overlaid with a thick layer of communist terminology. Thus, in his subordination to the new oligarchy, Feng was actually still following the basic values of traditional Confucian doctrine in the sense of loyalty (*zhong*) to the ruler, his ideologies and the state institutions (Rošker 2008, 158). Feng's main philosophical work, *The New School of Principles* (*Xin lixue*)[4] represents an elaboration and modernization of Neo-Confucian thought, as it had been developed by Cheng Yi, Cheng Hao and Zhu Xi. Despite his coherent application of Neo-Confucian terminology, Feng redefined the central terms of this classical Chinese system in the light of a formal analytical system based upon a logical metaphysical understanding of the nature of being (Rošker 2008, 158).

Carsun Chang (1877–1969) was also widely known as Zhang Junmai. He was an important twentieth-century Chinese thinker, who's participation in the aforementioned controversy on *Science and Metaphysics* of 1923 made a strong philosophical impression on an entire generation of Chinese intellectuals. In this controversy, he defended his modern Confucian views against those of Chinese progressives and scientists. He championed the value of traditional Confucian knowledge and asserted the limits of scientific proofs. Subsequently, Zhang's two-volume study of *The Development of Neo-Confucian Thought* (Chang 1957, 1962) cemented his identification with Confucianism and the view of Confucianism as compatible with Western modernity (Ciaudo 2014, 2). As previously mentioned, he was also the main author of the *Modern Confucian Manifesto* (*Declaration of Chinese Culture to the Scholars of the World*). Besides, Zhang was also influenced by Western philosophy, especially by the work of the French thinker Henri Bergson and exponents of German Idealism, particularly Immanuel Kant and Georg Wilhelm Friedrich Hegel. However, today, Zhang is best known not for his original philosophical work but rather his political activities during China's Republican era (1912–49), through which he and his "Third Force" party (Ciaudo 2014, 2) attempted to mediate between the polarized Nationalist and Communist factions in the Chinese political landscape, as well as his promotion of Neo-Confucian studies in the West. As Joseph Ciaudo points out (Ciaudo 2014, 12), his participation in both philosophy and politics makes him an exemplary Confucian and an embodiment of the Neo-Confucian ideal of *zhixing heyi* ("the unity of knowledge and action").

Although Liang Shuming (1893–1988) was a pioneer of the Modern Confucian revival, in Western academic circles he is better known as "the last Confucian".[5] John J. Hanafin, who introduces the philosopher in John Makeham's anthology on "New Confucianism", instead claims that his thought was not only Confucian, but even more Buddhist. Liang himself seems to have been of this same opinion, for in his study, *How Should We Evaluate Confucius Today?* (*Jintian women yinggai ruhe pingjia Kongzi*) he states that Xiong Shili should be considered a Confucian, whereas he himself was a Buddhist (Liang Shuming 1993, 19). However, such categorizations are always very problematic for, as we already noted, the Neo-Confucian system of thought which underlies the Modern Confucian movement was, together with other influences, deeply rooted in Buddhist philosophy. Hence, many Buddhist concepts can be found in almost all of the representatives of the first generation, and especially in the works of Feng and Xiong, where Buddhist and Confucian elements are inextricably interfused. Like Xiong, Liang was most probably originally a Buddhist. In 1917, he was appointed professor of Buddhism at Peking University, the first scholar ever to occupy such a position in a Chinese university. His interpreters are generally in agreement that his return to Confucianism in 1918 was prompted by his father's suicide.

Liang's most influential work, *Dongxiwenhua ji qi zhexue* (*The Cultures of East and West and Their Philosophies*), was based on his lectures at Peking University and expounds many of the Modern Confucian teachings. He became famous (or, in Maoist circles, infamous) for his critique of Marxist class theory, arguing that the class struggle could not be implemented in China because its society was based upon large clans, with a wide disparity in wealth. The class struggle advocated by the Maoists would thus lead to internecine conflicts within these clans, resulting in the complete destruction of traditional values.

He Lin (1902–92) is probably the least-known representative of the first generation. As a child, He Lin received a Confucian education and relatively early developed a strong interest in the neo-Confucianism of the Song and Ming Dynasties. In 1919, he enrolled at the Qinghua University, where he first met Liang Shuming, through who's influence he became a "devoted follower of the teaching of Wang Yangming" (Ci 2002, 189). In 1926, he moved to the USA to further study philosophy at the University of Chicago. However, he didn't like the pragmatic orientation which prevailed at that university and left soon for Harvard, where he developed a deep interest in Spinoza, Hegel and their followers. In 1930, after he obtained his master in philosophy, this interest has led him to Germany in search for a more profound understanding of the German Idealism. But only one year after that he interrupted his studies because of the Japanese invasion and returned to China. He was teaching at the Peking University until 1955, when he was put in charge of the study of Western philosophy at the Chinese Academy of Social Sciences.

In his entire life, he tried to find a unity of his philosophical interest in idealism (especially Hegel) on the one hand, and his political interest in national salvation and betterment on the other (Ci 2002, 190).

He was also profoundly interested in certain epistemological questions, especially in the problem of the nature of the relation between theory and praxis, i.e. between "knowledge and action" (*zhi xing*), which represented one of the central epistemological problems of traditional China. Although his theory of knowledge did not contribute anything fundamentally new in terms of forming new approaches to comprehension, He was one of several theorists who tried to revitalize those aspects of the controversies of ancient Chinese philosophy which could provide suitable elements for a specifically Chinese theoretical revival in the field of Confucian epistemology. Nevertheless, the crucial points of He Lin's epistemological renewal, in their modernized synthesis of knowledge and action, represent the foundations of the sinificated versions of Marxist theories, reiterating as they did the holistic aspects of the traditional inseparability of both concepts, which corresponded neatly with socialist ideals of connecting theory with praxis. Not surprisingly, similar approaches had already been formulated by earlier social-democratic thinkers, such as Sun Yat-Sen (Sun Zhongshan, 1866–1925). In his political theories, Sun also addressed the traditional question of the relation between knowledge and action and, like He Lin, he also argued for their inseparable unity (Rošker 2008, 298).

As already mentioned, the most important representatives of the first generation was probably Xiong Shili (1885–1968), who was the teacher of almost all philosophers belonging to the second generation. Here, the only exception was Fang Dongmei; however, even though he was never a direct student of Xiong Shili, their work showed numerous similarities. They both emphasized the importance of the traditional Chinese binary category of substance (*ti*) and function (*yong*) when determining the relation between the spheres of noumenon and phenomenon and both tried hard to shed some light on the relation between philosophy and science. Regarding the three other representatives of the second generation, we have to point out that, they remained true to their professor in their basic orientation and methodology, although they also significantly modified his teachings—of course each in his own specific way (Feng Yaoming 1992, 227).

Xiong is also important as one of the first Chinese philosophers who developed his own system of thought based upon classical Confucian concepts, but adapted to modern conditions. He was doubtless one of the most innovative and creative philosophers in recent Chinese thought, and also one of the first contemporary Chinese philosophers to create their own, specific philosophical system. In his work, this modernized tradition is primarily reflected in the fields of ontology, ethics and epistemology.

Xiong Shili was born into the poor family of a village teacher in rural Hubei province. As a child, he helped maintain his family, especially after his father's death, when Xiong Shili was only ten years old. Xiong was therefore never formally educated. As a teenager, he subscribed to revolutionary thought, advocating the overthrow of the monarchy and the founding of a Republic. In 1920, he finally began to study Buddhist thought systematically in Nanjing, and two years later he became a lecturer in Buddhist philosophy at Peking University. Here, he had the opportunity for a more detailed and deeper understanding of Confucian and especially Neo-Confucian philosophy, which made a profound impression on him. Soon after, he abandoned his Buddhist teachings, although his philosophical production, especially his ontology and theory of knowledge, remained strongly influenced by Buddhist, particularly Chan-Buddhist thought.[6] This "divorce" from Buddhism was quite already evident in his first serious philosophical work, *New Treatise on Consciousness-only* (*Xin weishi lun*), which appeared in 1932 and immediately gave rise to a storm of polemics. While many scholars believed that it represented the origins of an important, authentic new philosophy, which made possible a synthesis of Chinese tradition and modern streams of thought, Xiong was fiercely attacked by the majority of Buddhist philosophers, who accused him of being a "faithless apostate" and "traitor". (Feng Yaoming 1992, 302) The *New Treatise on Consciousness-only* originally appeared in ancient Chinese, but in 1944, Xiong published an expanded version written in modern

Chinese. In his second main work, *The Theory of Substance and Function (Tiyong lun)* Xiong explained the ontological presuppositions of his system. A number of important paradigms of renewed Confucianism can also be found in *The Original Confucianism (Yuan ru)* and *Clear Mind (Ming xin pian)*. Although his chief concern was the ideal renewal of Confucian tradition, he also made important contributions to Buddhist philosophy.

It was Xiong's belief that future philosophy would be based on a synthesis of Indian, European and Chinese traditions of thought. In his own work, he sought to rediscover and renew the most enduring elements of the Confucian ideal tradition, i.e. those elements which would not only help China to find a way out of the crisis of that time, but could also offer a specific and valuable contribution to the further development of world philosophy. Through the appropriation of some aspects of Buddhism and combining these with his sophisticated knowledge of the *Book of Changes*, Xiong tried to provide Confucianism—which has traditionally been regarded as only an ethics—with a more solid metaphysical basis and a more dynamic character (Rošker 2008, 213–5). After the founding of the PRC, Xiong remained at Peking University and continued to teach until his retirement. After his retirement, he moved to Shanghai, where he continued to study and write. In contrast to many of his colleagues, the "communist" oligarchy had always allowed him to work in peace and did not force him to compose "Marxist self-criticisms" or rewrite and "repair" his former theories. In fact, even after 1949, Xiong Shili was still able to obtain government subsidies for publishing his works. However, at the beginning of the Cultural Revolution, he still suffered some physical abuse. Seeing that Confucianism had suffered yet another disaster, he died in anger and despair in 1968 at the age of 84 (Rošker 2008, 213–5).

4.2 The New Moral Metaphysics: Mou Zongsan

Mou was the most important Taiwanese philosopher from 1980 to the time of his death. An innovative theorist, he was the best known second generation Modern Confucian. He wrote mostly on logic and metaphysics, but also occasionally delved into political theory. He was an open and radical opponent of Marxism and Marxist theory and thus of the dominant ideology in the P. R. China. In terms of general methodology, Mou followed his teacher Xiong, re-evaluating the Chinese philosophical tradition through the perspective of Modern European philosophy, especially Kant.

He was born in 1909, into a poor peasant family in the Chinese province of Shandong. Despite his unfavourable social origins, he managed to enrol at the University of Peking (Beijing daxue) in order to study philosophy. As is well known, (see for instance Lee Ming-huei 2001a, 65), Peking was then the cultural center of China and under Cai Yuanpei the University of Peking became the most important Chinese university. Its teaching methods were very open and it promoted free debate. This meant that a wide range of views could be heard at the university—from the most conservative to the most radical. Mou's gift for philosophy developed in this environment (Mou Zongsan, 1989a, 34–35).

In this very favorable setting, he not only studied traditional Chinese philosophy, especially Zhu Xi's School of Structure (*Li xue*), but also various Western philosophical systems. Initially, he was attracted by thinkers such as Bergson, Dewey and Darwin, who were "fashionable" among young intellectuals at that time.[7] None of these thinkers had a lasting influence on him, although Mou stuck to their systematic and structured thought that he encountered while reading their texts. Somewhat later he became interested in the philosophy of Bertrand Russell, mathematical logic and neo-empiricism. During this period he extensively studied the works of Whitehead and Wittgenstein, as well as the *Book of Changes* (*Yi jing*) (Mou Zongsan 1989a, 42). As a result of his studies linked to the *Book of Changes*, he published his first book entitled *Research of the metaphysical and moral philosophy of China from the aspect of the Book of Changes* (*Cong Zhouyi fangmian yanjiu Zhongguo zhi xuanxue yu daode zhexue*). This book was published in Tianjin already in 1935, i.e. soon after he completed his studies. His interest in the *Book of Changes* was induced by his research into the philosophy of Whitehead (Mou Zongsan 1988, 4), during which he ascertained that his views differ greatly from the views of this modern British mathematical philosopher, whose works were popular in China at the time. While Whitehead considered aesthetic perception and intuition to be two physical realities, autonomous and external to each other, in Mou's view, the opposite was true (Mou Zongsan 1988, 4).

Despite these basic differences, in his early years Mou was arguably the only modern Confucian to approach the original teachings through logic. And although his unconditional enthusiasm for the logical method was limited to his early works and he later acknowledged the imperfections inherent in this method, in a certain sense he never stopped using it (Tang Refeng 2002, 328).

Like Zhang Dongsun and other Chinese theorists of the early twentieth century, Mou Zongsan used logic to counter Marxism and refute dialectical materialism. But with his book *Logical paradigms* (*Luoji dianfan*) (1941), his interest in logic took a new direction. The book is an attempt to go beyond logical formalism, which Mou saw as not only conditioning but hindering true philosophy. In this work, he began to focus on the concept of the reason, its functions, operation and structure. Underlying this approach was a very close study of Kant's philosophy, especially the three critiques.[8] Mou's aim in reading Kant was to find a way that would lead him through logic to metaphysics. The results of his attempt to connect the two disciplines can be found in his work, *A Critique of Cognitive Heart-mind* (*Renshi xinde pipan*), which was written over a ten-year period and appeared in 1965. A basic premise of this work is that logic does not depend on actual reality and the relations within it. Ultimately, in his research he was seeking the ultimate origin or source of all logical methods. He later claimed that while writing it, he "knocked on the door that led to the subject of realization" (Mou 1989, 72). What was waiting for him behind this door and the impact this encounter would have on the further development of his philosophy—and of modern Confucian theory in general—will be described in greater detail below.

In 1939, Mou met his most important teacher, Xiong Shili, with whom he would remain in contact for as long as the political situation permitted. Xiong left a permanent mark on the young philosopher. Many years later, Mou remembered their first encounter as follows: "This was my first opportunity to meet a truly perfected person (*zhen ren*). For the first time, I could sense the fragrance of a scholarship linked to life itself"(Mou 1984, 134–5).

In his book, *The Teaching of Life* (*Shengmingde xuewen*), he cites the basic ideas that he was introduced to by Xiong. For Mou, these "teachings of life" were not based solely on a conceptual, but also on an "existential" understanding of life (Mou 1984, 134–5).

In late 1939, he got to know his best friend Tang Junyi (Chan 2011, 65), who was also Xiong's student, and this meeting led him to become interested in Neo-Confucian philosophy once again.

Following the second world war and the completion of his studies he moved to Nanjing, where he became a lecturer at Zhongyang University. After the founding of the P. R. China he escaped to Taiwan (Zhou and Yan 1995, 382; Tang Refeng 2002, 328). During his first years on the island, Mou—similar to other modern Confucians—dealt with the question as to why has traditional Chinese culture with its paradigmatic philosophical patterns and social interactions pushed the state to the edge of a ravine and led it backwards (Mou 1975, 439–42).

By this time, the majority of Chinese intellectuals had already been striving to understand the reasons for this crisis, and why China remains so backward with respect to the Euro-American cultures, for over a century. Here, too, the culprit was none other than Confucianism; "obsessed" as it was with moral cultivation, it was accused of hindering the development of pure knowledge, science and democracy. It is hardly accidental, therefore, that Mou often dealt with this problem in his writings, and tried to formulate arguments in favor of Confucianism. The most important of these arguments, innate knowledge, was developed quite late in his career. However, as Mou himself acknowledges, this idea was not original (Fang and Li 1995, 396), but was implicit in Wang Yangming's description of the functions of inborn knowledge (*liang zhi*), which led to the "self-negation" of the moral self (Mou 1975, 123).

To support this thesis, he turned to the concept of "the inner sage and outer ruler (*neisheng waiwang*),"[9] which views the moral self and political governance in a relation of complementarity. Like all advocates of tradition, Mou was convinced that the world of pragmatic action and politics should always be closely linked to the self-cultivation of individuals. This meant that the solution to all social problems was to be found in a higher level of moral awareness or maturity. These new-found convictions led him to focus again on classical Chinese philosophy. However, his research was not limited to Confucianism, but also included Daoist and Buddhist thought, especially their epistemologies. His study of traditional Chinese philosophy continued all through his years as a professor at The Chinese University of Hong Kong (Xianggang Zhongwen daxue). Following Tang Junyi's invitation, he has namely moved to Hong Kong in 1960; he officially retired from the Chinese University of Hong Kong in 1974, but continued to teach and lecture in Hong Kong and Taiwan until his death in 1995 (Clower 2014, 2).

His most important works were written after the age of 50. These include *Material Nature and Profound Principle* (*Caixing yu xuanli*, 1963), which examines the philosophy of the Wei and Jin, and the North and South dynasties,[10] and the imposing *Heart-mind as Reality and Nature as Reality* (*Xinti yu xingti*, 1968) and *From Lu Xiangshan to Liu Jishan* (*Cong Lu Xiangshan dao Liu Jishan*, 1979), in which he presented his interpretation of Neo-Confucian philosophy during the Song (960–1279) and Ming (1368–1644) dynasties, in terms of their central concepts, contents and historical development.

In his later years he rediscovered Buddhism; this interest is reflected in his book *Buddha Nature and Prajñā* (*Foxing yu bore*, 1977), which is dedicated to the epistemological aspects of the Huayan and Tiantai schools. In these works, he examined certain characteristics typical of specific periods, orientations or schools in the history of Chinese philosophy. However, they are anything but academic overviews, and instead represent the search for an original philosophical starting point and important steps in the development of his own philosophical system. Although in essence, these works grew from his earlier periods, they were also a necessary preparation for his later philosophical system of moral metaphysics. In this context, we should note that these many voluminous works on the history of Chinese thought, including those dedicated to Buddhism, should not be considered as mere academic exercises, for they embody Mou's very real efforts to develop his own philosophical system, a system which he would formulate with ever greater clarity over the course of his career.

In 1971, he published what is generally considered his most important work, *Intellectual Intuition and Chinese Philosophy* (*Zhide zhijue yu Zhongguo zhexue*), in which he examined the specific Chinese understanding of the structure of existence. In doing so, he drew certain parallels with Heidegger's ontology and pointed out inconsistencies in Kant's theories. Until the end of his philosophical career, Kant was both a fundamental source of inspiration and the object of harsh criticism. Due to the existential significance Kant ascribed to morality,[11] Mou considered him to be the pinnacle of European and Western philosophy. At the same time, he was convinced that his theoretical system was flawed and logically inconsistent. Indeed, one is sometimes left with the sensation that, for Mou, Kant's greatest failing was not having had a solid classical Confucian education, which would have helped him to fill the gaps in his worldview. Not surprisingly, much of Mou's work is dedicated to performing a series of "upgrades" and "repairs" on Kant's philosophy. Mou was convinced that along this line of thought he could build a valid moral metaphysics, which Kant did not succeed in building (Mou 1975, 37). For Mou, moral metaphysics' refers to the existence of things with moral substance that are reflected by moral consciousness. Thus, for him, this clear consciousness is the "moral substance, and, at the same time ontological substance" (Mou 1975, 40).

In working out his thesis, Mou relied on his earlier study, *Criticism of Cognitive Heart-mind* (*Renshi xinzhi pipan*), in which he had laid the groundwork for his Confucian rehabilitation model and his expansion of it, especially in the area of Chinese onto-epistemology.[12] Contemporary scholars generally consider *Appearance and the thing-in-itself* (*Xianxiang yu wu zishen*) and *On Summum Bonum* (*Yuan shan lun*) as his second most important works. In *Appearance and the thing-in-itself* he uses traditional Chinese philosophy to redefine the concepts of noumenon and phenomenon and their reciprocal relation. While writing this work, he also translated Kant's "three critiques" into Chinese.[13] Hence, Mou based his idea of "double ontology" on this new-found distinction between phenomena and "things in themselves".

> If we start from the assumption that "man is finite as well as infinite", we must apply ontology on two levels. The first is the ontology of the noumenal sphere, or the "detached ontology". The second is the ontology of the sphere of appearances, or the "attached ontology". (Mou 1975, 30)

Double ontology is thus divided into the noumenal and phenomenal, or the attached and detached ontology. Within the frame of these two ontologies, he defines detachment and attachment as follows:

> "Detached" corresponds to "the free and unlimited heart-mind" (in the sense of Wang Yangming's clear heart-mind of the cognitive subject)... "Attached" corresponds to the "attachment of the cognitive subject". (Mou 1975, 39)

Confucian metaphysics, which is also included in his noumenal ontology, is understood as not only "detached" (*wuzhi cunyoulun*) but also "transcendental" (Mou 1975, 39). A metaphysics of this kind is possible due to intellectual intuition (*zhide zhijue*). Hence, the "detached ontology" corresponds to the free and unlimited heart-mind (*ziyoude wuxian xin*).[14] Parallel to this ontology of detachment is the "attached ontology". Thus, both the "detached" and "attached" ontology are linked to the cognitive subject or cognitive perception.

In his work, *On summum bonum* (*Yuan shan lun*), Mou Zongsan examines Kant's moral philosophy, and its conclusion that happiness and the ultimate good (*summum bonum*; *yuan shan*) are impossible to achieve on earth, and can only exist in the perfection of god's world. In this context Mou emphasised the value and contribution of practical philosophy, upon which traditional Chinese—especially Confucian—philosophy is based. This is focused on the earthly life; on the here and now, in which there is no need to run into other, "supernatural" worlds. Of course, even Chinese philosophy could not "save" Kant's *summum bonum* problem, however in his work with the same title Mou exposes the problems linked to dealing with this problem in Western, especially Kantian discourses. According to Liu Shu-hsien (2003, 485), the Chinese people know only too well that in real life, happiness and the good rarely go together. However, in his *Yuan shan lun* Mou Zongsan exposed that they need not to look forward to another worldly kingdom of God. No matter what happens in human lives and how imperfect the earthly world is, human beings can always find fulfilment in this world. Consequently, they can always find fulfilment in non-fulfilment. In such view, *summum bonum* is realized here and now and there is no need to look for a kingdom of God in the other world.

According to Mou, the moral self that is expressed through the natural moral substance (*xingti*) unites in itself the three essential postulates of Kant's practical mind, i.e. free will, the immortality of the soul and the existence of god. "As soon as the infinite perception of substance materializes within me, free will, immortality and God can no longer exist" (Mou Zongsan 1975, 45).

Mou took Kant to task for the artificial division of his three postulates, for in his view all three are infinite and absolute. Since it is impossible for multiple, infinite and absolute entities to coexist, the three postulates are, in fact, a single substance, that can be epitomized in the term original heart-mind (*ben xin*), which is one of the forms of infinite heart-mind (*wuxiande zhixin*).[15] Mou concludes that the moral self, or original heart-mind, which is its essence, offers the only real possibility for merging happiness and goodness (Mou Zongsan 1985, 334–5). In Mou's view, Kant was "entangled" with the idea of God; and this idea constituted a superfluous and disturbing element in his theoretical system. Kant should have eliminated God, as in all coherent moral philosophies (e.g. Buddhism). According to Kant, given that the world was created by God, it could not change in accordance with the moral development of man. Kant was thus unable to explain the idea of *summum bonum*.

Contrary to current views of Confucianism as authoritarian, Mou argued convincingly that moral autonomy was implicit in Confucian philosophy (Mou 1979, 224). Even Kant was inadequate in this case. Limited by his Christian background, Kant treated free will as a postulate of practical reason, the other two postulates being the immortality of the soul and the existence of God. Hence, he could only establish a metaphysics of morals or, at best, a moral theology, but never a moral metaphysics. Mou felt that the Chinese tradition went further than Kant in this respect (Mou 1985, 330–5).

In Mou's later years, it became increasingly clear that his philosophical approach presupposed a moral metaphysics. As he clearly demonstrates in his work, *Nineteen Lectures in Chinese Philosophy* (*Zhongguo zhexue shijiu jiang*), this approach is also the main starting point of classic Confucian philosophy (Mou 1983a, 71–6). Like most Modern Confucians, he believed that the traditional *Tian* (Nature, Heaven) concept represents the origins of everything that exists, or the reason all (existing) things exist (Mou 1983a, 75). The merger of self with this proto-origin of all that exists can only take place through infinite heart-mind, i.e. when one allows the effects of their innate moral substance (*xingti*) to take control. When this takes place, one intuitively comes to know their true self (*neibude zhijue*, Mou 1971,

132). This experience or discovery is not a concept, neither is it the result of dialectical reasoning. However, this moral self, or self-intuition, which pours out spontaneously from one's inner self, is—through its conscious awareness—also permeating everything else that exists (Mou 1971, 200), for "it is omni-inclusive and the source of everything. It not only determines each individual's moral behavior, but also the existence of every plant and tree (Mou 1971, 191).

In this context, Mou's views regarding the existence of the concept of autonomy within traditional Chinese or Confucian thought is of particular importance, for he thereby refutes one of the key arguments of the May Fourth movement, which posited that personal autonomy was necessarily linked to individualism. In other words, Mou Zongsan demonstrates that Mencius' concept of innate morality (*renyi neizai*) corresponds to Kant's understanding of autonomy (Mou Zongsan 1985, 1–58). This conclusion is significant, for it shows that Weber's criticism of Confucianism is mistaken, rooted as it is in a misapprehension of the core tenets of Chinese philosophy. In Weber's view (and Hegel's before him), Confucianism was a kind of folk morality that did not offer any potential for speculative philosophy. It was basically an uncreative ideology that merely helped people adapt to the conditions of the external world. Instead, Mou's analysis unmasks the considerable bias and prejudice implicit in these views.

The emphasis on ethical issues, which is characteristic of modern Confucianism, is thus clearly evident throughout Mou Zongsan's work. However, Mou did not consider moral philosophy to be the only priority of ancient Chinese thought.

He argued forcefully against the idea that Confucianism is concerned only with morality and has nothing to do with existence (Mou 1983a, 71). Moreover, he believed that Confucian morality implied a moral metaphysics, that is, a metaphysics based on morality (Mou 1975, 37).

In his view, all three central philosophical Chinese classic discourses deal with metaphysics in various ways. However, they all are based upon a mental level, which surpasses mere rational recognition:

> Regardless of whether we are referring to Daoism, Confucianism, or even Buddhism, which entered these discourses much later, their most significant teachings all go beyond rational intellect.

> This means that insights and recognitions which in Western philosophy could only be obtained through divine consciousness, for the Chinese sages can instead be attained by the human mind. (Mou 1989a, 527)

Still, in this metaphysical field he sees Confucianism as the line of philosophical thought that added the most to the formation of these specific Chinese discourses. However, it is precisely this absolutization of Confucianism as the only truly important theory that disturbs most of his numerous critics; Fang Dongmei, who we will discuss in greater detail in the following chapter, and Chen Guying both reproach him for his arrogance that results from him being a member of this, what he assumes is the "only proper" line of thought (*daotong*), and the latter additionally reproaches him for his conceited advocacy of his absolute authority as a teacher. According to Chen, this dogmatism had harsh consequences also for the preservation of the beauty of the style and preciseness of the language used by Chinese humanistic sciences, for his students, who were used to uncritically accepting his thoughts, also accepted his style characteristics in the same uncritical manner which led to "an awful language pollution" (Chen Guying 1998, 95). Other critics, such as the well-known mainland New Confucian, Jiang Qing (2011, 42), have even repudiated Mou Zongsan, citing his wholesale acceptance of Western liberty and democracy as highly problematic.

Most scholars, however, stress his active and constructive role in the development of Modern Confucian theoretical thought. His many critics notwithstanding (some of whom are certainly very superficial), Mou definitely must be considered as one of the most sophisticated and creative Chinese language theorists of the twentieth century.

4.3 Fang Dongmei and the Philosophy of Creative Creativity

As we noted in our introduction, Fang Dongmei never considered himself to be a Modern Confucian, given that his philosophical interests also included traditional Buddhist and Daoist thought. Regarding this question, some scholars (i.e. Li Chenyang 2002, 269) claim that Fang's work stands beyond the Confucian tradition, because he did not regard Confucianism as the only legitimate philosophy and all others as heresies, as for instance Mou Zongsan. On the contrary, Fang Dongmei argued that Laozi's Daoism was the leading and most legitimate philosophical school during ancient times. Besides, they belive he saw Confucianism, Daoism, Mohism and Buddhism as mutually interacting and integrating components of a holistic cultural process, rather than as several distinct schools of thought.[16] However, he still acknowledged the preeminent role of Confucian thought:

> In Chinese philosophy, Confucianism is the body of thought that guides people through their lives. As for Daoism, it collapsed during the corrupt period of the Han Dynasty. Even though it was eventually revived, and with it the renewed striving towards ideals, in our view the real Daoists are those artists who consider the world to be useless. … After the Wei-Jin period, Buddhist thought spread throughout Chinese society, and compensated for certain Daoist deficiencies. The Buddhists, however, seek their own personal salvation, which has nothing to do with the world… (Fang Dongmei 1989, 1056)

These considerations aside, the content, concepts and methodological assumptions of Fang's own thought were to a great extent integrated into the framework of Neo-Confucian theories, which provided the "thought-base" for most of the modern Confucian discourses that appeared on the transition from the second to third millennia. However, here we encounter an additional problem with respect to Fang's classification, for he not only distanced himself from modern Confucians, but also from their historical conceptual base, i.e. from the Neo-Confucians of the Song and Ming dynasties. In his view—and regardless of their merit in preserving the classical Confucian tradition and its holistic worldview—these philosophers (especially Zhu Xi's school) relied too heavily on a mechanistic rationality, as exemplified in the structural logic of the li concept (structure, structural pattern). This resulted in a deformation of the holistic tradition in philosophy, in which the binary poles of rationality (li) and feeling (qi)[17] were harmonized, thereby preserving the harmonic unity of facts, values and the sphere of aesthetic experience. Due to these divergencies, Fang Dongmei did not consider the Modern Confucians as authentic heirs of Confucianism.[18]

In the category of Confucianism, Fang includes Confucius, Mencius and Xunzi. (Fang Dongmei 2004b, 155), while the Han Confucians he thinks were "lowly and unworthy of mention" and the Song Neo-Confucians were not authentic followers of Confucianism. He therefore criticized Neo-Confucian philosophy as "hybrid" and full of latent Daoist and Chan Buddhist elements (Fang Dongmei 2004b, 64) In his view, Zhu Xi's thought was little more than a compendium of the ideas of Zhou Dunyi, Zhang Zai and Cheng's brother (Fang Dongmei 2004b, 66), but without system, and full of logical contradictions (Fang Dongmei 2004b, 66).

Fang is indubitably an important and influential theorist, whose work made a significant contribution to the theoretical reflection on Chinese modernization processes and the effort to find creative solutions to the challenges posed by Western philosophy. However, as opposed to most modern Confucians, Fang Dongmei tried to revive the Chinese tradition based not on Neo-Confucian discourses, but primarily on classical Confucianism, enriched by the aesthetic and metaphysical concepts of classical Daoism and Sinicized Buddhism. Here, I should point out that my own understanding of the original Chinese expression *ru xue* (Confucianism; literally: "the teachings of the educated") is broader than Fang's own definitions. In my view, it has not been limited to the teachings of Confucius as a historical personage, but instead be seen as the dominant cultural discourse of the Chinese (and East Asian) tradition, and therefore as comprising a wide range of the prevailing philosophical discourses that combined to make up the history of Chinese (and East Asian[19]) philosophy over a period of over 2500 years. As a specific example of how these different views are applied in actual theory, we can point out that Fang always interpreted Daoism, which includes numerous critical, individualistic and free-thinking elements, within the framework of a neoconservative ideology that represents an essential, almost paradigmatic characteristic of modern Confucianism.

For these reasons, I believe that Fang Dongmei can be considered a representative of Modern Confucianism, especially within the context of the present study, which focuses on the members of that school who lived and worked in Taiwan and Hong Kong, where their contributions left an indelible trace.

While some scholars include Fang in the first generation of this intellectual movement, given that he was older than He Lin and the teacher of Tang Junyi (Liu Shu-hsien 2001, ii), others (e.g. Bresciani 2001) prefer to place him in the second generation. Because Fang Dongmei was also the teacher of the two most influential still-living representatives of the third generation,[20] and especially given his major influence on contemporary trends in Taiwanese philosophy, for the purposes of the present study (and notwithstanding his pioneering contribution to modern East Asian philosophy) I will follow Bresciani's categorisation and consider him as a member of the second generation of modern Confucianism.

Fang, who is also known to English speakers under the name Thomé H. Fang, was born into a family of intellectuals in the central Chinese province of Anhui. He was thus exposed to the Chinese classics at a very early age. After completing secondary school he attended Jinling University in Nanjing, where he was very active in the student movement. In 1919 he participated in the student demonstrations in Nanjing, which were organized in support of the May Fourth cultural reforms. In 1920, he met the American philosopher John Dewey[21] during his lecture tour of China, an encounter which awakened a keen interest in Fang for Western philosophy. After graduating, he went to America, where after only one year he earned his MA at the University of Wisconsin, and then two years later obtained his PhD at Ohio State University. Following his return to China, he taught at different universities, including Wuchang University (Wuchang daxue), Southeast University in Nanjing (Nanjing Dongnan daxue), the Political University (Zhengzhi daxue) and, briefly, Peking University (Beiing daxue). While Fang was in Nanjing, the Japanese invasion forced the university to move to Chongqing in the southwest province of Sichuan (Jiang and Yu 1995, 880). The difficult wartime conditions and the uncertainty and insecurity during this period led Fang to renew his interest in traditional Chinese culture and classical philosophy as a form of refuge and solace (Fang Dongmei 1959, 17). In 1948 he moved to Taiwan to teach at National Taiwan University (Guoli Taiwan daxue), where he remained until his retirement.

His principal works in Chinese were published in 2004 as the *Collected Works of Fang Dongmei* (*Fang Dongmei quan ji*), in 12 volumes. They include *Science, Philosophy and Human Life* (*Kexue, zhexue yu rensheng*, 1936), *A Survey of the Life Philosophies of Ancient*

Chinese Philosophers (*Zhongguo xian zhe rensheng zhexue gaiyao, 1937*), *Three Types of Philosophical Wisdom* (*Zhexue san hui*) and *The Ideal of Life and Cultural Types* (*Shenghuo lixiang yu wenhua leixing*). Under the name Thomé H. Fang, he also wrote a number of books in English, including *The Chinese View of Life: the Philosophy of Comprehensive Harmony, Creativity* in *Man and Nature* and *Chinese Philosophy: Its Spirit and its Development*.

Fang's theoretical works are characterized by his ability to combine a thorough knowledge of western philosophy, from the ancient to the contemporary, with traditional Chinese philosophy, especially Confucian, Daoist and Buddhist thought. His work also shows the influence of Indian philosophy. Among modern Western philosophers, Nietzsche had the greatest influence on his theoretical development (Fang Dongmei 1936, 195). Several of his works are dedicated to comparing Indian and European philosophy in order to define the characteristics of traditional Chinese philosophy.[22]

Fang believed that Chinese classical philosophy and epistemology were not based on mathematical or proto-scientific paradigms, but on aesthetic ones (Fang Thomé H. 1957, 195–235). However, his ontology is closely linked to the rational structure of the universe, as found in the ancient Chinese classic, *The Book of Changes* (*Yi jing*). Fang also described the process of cosmic change (constant creative creativity of existence) as an expression of rationality, which is rooted in (and at the same time encompasses) the minutely structured system of the "logic of creation" (Fang Dongmei 1936, 24–26).

In the centre of Fang's philosophy lies the concept of life or the living (*sheng*). According to Fang, all schools of traditional Chinese thought emerged from cosmology, which is defined by the all-prevailing instinct for life, survival, the vital impulse that constantly creates and recreates everything that exists. For Fang, the cosmos was a "living environment (*shengmingde huanjing*)", permeated by "circles of rational principles and feelings (*qingli tuan*)". While the structural patterns of existence remain fundamental, feelings (*qing*) represent the primary source of life (*shengmingde yuantai*): "Life is a world of feelings, and its essence is a continuous, creative desire and impulse" (Fang Dongmei 1936, 25). Life is thus "a flexible, extendable power" (Fang Dongmei 1936, 163).

The universe is a living entity that cannot be reduced to mere inertial physical stuff. Based on these premises, he then added a third category to the dualism of matter and idea, that of life: "We can see that life is a novel, original phenomenon; we cannot deal with it in the same way as with matter. Its system is predicated upon an organic wholeness" (Fang Dongmei 1936, 179).

This living universe is namely full of energy, and everything in it is structurally connected to the living process that penetrates the entire realm.

Human thought is also rooted in this colorful, sensitive and creative palette of life itself; it is not merely a product of rationality: "Life is the root of the thought, and thoughts are symbols or signs of life" (Fang Dongmei 1936, 164).

Hence, even science "is a symbol of the sentiments of life" (Fang Dongmei 1936, 138) and its value lies in "developing the human desire for life" (Fang Dongmei 1936, 160).

Life is thus the fundamental driving force of the universe. For this reason, Fang calls it the original (Fang Dongmei 1982, 149) or ultimate substance (Fang Dongmei 1984, 28) of the universe. However, he stresses that while this ultimate substance is transcendent (*chaoyue*), but it is not so supremely unique as to be an absolute (*chaojue*; Fang Dongmei 1984, 20). Fang Dongmei's ontology thus clearly belongs to the realm of immanent transcendence, which will be discussed in detail below.

According to most interpreters, (see e.g. Li Chengyang 2002, 265 or Fang and Li 1995, 895), such a view may be called a "life-ontology (*shengming bentilun*)". Li Chengyang also exposes that this life-ontology is more than a "Gaia hypothesis"; for Fang, it is reality. In this regard, the influence of Western philosophers such as Hegel, Bergson, and Whitehead on Fang is evident.

The second central concept of Fang's philosophy is the idea of "comprehensive harmony," which is characteristic of the traditional Chinese understanding of the world. In this understanding, the universe strives towards a harmonious unity of all the individual particles and entities within its system. In material terms, it is empty, or "void"[23] and expressed only through the richness and insight of its spirit.

In Fang's reading of the history of Chinese philosophy, he stressed the harmonious interplay of various schools of thought, rather than their differences and conflicts. One could argue that Fang was too idealistic and romantic in his understanding of these philosophies. However, for Fang, if harmony was not a reality, it still represented the Chinese "ideal" (Li Chengyang 2002, 266).

The belief in harmony and a harmonic universe is also reflected in his understanding of morality or moral philosophy. Because the cosmic tendency to establish and preserve harmony through the concept of *shengsheng* (creative creativity) is almighty and unlimited, it does not have merely ontological, but also ethical and epistemological dimensions. For him, the natural life order is tightly linked to the moral order (Fang Dongmei 1979, 351). This means that Fang's philosophy has no room for a division between facts and values. The universe is enriched by goodness, which derives not only from the pragmatic postulates of human co-existence, but is *a priori* a part of its essential structure, as reflected in the sphere of pure aesthetics. Fang thus views morality as the essence of life and a concrete embodiment of the deepest human values. Human existence is not merely about survival, but presupposes the search for meaning and purpose. The aesthetic side of culture and art is the expression of human creativity (Fang Dongmei 1984, 149), which is always oriented towards perfecting the deficiencies of the world into which we are thrown; Dao represents the path that leads to perfection as well as the path upon which facts and values are merged into an organically structured harmony (Fang Dongmei 1984, 158). In this way, he strove to unite the three ideals of epistemology, ethics and aesthetics, i.e. truth, goodness, and beauty. He also thoroughly emphasized that *qing* (the emotive reactions) and *li* (the rational principles) cannot be separated. Although Fang's philosophy is established, as we have seen before, on his "life-ontology, it can thus also be called "value-centered-ontology", because, for him, life is the basic value of existence and both life and value are rooted in the *dao*. In his view, dao represents the ultimate, all-encompassing and all-pervading unity, which is the primary source of life, value, and their harmonious fusion.

In Fang's previously mentioned work *Zhexue san hui* (*Three Types of Philosophical Wisdom*) he defined philosophy as a synthesis between the rational structure of thought (*li*) and emotions (*qing*). According to the *Book of Change* both originate from the extreme pole (*taiji*), i.e. the onto-epistemological, indescribable and unexplainable ancient origin of all existence. Thus, for him *qing* and *li* are not merely the base of all philosophy, but also the fundament of existence as such. Fang believes that the two elements represent a binary category, for their reciprocal relation is correlative and complementary. Li Chengyang (2002, 264) exposes that Fang sees the mutual, reciprocal interaction between *li* and *qing* as a process that pervades facts as well as possibilities, and from which philosophy draws its origin, truth and mystery.

He based his interpretation of traditional Chinese philosophy on the holistic view, according to which man forms a unity with space and time. In the forefront of his interpretation we can find the traditional unity of values, which through constant creativity includes the activities of Heaven, (*tian*), and man. Regardless of his declaratively broad starting points which included all the most influential discourses from ancient and classical Chinese philosophy, it was precisely this very central point through which he proved that his thoughts were grounded in the classical Mencian viewpoint of four natural origins (*si duan*) of human goodness; in this way, he (regardless of his—also clearly stated—detachment from Neo-Confucianism of the Song and Ming dynasties), also proved that in fact, he did followed precisely this very tradition that formed the foundations of this pre-modern Confucian reform.[24]

> The universe is a place to live in, and not a place to escape from, because it is a realm of value. Similarly, human nature is something to rely upon, and not something to dispense with, because it has been proved to be not sinful but innocent. (Fang Dongmei 1980, 99)

However, he detached himself from this line of thought by constantly emphasising that the natural goodness of man is a common characteristic found in all traditional Chinese philosophers (Fang Dongmei 1980, 87–115). He even tried to convince the readers that even Xunzi, who is considered to be Mencius' main opponent, in essence shares this opinion, the only difference being that he had swapped the roles of nature and emotions:

> We can find no valid reasons for the theory of evil nature. Even Hsüntze[25] held the belief that "human nature is a natural achievement" or "human nature attains itself after the pattern of constant nature". The reason why Hsüntze considered human nature to be evil is that he confused it with emotion which, logically speaking, is of a lower type than original nature. The evilness of human nature is here inferred, a posteriori, from the evilness of emotion. Here Hsüntze commits a fallacy of the confusion of logical types. (Fang Dongmei 1980, 109)

In his comparative aspect and endeavour to come up with a harmonious synthesis of his own work, Fang mainly focused on the common points of the three central schools of classical Chinese philosophy. He ascertained that they are all connected by the Dao concept, which each treats from a slightly different aspect and in a slightly different way, but all three are basically describing the concept of holistic harmony and the tendency for perfection. As Dao is possible only in the context of holistic worldviews, it can reflect the method of immanent transcendence as well as the unity of facts and values, absoluteness and relativity.

Xu Fuguan, the life and work of whom we will look at in the following subchapter, attributed to Dao a similar importance in the formation of the classical Chinese thought tradition.

4.4 Xu Fuguan: A Philosopher of Culture, Philology and Politics

If we wish to start this chapter at the point where we finished with the previous one, we have to start with Xu Fuguan's vision of the Dao concept. In his opinion the *tian* concept was in the forefront of the teachings of Confucius, however this concept was not understood in the sense of a concrete anthropomorphic being, nor as an idea of an attached higher force with its own will, but more in the sense of (external) nature, which Xu Fuguan understands in the same way as Dao. He believed this was a concept that somehow embodied or recapped all teachings of Confucius (Xu Fuguan 1979b, 10). Confucius mainly used this term in the sense of the "proper way" or "walking along the proper way".[26] Emphasising and revealing the traditional meaning of this practical orientation did not mark merely Xu Fuguan theories; this Modern Confucian scholar always introduced the practical principle into his social and political activities. His importance for the development of the modern Confucian movement can thus also be seen in the constant active publicity, in which he stood for the values and ideals of this philosophical school. He was a very prolific theoretician, mainly focusing on philosophy and sociology of culture; he was also a penetrating journalist, who believed that Confucian values represented the central foundation of true democracy (Fang and Li 1995, III/727). Perhaps even more significant was his contribution to the promotion of Confucianism in everyday life and politics. As Bresciani points out (2001, 354), he helped many people to go beyond the stereotype image of a Confucian as a person without a moral backbone and sold to the political rulers. A strong concern for the immediate social and political reality has—through his contributions—become a typical characteristics of later generations of the Modern Confucianism.

Born to a poor provincial teacher in the countryside of the present Hubei province (Xu Fuguan 1980a, 75), this student of Xiong Shili has after graduating from high school first studied at the Meiji University in Japan, where he—through Japanese translations—obtained fair knowledge of the main elements of Western political sciences and the bases of economy. The Japanese Marxist theoretician Kawakami Hajime was also a great influence on the young student; his enthusiasm for Marxism lasted until the early 1940s, when he met Xiong Shili (1942) and became one of his most enthusiastic students.[27] The meeting with this philosopher caused Xu to rethink the values of traditional Chinese philosophy and importantly influenced his later work.

Already during his life in Japan Xu has focused on a military career. As he could namely not afford the high study fees, he was forced to cut his University studies short and to enrol into the Junior Officer School for Japanese Infantry. In 1931, when Japan invaded Manchuria, Xu Fuguan protested sharply with the Japanese government, ended up in jail and was forbidden to continue with his studies. Thus he returned to China in the following year, where he (also in 1942) met Jiang Jieshi;[28] soon after their meeting he became his expert adviser and a zealous member of the Nationalist Party (Xu

Fuguan 1980a, 314). At the end of WWII he stepped out of the military as a major general and moved to Hong Kong, where he spent his time writing essays and working as a journalist. He moved to Taiwan even before the civil war ended, i.e. before the Communist Party took over power on the continent;[29] at first he found employment as a lecturer at the Agricultural Institute in Taizhong (later State University Zhongxing), and then he became a full professor of Chinese literature at the Donghai University in the same town. He soon gained reputation as a notorious civil and political personality, whose critical attitude towards the West and against the domination of pro-American cultural and material goods soon received a number of followers as well as enemies. He often criticized the Westernizing trend, which used to prevail in intellectual circles in Taiwan in his time. This trend was especially strong in the early sixties, fostered by Hu Shi, who had returned to Taibei as head of the Academia Sinica. Xu Fuguan, on the other hand, firmly believed that he was fighting for the survival of his country's culture. He was trying to wake up his countrymen to the danger of becoming a cultural colony. In his romantic manner, Bresciani even sees him as "a knight fighting for his ideals, afraid of nothing" (2001, 333). Thus, it was by no means coincidental that he eventually managed to enrage several influential figures and was consequently fired from his job.

While he was unemployed, he made most of his money as a freelance essayist and lecturer. Similar to most other neo-conservative Modern Confucians he saw the domination of "communist" China to be much more than merely a change of the political regime (Xu Fuguan 1951, 16). He saw it as a heavy strike for Chinese culture and as the beginning of its decline. In order to combat this he received financial and political support from the People's Party and established the periodical "*Democratic Criticism*" (*Minzhu pinglun*), the main goal of which was to criticise the Communist Party and the government of the People's Republic of China "from the viewpoint of Chinese culture" (Xu Fuguan 1951, 16).[30]

Most Modern Confucian theoreticians published contributions in this periodical. In 1955, Xu Fuguan started lecturing at the Donghai University (Donghai daxue) in Taizhong, where he remained for fourteen years. In 1970 he left this job ("due to personal disagreements", Xu Fuguan 1951, 16) and moved back to Hong Kong, where he was offered a job in the stronghold of Modern Confucian philosophy and ideology, i.e. in the New Asia Academy (Xin Ya shuyuan),[31] where he mostly lived and worked until his death in 1982.

After the end of Cultural Revolution and during the gradual liberalization which followed, he also changed his attitudes regarding mainland China and even praised Deng Xiaoping's pragmatic politics, which took as their slogan the traditional motto "Shishi qiu shi",[32] i.e. "To seek the truth in facts":

> The four characters which signify: "To seek the truth in facts", have a great general value, and are both effective and original. Applying this phrase, which was first expressed during the Han Dynasty by King Xian of Hejian, in a period of intellectual chaos and ideological confusion, assumes great importance in terms of distinguishing true from false, clarifying a situation and then moving forward. (Xu Fuguan 1979a, 335)

He also advocated the reunification of Taiwan and mainland China, arguing that: "the mainland is China's eternal essence, and Taiwan can never be separated from it" (Xu Fuguan 1981, 85).

Apart from his historic, cultural and socio-philosophical studies, Xu Fuguan is also known for his good philological analyses of ancient Chinese sources. In this frame his brilliant philological analysis of the classic work *Debate on Salt and Iron* (*Yan tie lun*) is worth a mention. In this work he proved the ideologists from the "Gang of Four" that their propaganda as regards the main message in this work is untrue, and that it merely serves the anti-Confucian political ideology of new legalism, which stood behind the Cultural Revolution (Xu Fuguan 1976, 416). In most of his works Xu, who considered himself a historian, dealt with the question as to why traditional Chinese culture, which was credibly defined by Confucian thought, never really managed to totally free itself from the tendencies that led the state into despotism. In his work *The Intellectual History of the Two Han Dynasties* (*Liang Han sixiang shi*) he explains how the despotic system in China established itself only after the pre-Qin period and how it totally suppressed or eliminated most democratic elements of original Confucianism.[33] In this context Xu Fuguan developed the thesis of the "double subjectivity" (*shuangchong zhutixing*), which should appear as the key element of traditional Chinese political thought. This concept means that in the Chinese philosophical tradition (with the exception of the legalist school) the people were seen as the subject, however in the social reality of the despotic system the ruler always—without fail—appeared as the sole subject. In this way the unsolvable basic contradiction between the Confucian ideal and the despotic reality was reproduced throughout Chinese history. Because of this Xu decisively stood up to Qian Mu's interpretation of Chinese history (Xu Fuguan 1976, 416). This important modern Confucian historian tried to prove that the basic orientation of the Chinese state was not despotic ever since the Qin dynasty.

His best known work regarding the history of philosophy is his book *The Chinese History of Human Nature Theories* (*Zhongguo ren xing lun shi*) which was published in two parts. The first discusses the period of pre-Qin philosophy, while the second discusses the philosophy of the two Han dynasties. In his opinion the following factors play an important role in defining Chinese philosophy:

a) Pragmatic orientation

b) Autocratic political tradition

c) Agricultural culture

The first characteristic[34] was linked to the original Confucian rejection of metaphysics,[35] which we will discuss in greater detail a bit later.[36]

As regards the autocratic political tradition, which played an important role throughout Chinese history, and which is often totally unreflectively ascribed to Confucianism, Xu wrote:

> If we compare the philosophy of the two Han dynasties with the Qin dynasty philosophy, a great change can be noticed. The reason for this change can be found in politics and society. A joined, autocratic ruling system with an absolute ruler and the formation of family clans emerged simultaneously. This had a great influence on the later development of our state and represents the key to the understanding of the basic problems of our two thousand year history. (Xu Fuguan 2001b, 13)

In the centre of Xu's philosophical reflection is the notion of concern, anxiety or distress (*youhuan yishi*):

> After the Zhou people managed to rid themselves of the Yin domination, they became the new rulers. But sources from the early Zhou dynasty suggest that they differed from other nations that generally become arrogant and overbearing after a conquest or victory. Instead, the Zhou could be described as having what the *Book of Changes* describes as a "concerned" consciousness. (Xu Fuguan 1995a, 659)

In the following, he positions this kind of consciousness in contrast to the concept of curiosity, which represents the origin of European philosophy. In his research he tried to find the consequences this statement has on the understanding of human life and the traditional Chinese concept of heart-mind (*xin*).[37] Xu Fuguan believed the ethical values that are in the forefront of most classical discourses were the values of an agricultural society. According to him, the Confucian teaching is primarily the philosophy of farmers; the elite classes that ruled China in a more or less despotic fashion throughout its history did not implement policies that would be based on such values.

For Xu, it was important to clarify these issues, because the trend in Chinese intellectual circles since the May Fourth Movement was to put blame for the backwardness of China on the Confucian heritage, and to attribute the dominance of Confucianism to the Han emperors who adopted it as the state religion (Xu Fuguan 1995b, 673). Therefore, he often exposed that the Han emperors were not necessarily honoring Confucius and favoring Confucianism (Xu Fuguan 1995b, 701). It was the society at large, the scholars and the people, who honored and exalted Confucius (Xu Fuguan 1995b, 702), so that at a certain point Emperor Wu of the Han dynasty considered it an advantageous political move to officially opt for Confucianism in establishing what classics should be studied. As for the Confucian scholars, they were navigating in the perilous waters of autocratic politics and trying, often at risk of their lives, to expound Confucian values and to influence the emperor accordingly.

I consider this understanding of the beginnings of the state doctrine to be slightly simplified, even though it is true that Han period "Confucianism" differs greatly from the original teachings, which emerged in the pre-Qin period. This new Confucian state doctrine was more rigid and autocratic and much less democratic than original Confucianism, which was supposed to serve as its basis. The new ideological formation was a Confucian doctrine on the formal, i.e. declarative level, but also included numerous rigid Legalist elements. However, at the decision regarding the question which pre-Qin philosophical school could provide the most appropriate teachings for the new state doctrine, most likely other factors (and not their general popularity) were taken into account. As we namely know, Confucianism did not stand out in popularity compared to other philosophical schools of the pre-Qin period. Because the new Han dynasty authorities succeeded the Qin dynasty government, under the influence of which China was unified into a centralised Empire for the first time in its history, they—similar to their predecessors—needed a centralised and absolutist ideology, for it was impossible to efficiently control such a large state formation in any other way. Legalism was not appropriate, for it was a doctrine of the defeated. Once cleared of all the democratic and anti-monarchy elements, the Confucian teachings were the most appropriate simply because they emphasised the importance of social hierarchy.[38]

On the other hand, Xu Fuguan believed that in the core of any "true" Confucian teaching we can find Chinese humanism (Xu Fuguan 1995b, 711), justice and democracy in the sense of political participation or the possibility of direct political decision-making by individuals.

In this respect we should agree with Xu Fuguan, for even though these elements of Confucian ideas are not too well known in modern Sinology, they were indeed extremely advanced for a period of feudal transition, especially given the fact that such orientation can actually be found in almost all ancient Confucian classics. Even Xunzi, one of the most rigid and rationalist representatives of pre-Qin Confucianism, who is often described as a link between Confucianism and Legalism (Rošker 2010, 60), stated that the ruler is like a boat and the people like water. The latter is the one that carries the boat, but also the one that can tip the boat over. Mencius, the second main successor of Confucius, also stated that people are to be put first, and the ruler last. The Confucian classic *Book of Rituals* (*Li ji*) emphasises, that everything under the sun belongs to everyone, and is thus in joint ownership of the public (*gong*). The values of classical Confucianism are clan defined social and political orders. Thus, in Xu's view, they did not have any direct connection with the despotic system of the autocratic "Confucian" state.

Even though Xu Fuguan was primarily an essayist who had shown his excellent knowledge in the development of the ancient Chinese society (especially its socio-cultural characteristics), and thus never published deep philosophical debates, he is interesting for his basic methodological orientation, which defined his vision of the development of thought in traditional China. As previously mentioned almost all modern Confucians emphasised the importance of constructing the new ontology, which could serve as the basis for the Confucian reform (cf. Chapter 4.2). Xu Fuguan was one of the rare second generation representatives who believed that ontology and metaphysics do not represent an appropriate tool for understanding, let alone developing, classical Chinese thought (Xu Fuguan 1982, 589), for their pragmatic core never led to the composition or conception of a coherently structured metaphysical system, as established by the ancient Greeks (Xu Fuguan 1979a, 58–59). Instead, it developed the idea of ethics based on the divine core of human inner self[39] directly from a "primitive" stage of a religious and mythological society. In his view, Chinese traditional ethic is very different from the Western one, for it relied neither on metaphysics nor on religion. Instead, it was based upon the internalization of morality:

> Based upon the nature and heart-mind of a single human being, it is possible to reflect upon, comprehend and determine the fate of all of humankind. And every person can attain a complete self-sufficiency in their own nature or heart-mind, without recourse to the aid of some external force or entity. (Xu Fuguan 2005, 182)

Thus, in the Confucian tradition, knowledge of external things and knowledge of one's intimate personality are closely related, and the object and the subject are therefore united. There is no concern of metaphysical objections, or need to escape this world.

As we have already mentioned, most modern Confucians were of the opinion that the Western concepts of "freedom and democracy" could be easily merged with traditional Chinese culture. Xu went a step further, for he believed that a democratic social system is the only one in which the Confucian teachings can actually be realised (Xu Fuguan1995b, 711).

He did not stand alone in this general view, which caused a division between the liberal and modern Confucianism schools. Apart from the periodical *Democratic Criticism* (*Minzhu pinglun*), which he founded, Chinese intellectuals outside the People's Republic of China were also influenced by the magazine *Free China* (*Ziyou Zhongguo*), which was established in Taiwan in November 1949 by liberal intellectuals under the leadership of Hu Shi. At first the authors of the two publications cooperated and supported each other in their joint criticism of the communist regime. But already in the mid-1950s a vile debate sprung up between the new Confucians who represented the first magazine and the liberals who worked for the latter. This debate was rooted in their opposing views on traditional Chinese culture and especially on Confucianism (Lee Ming-huei 2001a, 77). The debate focused on the following two issues:

1. Does the Confucian tradition hold back the development of science and technology and the appearance of a modern democratic system?
2. Is a moral base necessary when establishing a modern democracy? In other words: does political freedom have to necessarily be conditioned by the moral freedom on the theoretical level?

As regards the first issue Modern Confucians headed by Xu Fuguan believed that science and democracy are not directly present in traditional Confucianism, but traditional Confucianism included valuable thought processes that enable their development. They emphasised that external cultural factors should not be brought into China without a reason; they can only be integrated on the basis of the internal development of Chinese tradition itself. His liberal opponents stated that already the fact that the Confucian tradition did not directly led to modern science and democracy is enough to lead us to the conclusion that this tradition does not include elements that would be favourable for such development. The Chinese liberals of the period were (similar to classical western modernisation theoreticians) also convinced that China had to renounce this tradition and bid it farewell, if it wishes to develop into a modern democratic and technologically developed state.

As regards the second issue, Modern Confucians acknowledged the difference between politics and morals, and stated that moral freedom is not a sufficient precondition when attempting to construct a democratic system. On the other hand, they explicitly emphasised that every democratic political system needs to be based on morals, thus political freedom has to be conditioned by moral freedom. The liberal camp denied this connection between politics and morals; the liberals were convinced that this connection can—"in the best case scenario—lead merely to a totalitarian democracy as defined by J. L. Talmon" (Lee Ming-huei 2001a, 77).

The liberal Taiwanese intellectuals were led by the noted thinker and politician, Hu Shi. In fact, this debate was mainly concentrating on the question of whether traditional Chinese culture, and primarily Confucianism, was capable of developing science, technology and Western-style democracy. While Modern Confucians acknowledged that traditional Confucianism did not include these elements, they still argued that this tradition did by no means hinder the development of a modern society. The liberals instead insisted that China had to eliminate all traces of Confucianism if it wished to become a modern, technologically developed and advanced democratic state. Although Modern Confucians accepted the difference between politics and morality, they still believed (on the theoretical level) that political freedom was conditioned by moral freedom. The liberals instead refuted this position, declaring that at best this would lead to a "totalitarian democracy" (Lee Ming-huei, 2001a, 89–129). Indeed, Chinese liberals and Modern Confucians did not have a consensus about what "freedom" meant in their specific time and place. While "individual freedom" was a notion generally acknowledged, the term "national freedom" was embraced by the Modern Confucians, yet severely objected to by the liberals. Furthermore, the liberals understood freedom as "specific liberties" in the political sphere only, whereas the Modern Confucians insisted that "inner freedom" was integral to a sound understanding of the term (Lee Su-san 1989, 247).

Although Xu Fuguan is most famous for his political thought and his cultural studies, he also wrote a lot on literary and art criticism and is one of the founders of theoretical aesthetics within the frame of Modern Confucianism (Xu Fuguan 2001a, 23–31). Thus he became a part of modern Chinese history also as one of the early theoreticians of specific Chinese aesthetics; he was also an extremely well educated and talented philologist, which can clearly be seen in his (previously mentioned) precise analysis of the intellectual history of the Han dynasty. Xiong is also known as an extraordinarily knowledgeable and insightful philologist, and one of the first Chinese theorists who tried to systematically link the development of Chinese philosophy with the semantic development of its basic concepts (Xu Fuguan 1995b, 667–9).

4.5 The Voice from Hong Kong: Tang Junyi

Tang was born into a bourgeois family and was raised and taught by his father who lectured at various Chinese universities. Tang was born in the province of Sichuan in 1909, where he also attended primary and secondary school. He started his philosophy studies in Peking, where he was a student of Liang Shuming for a short while. However, after a single year he switched to Zhongyang University, where he met a series of excellent lecturers who decisively influenced his later development. Amongst them was Fang Dongmei, who got him interested in British or American new realism which was popular at the time. As he became more seriously interested in the works of Kant and Hegel, he dropped this realism, and focused on idealistic philosophies. In 1927 he started attending Xiong Shili's lectures *New Treatise on Consciousness-only* (*Xin weishi lun*) and soon became one of his enthusiastic followers. A year after he graduated (1933) he started lecturing at the same university, at first as an assistant professor, and in 1944 he became a full professor and the head of the Department of Philosophy at the Zhongyang University, even though he lectured at other universities for a few years in between.[40]

He retreated to Guangdong at the beginning of 1949 (even before the People's Republic of China was established), and later that year he moved to Hong Kong, where he—together with Qian Mu and some other colleagues—founded the previously mentioned Academy Xin Ya shuyuan, which became the revitalisation centre for traditional culture and a space in which numerous renown intellectuals in exile met.

Tang was the main author of *Declaration of Chinese Culture to the Scholars of the World* (*Wei Zhongguo wenhua jinggao shijie renshi xuanyan*). While stationed in Hong Kong Tang travelled a lot; from the work aspect his greatest interest lay in the methods of university lecturing and research in USA, and he often visited Europe and his Asian neighbours, especially Taiwan, and of course Japan and Korea. In 1963 the Chinese University of Hong Kong (Xianggang zhongwen daxue) was established (specialising in Chinese language and culture) and the Academy Xin Ya shuyuan became a part of it. Tang became the head of the postgraduate institute at this Academy, however his views grew further and further apart from those of the university management, thus he co-founded the private postgraduate and research institute, which he led until his death in 1978.

His works reflect the following three main fields of his theoretical endeavors:[41]

1. The inseparable connection between metaphysics and ethics or morality;
2. Comparative studies in Western and Chinese cultures and problems, linked to the modernization of Chinese culture;
3. The in-depth compilation of the central approaches and methodological characteristics of traditional Chinese philosophy.

Even though Tang was an exceptionally productive writer, we will mention merely his main work in each of these categories by which his intellectual development is summarized. The research from the first category is most likely best summed by his book *Heart-Mind, Objects and Human Life* (*Xin wu yu rensheng*). In this work Tang started to establish his ethical idealism. It offers an interpretation of his concept of moral self, and the relation between this self, the universe and the humanistic ideal in society. In this book, Tang has tried to solve the problem of alienation in modern humankind, which he saw as a by-product of the decline of established social values. In modern times, people loose themselves too often in abstractions, and are thus led astray from the concrete reality of their existence: The human soul longs for truth, goodness and beauty and people want to be absorbed by and focused on the concrete reality of their lives.

He argues that the universe is not senseless, but a creation that is deeply permeated with ethical values and hence meaningful. In this context, he defines the concept of the moral self (*daode ziwo*), which he also denotes as a spiritual or transcendent self (*jingshen ziwo, chayue ziwo*, Tang Junyi 1986, 9). He places this moral self, which transcends the phenomenal world, in direct opposition to the so-called real self (*xianshi ziwo*), or a self-limited by reality:

> The "real self" refers to the self as an object of reality, fixed or captured within time and space. It is limited and determined by things and events pertaining to a certain time and space. It is a phenomenal self. (Tang Junyi 1986, 9)

He developed and theoretically upgraded this concept in his book *Establishing the Moral Self* (*Daode ziwozhi jianli*), which will be discussed in greater detail in Chapter 6, for in it he focuses on the analysis and sinicization of the key concepts of modernisation, i.e. the subject and reason. In both of these works he also began to develop his thesis regarding the substance or subject of the heart-mind *(xin benti, xin zhuti)*, which became one of the core concepts of his entire philosophical system. Tang Junyi argued that there cannot be any physical substance, for all matter exists merely in the phenomenal sphere. Thus, substance can only be immaterial, and belongs to the realm of spirit or human heart-mind (Tang Junyi 1977, 2/322).

The questions concerning the link between the mysterious dimension of the human spirit and spirituality and the physical substantiality of the universe in which that dimension exists, would occupy him throughout his career, and he would continue to produce new theories on the problems of transcendence, morality, and metaphysics throughout his many publications.

In his last book entitled *The Existence of Life and the Horizon of the Soul* (*Shengming cunzai yu xinling jingjie*), which was published less than six months before his death, Tang established his own system of philosophy. In this work, he tried to connect metaphysical, ontological and ethical elements into a coherent unity, combining methods and paradigms from Western, Indian and Chinese philosophy (Tang Junyi 1977, 1/12–15, 48). He explores and explains the activity of human spirit and tries to place it in dynamic mutual inter-relation with various realms or spheres (*jingjie*) of existence (Tang Junyi 1977, 1/393, 2/256). According to him, these inter-relations represent everything that makes up the object and the contents of human knowledge. He certainly acknowledges that the activities of human spirit are of utmost complexity and extremely multifarious. Nevertheless, he succeeds in categorizing the whole of it inside nine spheres.[42]

Tang tried to connect these nine spheres or horizons and to categorise them into three areas, i.e. the area of the objective world (the area of the structural order *li*), the area of the subjective world (the area of heart-mind *xin*) and the area of the world that transcends the object/subject division (the area of creativity). He combined these three areas with the concepts of substance (*ti*), modality (*xiang*) and function (*yong*).

Tang's comparative cultural studies were also permeated by ethical and moral issues. Proceeding from the above-mentioned concept of the substance of the heart-mind, he emphasized that all different cultures were manifestations of specific features of their dominant moral rationalities. As regards moral behavior, Tang Junyi distinguished between intuitive and non-intuitive ethics, at which the latter would serve as a specific base for any culture, while the former would represent the totality of all cultural factors (Tang Junyi 1986, 30). According to Tang, all concrete cultures, culture in general and human action as such are based on the existence of the moral presence to the same extent (Tang Junyi 1975a, 82).

The second field of Tang's work was thus defined by comparisons between Chinese and Western cultures, and by his attempts to find a wholesome reflection of traditional Chinese culture in order to place it into the context of modernisation and its specific values. Of central importance for this aspect are the books *Spiritual Values of Chinese Culture* (*Zhongguo wenhuade jingsheng jiazhi*) and *The Reconstruction of the Spirit of the Humanities* (*Renwen jingshen zhi chongjian*). While the first is a relatively populist work that Tang wrote in Hong Kong as soon as he escaped from the newly emerging People's Republic of China, and was thus written "from memory", without numerous references, the second attempts to save mankind through the moral self, which supposedly represents the base of Chinese as well as Western culture. He argued that traditional Chinese culture was based on humanistic approaches (Tang Junyi 1975b, 418), while Western culture was too materialistic (Tang Junyi 1975b, 414):

> I can describe the spirit of Chinese philosophy as follows: it establishes the human way through the way of heaven (meaning that the divine virtues are directly reflected in each individual). It achieves co-humanness in human nature, in human relations and in its humanistic spirit. (Tang Junyi 1953, 478)

He nevertheless believes mankind can be saved if both cultures (and possibly some other cultures that might be worth a mention) are harmoniously merged under the flag of peace, permanent stability, freedom and democracy. While the tradition of freedom and democracy would be supplied by the Westerners, the Chinese contribution to this excellent project would of course be to offer the method of harmonious merger (Tang Junyi 1975b, 703).

As regards the third part of Tang Junyi's theoretic creation, we should mention his collection entitled *Treatise on the Origins of Chinese Philosophy* (*Zhongguo zhexue yuanlun*) in six volumes, in which he researched the development of Chinese philosophy through the optics of moral philosophy. In the first book he focused on the methodological characteristics of the Chinese philosophical discourses, in the second on the concept of *xing* (human nature or inborn qualities), which is more or less in the forefront of all Confucian debates throughout the history of Chinese philosophy. The following three books are dedicated to the analysis and interpretation of what is most likely the most important concept in traditional Chinese philosophy, i.e. the concept of the Way, the elementary principle or the method (*Dao*). The sixth, i.e. the final book in the series, focuses on the concept of the teachings or doctrine, mainly within the Neo-Confucianism framework.

As an advocate of the Confucian tradition, Tang was worried about its position in the modern world. He considered the domination of socialism in the People's Republic of China to be a product of anti-traditionalism, the roots of which reached into the time before the May Fourth Movement (Tang Junyi 2000, 283–4). His neo-conservatism is based on the conviction that the values of his tradition do not need to be especially founded, for they supposedly represent the basic ingredient of every individual existence. In accordance to this view, we should not treat our tradition as an object of external research, as is the case with most Chinese intellectuals—for this leads to the self-alienation of one's own existence. Tang thoroughly exposed that the Chinese do not need a reason to preserve their habits and rituals. In order to change them, they need to state the reasons, which are based on the reflective value consciousness. Tang was not in favour of conservatism in the sense of unreflectively preserving tradition, but he also opposed blind faith in progress (Tang Junyi 2000, 309). He emphasised that preservation and progress have common roots in value consciousness. Only one who knows the true value of his tradition can understand where progress lies. According to Lee Ming-huei (2001a, 62) such viewpoints can be read as a "Manifesto of cultural conservatism".

Tang's essays also reveal the influence of Buddhism, especially the teachings of the Tiantai and Huayan schools. He updated the *panjiao* concept, which attempts to systematically sort Buddha's teachings by incorporating into it certain parts of Chinese and even Western philosophy.

Tang's philosophy represents a great contribution towards the modernisation of Confucianism. He expanded and modernised several important concepts and ideas found in Neo-Confucian philosophy. His ethics did not bring anything totally new per se, however he did try to place them in a dialogue with Western philosophy. His disclosure of the differences and similarities between Neo-Confucian and Western philosophers revealed those elements of Confucian thought that are interesting also for the contemporary man. In this sense Tang successfully rejected the prejudice according to which Confucian philosophy is merely an archaic and outdated ideology. It is especially important that his depiction of Confucianism is freed of the—allegedly necessary—connection with institutions and conventions. He emphasised the significance of the concept of humanity (*ren*), and did not focus as much on the concept of rituality (*li*), which was always closely connected to established social practices and institutions. Instead, he laid stress upon his conviction that the central Confucian virtues are representing the core of the moral self (Tang Junyi 1986, 54). Through his extraordinarily productive work he established an open space for new debates on the Confucian values and their social dimensions.

5. Science and Democracy

The representatives of the second generation of Modern Confucianism generally believed that if China intended to undertake a process of modernization while also preserving its cultural identity, it had to strengthen and develop those elements of its own tradition that represented potential seeds of science and democracy.

This view was the object of severe criticism by their many opponents, who claimed that Confucianism was an outdated ideology that was not only unsuited to the development of modern science and democratic societies but was, in fact, chiefly responsible for the profound social and political crises which had afflicted China in the previous two centuries. The Modern Confucians denied this historical responsibility, and claimed that Confucianism was fully compatible with science and democracy. Many of these thinkers (with Xu Fuguan appearing as, perhaps, the most radical in this regard) even went so far as to sustain that, given their specific social features, East-Asian cultures would be unable to develop democratic structures if they did not rely on corresponding elements of the Confucian tradition.

Despite this general view, the members of this school were hardly uncritical of the tradition they advocated. They were fully aware of the fundamental differences between the democratic elements within Confucianism and Western models of democracy, and that these differences were not marginal but fundamental to the problems emerging in the course of China's transition into a "modern society". Foremost among these problems was the fact that the Confucian morality which underpinned the idea of a righteous society was understood as an internalized concept that demanded a high degree of personal responsibility. It was thus subjective and could not be universalized by applying formal or normative criteria. The core of this traditional, moral Self (*daode benxin*) could not be objectively defined, for it functioned differently depending on the specific socio-political context, by which it was conditioned. At the same time, Modern Confucians stressed that even the Western concept of the individual, which is grounded on the use of reason and posits a rational, autonomous being with inalienable rights, was not without its contradictions. This concept was, in fact, based on an abstraction which, in terms of the actual reality, did not coincide with real individuals, the social relations in which they are enmeshed, and the various value systems which influenced or conditioned them. This conceptualization of the relation between the individual and society thus often resulted in dilemmas and conflicts linked to a general inequality in the original conditions of individuals, which could not be fully taken into account or reconciled by laws purported to be "equal for all".

Another important difference between Western models of democracy and the Confucian concept of a righteous (democratic) society is found in the latter's belief in the moral equality of all people, while the Western model instead advocates an equality which is political. This constitutes a key distinction, for even given the difference between the autocratic (Xunzi's legalistic line) and the democratic (Mencian) elements within Confucian discourses, their common denominator can still be found in the principle of a hierarchically structured society. This structure represents the core of original Confucian political theories, and proposes a verticalization of power in which the superior hierarchical element possesses authority, while the subordinate position is defined by its general obedience. However, it is important to recall that this model was originally (especially in the classic Confucian teachings) rooted in the principle of complementarity and reciprocal responsibility. And while the autocratic model of hierarchy, by which the ruler's authority was absolute and their responsibility towards their subordinates reduced to a mere formalism or symbolic icon, has undeniably held sway in Chinese history, we must also bear in mind that Confucianism in its role as the state doctrine represented the doctrine of the ruling class, and as such was defined by legalistic elements that are not found in original Confucianism. Hierarchic structures are also present in Western democratic systems and, in any case, an authority based on experience, education and abilities is not necessarily negative, or a threat to the autonomy of individuals.

Modern Confucians also share a general skepticism regarding "Western models of science and democracy". In particular, they find themselves at odds with the exaggerated normativity of these models, and the dominance of a mechanistic rationality and non-reflexive scientism which, they argue, may lead to the loss or abandonment of the fundamental principles of social ethics.

5.1 The Old Holism in a New Disguise

Despite these shared views, the individual members of the second generation of Modern Confucianism had very different ideas on how to actually go about realizing a form of Confucian democracy.

For Fang Dongmei, the most important principle in a democratic society was tolerance. For this reason, he criticized Mencius for his harsh attacks against the Mohist school which had contributed greatly to the Chinese intellectual tradition, especially in terms of offering new insights and establishing a basic framework for the growth of science in China (Fang Dongmei 1992, 437). Fang was also convinced that the principle of creativity, which is central to his theories (Fang Thomé H. 1980a, 36), could represent a key element for the future development of Chinese science and democracy. Furthermore, man's mission of cultural creation in the different realms of art, literature, science, religion and social institutions is being carried forward, so that any imperfections existing in Nature and Man may be brought to ideal perfection (Fang Dongmei 1980, 11). However, an important premise which preconditions such perfection is the revival of tradition, for the realization of contemporary ideals must be based upon a humanistic spirit: "Only if we work hard and never forget our ideals, will we be able to water the sere tree of life, so that it can grow new roots and put forth luxuriant foliage" (Fang Thomé H. 1980b, 6).

Like other Modern Confucians, Fang acknowledged that the Chinese intellectual tradition had failed to lay an adequate foundation for the development of science (which he generally supported). In this context, he claimed (Fang 1980b, 19), that science has not yet gained the dominant position in Chinese culture that it should have. He explained this failure with the holistic nature of the Chinese intellectual tradition:

> Regardless of the stream of thought to which its actual contents may belong, or whether it deals with man or the cosmos, Chinese philosophy is always founded upon a holistic wholeness. In Confucian terminology, this is called "the doctrine of pervasive unity", and it is common to all Chinese philosophy. (Fang Dongmei 1978, 45)

For Fang, the reason is not far to seek. The Chinese can easily realize the importance of Science as a form of knowledge. But in the West, several meanings have been attached to it. The Greeks, for instance, saw it as a rational explanation of the intrinsic order of things in the universe to which human beings are harmoniously related. Science in this sense we can also find in China—but science naturally means more than that (Fang Thomé 1980b, 19). And even if we could equate the Greek conception to the science as such, there would still be a problem. The Greek thinkers have namely conceived of things behind the forms of the specious present as eternity. They have explained nature only quantitatively as a mechanical process of combinations and separations. Fang Dongmei pointed out that the Chinese people usually think differently. For them, nature is permeated with life and charged with value. Any process of change in nature is necessarily qualitative and creates novelties. In this framework, nature and human beings are also in a mutual relation. Thus, in terms of creating culture, nature is a help, not a hindrance (Fang Thomé 1980b, 19).

Fang ultimately concluded that the current forms of scientific development should not be pursued. Because modern science was rooted in Cartesian dualisms and viewed human beings only as mechanistic components of a society that was separated from Nature, he considered it essentially dogmatic and incapable of providing the basis for real democracy. It was, in fact, an obstacle to democratic development, because:

pure science arises out of the desire for knowledge; through the application of abstract laws it seeks to arrive at purely logical conclusions, and absolute justice, without taking into account their effective reality. Its line of reasoning always transcends human life. (Fang Dongmei 1936, 194)

Hence, for him, modern Europeans have viewed science as a systematic study of Nature, organic as well as inorganic, separate from the concrete human beings. Fang Dongmei believed that the distinction between primary and secondary qualities tends to exclude humans from *real* nature. Science seeks pure objectivity while men, according to modern psychology and epistemology up to the mid-nineteenth century, is essentially subjectivity. In such a realm of "pure objectivity", science tries to analyze the abstract. It remains limited, however, to what is mainly quantitative and to determine what is exact. In order to reduce everything, it works with formulas of identity. In Fang's view, humans should not be treated in this way (Fang 1980b, 19).

Hence, Fang Dongmei believed that the Chinese tradition not only implied certain seeds that could grow and develop into a democratic system, but also possessed certain characteristics that could lead society towards a true democracy which, thanks to the organic connection between Man and Nature, would be much more reasonable and legitimate than Western-style democracy. This view arises out of Fang's general conviction that Chinese philosophy could help resolve the current crisis of the prevailing Western philosophies and empirical sciences, a crisis which derived from their dualistic, rationalistic and scientific nature.

5.2 People as the Foundation of the State and Man as a Basis of Science

While Xu Fuguan was much more critical of the Chinese intellectual tradition, he also argued that it should not be treated as a "dead thing", but as an eternal, living entity that had a great impact on all cultures, including cultures of "modernity".

> The tradition which we are dealing with implies different lifestyles and concepts that have been transmitted from generation to generation within a certain community or nation. Traditions, being inter-generational, thus imply a certain temporal continuity. But because we are also dealing with communities, when considered in terms of space, traditions imply functions of unity and homogeneity. (Xu Fuguan 1979a, 92)

In criticizing his own tradition, Xu accepted the premise that throughout its long history, the Chinese Empire had opposed rather than encouraged the development of science and democracy. But the reason for this opposition was to be found in the misuse of original Confucianism by the political interests of the ruling classes.

> Confucian thought was not only deprived of a normal development in the field of politics, but was also often modified in its essence due to the pressures of an autocratic ruling class. The most important change was substituting the central idea of "controlling the ruler" with the legalistic idea of worshipping him. (Xu Fuguan 1955, 3)

According to Xu Fuguan, the Confucian discourse was essentially compatible with democracy, for it considered the people to be the basis of the state (*bang ben*). Xu claimed that this idea could be found in one of the earliest Confucian classics, the *Book of Documents* (*Shu jing*): "The people should be close to us, and not looked down upon. The people are the basis of the state; when this basis is solid, the state will be peaceful" (*Shu jing* 2012, Xia shu, Wu wizhi ge 2).

Similar sayings in original Confucianism suggested that the people were not to be seen merely as subjects who had to blindly obey the ruler. These ancient classics stress the importance of the connection between the People and Heaven: "Heaven sees as the people see, and hears as the people hear" (*Shu jing* 2012, Zhou shu, Qinshi zhong 2).

In these citations[1] Xu found an even more convincing proof that the state-making role of the people in classical Confucianism was of the utmost importance. The people were not merely subordinates, but representatives of Heaven and the Deities and thus above the ruler. (Xu Fuguan in Ni 200, 294) This original spirit of Confucius was then elaborated in the works of Mencius, who states quite clearly: "The people are the most important; the spirits of the land and grain are next in importance, followed by the ruler" (Mencius 2012, Jinxin xia, 60).

According to Xu, Mencius clearly stated that the people had the right to overthrow the ruler, if his rule was not in accordance with the principles of humanity (*ren*) and justice (*yi*).[2]

In Xu's view, the acceptance and development of these classical elements could thus contribute to modernization and the construction of a democratic system in China. He believed that in the Confucian model of an ideal social system, the relation between the ruler and his subjects was reciprocal and not defined by any constraints upon the subjects. Morality naturally plays an important role here, because morality is what makes people human. The concept of the cultivation of personality is thus of paramount importance, for the higher the level of cultivation, the better the nature of interpersonal relations, which in this case would be defined by a shared humanity. When this concept is fully and properly applied, people no longer see their fellow human beings as "Others" (Xu Fuguan 1980b, 49). While Xu saw the rule of law as an indispensable mechanism for the regulation of social relations, he emphasized that its basic nature remained that of a set of external norms imposed upon the individual from outside. In his view, this constitutes one of the main defects of this system, as such external relations would contribute nothing to the free development of individuals, unless they were founded upon intrinsic or concrete psycho-physical relations. The Confucian ideal of moral rule (*de zhi*) was a model which sought to regulate these intrinsic relations among individuals by emphasizing the moral values possessed by every human being in the social sphere (Xu Fuguan 1980b, 50).

He also stressed the Confucian principle of human equality, first expressed by Confucius himself and then developed further by Mencius. In these discourses, even human desire was not something to be negated or suppressed, but instead transformed through the guidance of moral reason. In the Confucian idea of the internalization and transformation of desire, likewise elaborated by Mencius, Xu saw the basis for a specifically Chinese concept of human dignity.

According to He Xinquan (1996, 136), Xu Fuguan's reinterpretation of the Confucian theory of the goodness of innate human qualities (or of human nature, *xing shan lun*) not only confirmed that the concept of justice was based on (the idea of) human equality, but also clearly showed that this theory, which was rooted in refining moral practice and establishing the concept of the moral Self, tended towards a democratic political outlook that was in accordance with the requirements of human nature. This democratic political view was based upon human rights and freedom. But on the other hand, Xu Fuguan also marked some important differences between these Confucian "seeds" of democracy and the concept of liberal democracy prevalent in the Western world. While democracy was based upon individualism, and socialist or nationalist ideologies on a collective ideal, traditional Chinese (or Confucian) state theory was neither collectivistic[3] nor individualistic, but could instead be defined as a theory of communitarianism (*quntizhuyi*), and thus rooted in a sense of the importance of human communities. As opposed to collectivism, which is based upon mechanistic and externally determined relations between individuals, communitarianism proposes an organic network of interpersonal connections in which the people (and not the ruler) uphold or underlie the state.

For Xu, the moral rule (*de zhi*) could not be separated from the refinement of (a ruler's) personality. He saw both elements in a complementary, mutually interdependent relation, and manifested in the traditional binary category of the internal sage and the external ruler (*neisheng waiwang*) (Xu Fuguan 1980a, 48). He also evaluated this moral rule through the lens of the concept of non-action (*wuwei*):

> In his political thought, Confucius has applied the concept of non-action (*wuwei*) in a way, in which education should ultimately replace politics and would, after all, even eliminate political thought. This is the substance of his moral rule (Xu Fuguan 2000, 192).

Xu's views were severely criticized by other scholars. Qi Liang, a noted expert in Chinese intellectual history from the P. R. China, claimed that the traditional idea that people were the "basis of the state" was fundamentally anti-democratic, for it was based upon the assumption that the people were—whether in this or other ways—still subject to the ruler. Qi stressed that in these early Confucian sources there is no trace of the idea that the people could determine their fate on their own, and that these specific citations were merely guidelines for the ruler, advising him to take into account the people's interests if he wished to retain power (Qi Liang 1995, 438–40). However, Xu Fuguan was obviously following several passages in which Mencius seems to affirm that the people should participate in the process of choosing the governments (Qi Liang 1995, 50).[4]

In any case, Xu stressed that these democratic elements deriving from original Confucianism had never been developed throughout the whole of autocratic Chinese history, and that therefore Confucianism failed to develop the idea of the subject as an active political agent or factor:

> Because Confucians were responsible for interpersonal relations, they were also responsible for political ones. However, due to historical conditions, and despite the beauty of its theory, Confucian political thought has been limited to justifying the position of the rulers. It never focused on the position of the subjects or allowed them to put these theories into action. Thus, Chinese history never developed a political subjectivity and (the principle) of the people as the basis of the state was never developed democratically. (Xu Fuguan 1952, 3)

He thus proposed a dual (political) subjectivity (*er zhongde zhutixing*) to express the dichotomy between democratic theory and autocratic practice, a dichotomy that could be resolved by the ruler's "self-negation" (*ziwode fouding*, Xu Fuguan 1980a, 224) or "non-action" (*wuwei*). This element could thus provide a socio-political foundation that would enable the people to actually carry out practical political decisions, since the function of the ruler would be reduced to that of a symbolic arbiter. Moral rule (de zhi) underpins this "limited government" for the moral qualities (including the cardinal virtues) innate to every human being (Xu Fuguan 1988, 232), and which form part of the innate knowledge and subjective potential common to everyone (*ren xin suo tongran*),[5] are what make this limitation possible.

Xu also realized that the development of science was likewise important for creating a democratic society. The fact that science, in the sense of gaining "objective" knowledge, had never developed in traditional China could be explained by the very different conditions obtaining in ancient China, as opposed to ancient Greece (Xu Fuguan 1988, 232). These differences led to a spirit of curiosity prevailing in Greece, while China was dominated by a sense of anxiety or concern (*youhuan yishi*). This fundamental difference influenced the way knowledge was acquired within the two cultures: the Greeks held rationality to be Man's defining characteristic, and the love or contemplation of wisdom the true source of happiness (Ni 2002, 283). They viewed the pursuit of knowledge as a goal in and of itself. According to Xu Fuguan, these features of Greek culture led to the search for objective knowledge, especially in metaphysics and science. Modern Western thinkers inherited this tradition. However, while the Greeks saw "knowing" as a form of education, modern Western thinkers shifted towards a concept of knowledge as power, through the possession and control of the external, material world (as in Francis Bacon's famous motto "knowledge is power").

A major consequence of these very different approaches was that Western science saw human beings as mechanistic compounds of nature, while Confucianism kept human beings at the centre of its focus, even interpreting nature through the lens of human conditions (Ni 2002, 288). In this context, Xu pointed out certain autocratic elements implicit in the Western model of science, and which were present in all modern cultures deriving from it:

> In general, we can say that this tendency was formed because every human being became involved with this omnipotent technocracy and the bureaucratic system. This meant that human beings were no longer "individuals", but merely parts of the "mass". ... Because modern man has lost the subjectivity of his true "Self", which has been overwhelmed by the dominance of technocracy and bureaucracy, he lives a thoughtless, unreflective life... Science is one of the most magnificent products of human thought. But today its proponents have greatly increased modern thoughtlessness in the name of Science. This phenomena is truly paradoxical. (Xu Fuguan 1960, 2)

While Xu acknowledged that Confucianism did not imply a scientific dimension, he laid stress upon the fact that this did not mean it was opposed to science (Ni 2002, 293). And although the Chinese tradition, as such, had never developed an adequate methodology for scientific research, he denied that this was due to the "naive" nature of this tradition. He pointed out that Confucianism had simply developed a different methodology, based upon the preservation and cultivation of personalities. The Confucian tradition was never interested in abstract laws for the objective world, but instead sought a world of objectivity within moral virtues.

Xu Fuguan's views regarding these two extraordinarily complex and heterogeneous traditions can certainly be criticized for their excessive generalization, while his conclusion that the Confucian tradition never developed any methodologies for developing the empirical sciences, is likewise open to debate:

> I am not sure that Xu has assessed Confucianism fairly in this respect. Xu seems to overlook the fact that Western science may also be value-laden, and thus also objectifies human values and assumptions. Secondly, he never mentions the holistic and correlative way of thinking that characterizes the Chinese philosophical tradition, including Confucianism. Whether this mode of thinking offers an alternative way of scientific thinking is open to debate. If one defines science in terms of the model developed in the West, one can argue that China has never produced any scientific thought. Yet the Chinese, including the Confucians, used correlative thinking to understand nature and achieve remarkable insights into how the universe functions, as best exemplified by Chinese medicine. In this regard, Joseph Needham's work on science and civilization in China and more recent discussions of Chinese correlative thinking by A. C. Graham and others, merit serious attention. (Ni 2002, 294)

But, on the other hand, we certainly have to acknowledge that even though Xu Fuguan's extensive philosophical production contains inconsistencies, his analyses of Western science and the democratic elements within Confucian teachings, together with his original proposals for the founding of a Chinese theory of modernization, definitely constitute important contributions to Modern Confucian researches in this area. The theoretical foundations of his thought certainly deserve further investigation and analysis.

5.3 The Heavenly Mandate and the Analysis of the Basis of Integration

Tang Junyi's recipe for China's modernization differs completely from Zhang Zhidong's view that China should "preserve its own substance" (i.e. its traditional thought) and assume Western functions (Western technology) (*Zhongxue wei ti, Xixue wei yong*). Tang criticized this position, arguing that merely adopting Western technologies was not enough to guarantee China's modernization, for these technologies were based on complex, multilayered ideas that had been developed by Western cultures over many centuries. Of course, this did not mean that Chinese culture should be abandoned completely and replaced by the Western model, as had been proposed by the radically iconoclastic scholars of early Chinese liberalism. In terms of introducing science and democracy into China, Tang agreed with scholars such as Hu Shi and Chen Duxiu, but opposed those who wanted a complete Westernization, he argued for a partial Westernization that remained grounded in Chinese culture (Tang Junyi 1986, 5–6; 1953, 482–9):

> Thus, if China chooses to accept Western culture in the future, it must change its attitude completely, as hitherto it has been both excessively modest and overly envious. China should learn to view itself in a healthy and sophisticated way. It should ground itself in its own spiritual origins. (Tang Junyi 1953, 476)

As noted, Tang believed this synthesis was possible because Chinese culture also possessed its own indigenous seeds of science and democracy, a view which accords with the other second generation thinkers. Another, less positive aspect he shares with this group is that his theoretical assumptions regarding the specific features of Chinese modernization were often based on superficial and generalized comparisons of Chinese and Western cultures (see for instance, Tang

Junyi 1986, 5–8, 10–18). In his view, Chinese culture is humanistic and focuses on ethics, arts, and human relations. Western culture, on the other hand, is materialistic and emphasizes science, religion and individual freedom (Tang Junyi 1975a, 414). In spite of such critical remarks, Tang still believed that Chinese culture should reinforce its assimilation of science and democracy, for in order to modernize itself successfully it had to proceed from its own traditions. He even went a step further, claiming that Chinese culture could become the leader in the search for a perfect culture through the integration with other cultures (Tang Junyi 2000, 293).

Given that the Western model of science was defined by distinctions between the subject and object of comprehension, the idea of modernization would have to infuse a spirit of objectivity and analysis into the aesthetically and spiritually oriented Chinese tradition. Tang also claimed that science, as such, could be found in various forms in the Chinese intellectual tradition. He pointed out that the Chinese had developed certain advanced technologies before the West, but that these technologies had never led to actual scientific progress. Tang explained this limitation with the traditional Chinese focus on the moral refinement of individuals within the system of formalized social ethics, a factor which tended to reduce epistemological investigation.[6] Tang noted that many traditional Chinese scholars had recognized this problem,[7] and had sought to broaden their epistemological methodology to include aspects of the external, material world. While their efforts were mostly limited to philological research and textual analyses, the Confucian scholars of the Ming and Qing Dynasties had shown great interest in irrigation systems and other agrarian technologies, as well as medicine and astronomy, indicating a desire to improve the general welfare through a better understanding of Nature. But as Sin yee Chan (2002, 323) points out, all the examples Tang Junyi musters in order to demonstrate the traditional Chinese interest in exploring the external world, reveal a purely instrumental relation to Nature. This interest was therefore defined by its applicability and not by a curiosity as to how Nature "works". Further, given Tang's general definition of culture as the manifestation of a certain awareness directed towards certain aspects of reality, it is doubtful whether science could ever have developed in traditional China. An awareness which is focused on integration is namely something quite different from one which emphasizes distinctions and analysis. It is thus difficult to see how using science to achieve modernization could be reconciled with the traditional Chinese awareness that viewed integration as paramount. And while Tang argued that it was possible to suspend or set aside integrative reasoning when thinking scientifically, Sin yee Chan (2002, 323) expressed scepticism regarding this solution, concluding that Chinese culture would be forced to pay a high price for its scientific development, as this would inevitably result in an erosion and weakening of its own spiritual nucleus.

Most Modern Confucians were aware, to varying degrees, that understanding modernization also meant taking into account the consequences and possible negative collateral effects of this process. In any case, Tang Junyi's belief that modern science could somehow be based on traditional Chinese values (Tang Junyi 2000, 293) was probably too optimistic.

Using similar arguments, Tang also tried to demonstrate that the Chinese intellectual tradition contained the seeds of a democratic system. He thus proposed a series of democratic reforms for modern China, arguing that such reforms had to be grounded on morality and on raising the ethical awareness of Chinese citizens.

> This democratic system would form and improve the political awareness of the people, based on a moral culture. This system would not be in contradiction with the people's trust in such a wise political spirit. (Tang Junyi 1986, 283)

As a genuine Confucian, he was convinced that this reform, which could direct the Chinese transition towards a mature democratic system, could only take place by means of the moral education of the Chinese people, an education which also had to be grounded in a moral culture:

> Human political awareness could thus merge with human cultural awareness, and the respect of rituals and moral personalities. If political awareness were guided by moral awareness, it could—through genuine dedication—assume an elite, political role which would once again develop an awareness of cultural formation and education. (Tang Junyi 1986, 285)

In this context, Tang Junyi did not concern himself with the issue of who should define the axiological contents of this "cultural formation and education". His paramount concern was that this democracy should be based on authentic Confucian foundations and thus, by implication, on all the main elements of the traditional idea of moral rule (i.e. moral guidance and ordering society): "This ideal form of political democracy would still imply the traditional Chinese ideals of rituality, humanity and morality" (Tang Junyi 1986, 289).

This new democracy would be based on the Confucian concept of the Heavenly Mandate (*tian ming*). In Tang's interpretation, the will of Heaven essentially expressed the will of the people. Like Xu Fuguan, Tang emphasized that the mythological Emperors Yao and Shun, who in Confucianism represent the supreme models of moral rule, did not leave their thrones to their sons, as ordained by the laws of succession, but to successors chosen from among the most capable people (who were, needless to say, all male). The famous Confucian maxim that "everything under Heaven is public and common" (*Li ji* 2012, Li yun 1), was also interpreted by Tang Junyi as endorsing a "Chinese type" of democratic order. Here, he invoked the Confucian principle of the moral equality of all people, which affirmed that every human being has the possibility of becoming a sage (*sheng ren*). Tang even detected the seeds of a democratic order in some of the historical Confucian institutions and practices which were intended to keep the emperor informed concerning the views of his subjects.

Tang Junyi also focused on issues linked to the concept of human freedom, and compared various Western theories of liberty to the traditional Confucian idea of personal freedom, which is rooted in the individual practice of humanism:

> However, in traditional Chinese thought, the values of self-completion, self-seeking, self-realization and self-achievement were paramount. The efforts of the individual were not directed towards society per se, or engaged in a struggle with others for forms of personal freedom. (Tang Junyi 1953, 488)

While he believed that this kind of informal, morally conditioned freedom had become a reality in traditional China, he criticized this concept precisely for its informal structure. This informality meant that personal freedom never acquired a constitutional protection and was thus constantly in danger of being eliminated by autocratic rulers. Tang Junyi distinguished eight stages of individual and social freedom, with the latter being more important, given that personal or individual freedom was necessarily conditioned by social, i.e. communitarian or political freedom (Tang Junyi 2000, 335–8). Another important democratic element implicit in traditional Confucianism was the concept of tolerance, which Tang considered to be one of the most important features defining the specific Confucian spirit of humanism (Tang Junyi 1953, 480–1).

Tang's claims as to the seeds of democracy within the Confucian teachings must be viewed with reserve, for a ruler's interest in the will of his subjects does not necessarily endow them political sovereignty. Indeed, the concept of political sovereignty is precisely what defines and conditions the common idea of democracy, whereas in Confucianism, the concept of the Heavenly Mandate precluded the people from any active political role, which remained the exclusive prerogative of the Heavenly ruler.[8] The origins of Confucian political authority are thus completely different from those of Western cultures, which are grounded in the idea of the social contract, and with the people delegating their political power to the ruler (or government). Their role as political actors is thus based upon a contractual relation—as equals—with the ruler or government.

Even Tang Junyi is forced to admit that the principal defect of the traditional Chinese ideal of social order is that political power is concentrated entirely in the person of the ruler:

> Here, it is important to note that any realization of the traditional Chinese rule of humanity, rituality and morality has, in the past, always depended on the subjective moral will of the ruler. (Tang Junyi 1986, 289)

Despite the positive aspects of the seeds of democracy, such as the Confucian respect for all people and a general spirit of equality which, according to Tang, was rooted in a positive view of innate human qualities (or, "human nature"), (Tang Junyi 1991, 420), in traditional China these seeds referred to a moral and not a political democracy. While Tang believed that this major shortcoming could be resolved by strict legislation and the rule of law (Tang Junyi 1975a, 889), this legalistic remedy would still be subordinated to the criteria of traditional morality:

> What I imagine and what I want, is an ideal based on rituality, humanity and morality. Such a system transcends laws while still including them, and thus most certainly must include legislation and democracy. Although the past ideal of traditional China is, in many respects, superior to the Western social order based on law and democracy, in practice it represents an inferior stage with respect to the social and political systems of modern Western societies, precisely because it does not include a legal system. (Tang Junyi 1975a, 889)

Tang Junyi's conclusion that the rule of law constitutes the foundation of modern societies is certainly true. His critique of such systems is also credible. However, and granting that there is always the possibility of an abuse of power in both systems, Tang was unable to formulate a new theoretical model which could provide a creative and functional link between the two very different social orders. However, there are some significant elements in Tang's thought, which differ from the basic political paradigms proposed by other second generation theorists. For instance, Mou Zongsan and Xu Fuguan both stressed the difference between the two aspects of personality cultivation and regulating others (*neisheng waiwang*), claiming that the former had to be evaluated by the highest (maximal) criteria, and the latter by the lowest (minimal). This contrasts with Tang Junyi's view that the value of humanism represents the fundamental level for achieving freedom. Such distinctions between ethical and political categories could certainly help clarify the many conceptual problems linked to the relation between Confucianism and democracy.

We can conclude, therefore, that none of the representatives of the second generation succeeded in resolving the general (and most significant) question of the relation between law and morality in modern (or post-modern) societies. But a first step towards such a solution might be found in the concept of two truths, which we will now examine.

5.4 Two Truths, Two Subjects

As we shall see below, the link between reason and intuition was the element which the thinkers of the second generation of Modern Confucianism, based on very similar hypotheses already elaborated by the first generation, used as a key criterion for defining differences between philosophy and science, and Western and Chinese philosophy. In his evaluation of the May Fourth Movement and its proposals regarding a liberalistic Westernization (Han and Zhao 1994, 247), Mou Zongsan explains how the scholars who had gathered around Hu Shi had produced a rational, theoretical elaboration of their views on science, in contrast to previous approaches which were little more than emotionally colored and often even irrational declarations of pure admiration. Despite this ostensibly rational approach, the formulations of this new generation of intellectuals adhered even more closely to the domain of one-dimensional scientism and the monopolistic position of scientific discourses. This approach gradually became an indispensable aspect of their theoretical endeavors, not only in the controversies surrounding science as such, but also in their more general theoretical discourses. Mou has criticized the predominance of such discourses, accusing them of "annihilating meanings and values" and of propounding a philosophical perspective "limited to objects without seeing human beings" (Han and Zhao 1994, 247). In his view, this one-dimensional scientism and the monopolistic dominance of pure rationality has been preserved in Chinese academic circles until the present time. Mou also claims that these discourses—together with others—why many Chinese theoreticians continued to look down upon traditional Chinese culture and its intellectual achievements, thereby hindered the adaptation of these traditional discourses to the requirements of the modern era.

> When morality goes blind, people are even more inclined to turn to the omnipotence of science. They are convinced that science, if sufficiently developed, can solve any problem. There is no longer any place for fate in this situation. This view is based upon the unreasonableness and stupidity of shallow rationalists who have never experienced the meaning of a moral life. (Mou Zongsan 2010, 157)

Mou's interpretation of the traditional concept of the "external ruler" (*wai wang*) is rooted in the inseparability of science and democracy (He Xinqian 2000, 75). In this context, Mou Zongsan emphasizes that while science as such is rooted in human desire (in terms of comprehension, wellbeing, material progress and the ability to control nature and the outside world), it does not possess any mechanisms for controlling this desire. Even if science could actually solve all the world's problems (as the "shallow rationalists" like to think), it would still not be possible to do so because the world's resources are limited, while human desire as such has no limits. And this is precisely where the advantages and specific contributions of Chinese philosophy, with its focus on moral and ethical questions, becomes more clearly evident. If we wish to establish a harmonious relation with Nature we must somehow control human desire (Tang Refeng 2002, 343). In contrast to Buddhism, indigenous Chinese philosophy does not negate human desire, but understands the world in a way that enables the transcendence of desire, thereby freeing human beings from their obsessive pursuit. In his efforts to define a formal boundary between science, which is rooted in instrumental reason, and philosophy, Mou Zongsan often characterizes philosophy as a form of "teaching" (*jiao*):[9]

> Speaking in very simple and approximate terms, we can denote anything that was declared by the old masters as a form of teaching. Even without referring to these masters, we can say that anything which moves human beings to develop their reason and purify their lives through specific practices, or which enables them to reach their culmination, can be denoted as a teaching. If philosophy is more than a pure profession, while still differing from science, it can also be seen as a form of teaching. (Mou Zongsan 2010, ii)

In defining fundamental differences between Chinese and Western philosophy, Mou Zongsan distinguishes two kinds of truth: the intensional (*neirongde zhenli*) and the extensional (*waiyande zhenli*).

> Roughly speaking, truth can be divided into two kinds: I denote the first as extensional, and the second as intensional truth. The

> extensional truth can be explained roughly as a scientific or mathematical truth... Extensional truths are detached from subjectivity and can thus be objectively valid. All truths which do not belong to the domain of subjectivity and can thus be verified as being objectively valid, belong to extensional truths. (Mou Zongsan 1983a, 20–21)

Intensional truths instead have the form of intensional propositions and represent intensional relations within a subject. Strictly speaking, they do not belong to scientific truths, but rather to the truths of the humanities and cultural studies.[10] Mou argues forcefully for the acknowledgement of this type of truth, which also appears in Buddhist, Daoist and Confucian discourses. Such truths are universal in the intensional, rather than extensional sense:

> In addition to the extensional, we must also recognize the existence of intensional truth. But in this regard, how can we respond to logical positivism which claims that everything implied in metaphysics is nothing but a set of conceptual poems which, at best, can only satisfy our emotions? If metaphysics is only a set of conceptual poems, and if it can only satisfy our emotions, then we cannot claim that it implies a truth, or truths. But are metaphysics, and the messages of Buddhism, Daoism and the Christian faith really only limited to satisfying us emotionally? While one can certainly claim that they are not extensional truths, this certainly does not mean they are not truths at all. They are, in fact, all intensional truths that cannot simply be dismissed as "conceptual poems". (Mou Zongsan 1983a, 23)

This is why Mou Zongsan considers it wrong and harmful to denote Chinese philosophy, which is based upon seeking intensional truths, as a science and to look for extensional truths within it. Furthermore, the universality of both kinds of truth also differs, for extensional truths are universal on an abstract level, while intensional truths are universal on the concrete level. In fact, the term "concrete universality" is Hegelian. Tang Refeng (2002, 342) points out that on the one hand, Mou Zongsan views Hegel as a philosopher who can go beyond the limitations of Western orthodoxy. On the other, however, he does not agree with Hegel's way of expressing this idea. Mou is convinced that concrete universality is more clearly expressed and thus more evident in Chinese philosophy.

For Mou, concrete universality is flexible or "elastic" (Mou Zongsan 1983a, 23), and therefore cannot be seen as eternal, in the sense of being unchangeable. In Mou's view, Western science has generally developed the extensional, while Chinese thought has mainly focused upon intensional truth. Due to the universality of both types of truth, the two cultures can learn from each other in multiple ways.

In the intellectual and cultural crisis which produced the May Fourth Movement, Chinese intellectuals recognized their limitations in seeking and using extensional truths. For this reason, Zhang Zhidong's dictum on preserving the Chinese substance while simultaneously applying Western technology (*zhong ti xi yong*) appears as inappropriate. If we wish to obtain a proper tool for comprehending extensional truths, it is not enough simply to acquire and accumulate knowledge, but we must also obtain a more profound understanding and mastery of the intellectual and cultural discourses which have made certain developments possible. As opposed to the Chinese, who by the end of the nineteenth century had begun to realize the necessity of gaining extensional truths, Western theoreticians never fully understood their own inability to comprehend intensional truths, for the simple reason that they did not see them as truths (Tang Refeng 2002, 342). In Mou's view, this defect clearly manifests itself in the problems affecting modern and post-modern (Western) societies.

In the field of epistemology, there are two forms of reason that correspond to intensional and extensional truths: the functional and the constructive. These will be discussed in detail in the chapter on reason and intuition below.

According to Mou Zongsan, it was precisely this recognition of the need to establish extensional truths which produced the Chinese "enlightenment", and with it the May Fourth cultural renewal movement and the interest of Chinese intellectuals in science and democracy.

Mou Zongsan also concurs with those who claim that Chinese culture has quite successfully developed morality and ethics, but has failed in establishing democracy and science. Like other Modern

Confucians, he does not think this means that Chinese culture was incompatible with science and democracy, but that this failure was due primarily to the specific historical conditions that determined the development of Chinese culture. These conditions also naturally determined the specific features of traditional Chinese epistemology (He Xinquan 2000, 76–77). An important factor here is that the structure of traditional Chinese society was not defined by class struggle; in philosophy, this resulted in the lack of individual self-awareness (He Xinquan 2000, 75–76). According to Mou, this also led to the development of universal principles, but without establishing principles of particularity. These specific characteristics also resulted in the integrity of all dual oppositions defining traditional methods of reasoning; in this sense, they failed to mark a separation between subject and object:

> These two entities were not in mutual opposition: either the object was incorporated into my own subject, or I was integrated into the object... In my inwardness, all objects were part of my heart-mind, and the heart-mind was part of the (external) objects. Both were actually one entity. If we want to forcibly divide the subject from the object in order to establish some kind of relation between them, then this can only lead to a relation of sub-ordination. So too with the "transformation" of saints and sages. In such a wise government, the relationship between the ruler and his people was seen as a relation between parents and their children. In this view, children cannot be the enemies of their parents. (Mou Zongsan 1987, 52)

Hence, Chinese intellectual history developed the moral (*daode zhuti*) and the artistic (*yishuxing zhuti*), but without establishing a concept of the cognitive subject (*renshi zhuti, zhixing zhuti*). Mou concludes that a cultural spirit of this sort could not provide the basis for the development of science and/or democracy.

In order to incorporate the concept of an active cognitive subject, which was essential for both the development of science and a democratic social system, the traditional concept of the moral Self had to be transformed through the process of so-called self-negation[11] (*ziwo kanxian*), which will be discussed below. For now, let us assume that this self-negation was necessary, for goodness and truth are not necessarily the same thing (He Xinquan 2000, 93). However, the self-negation of the subject was seen as a temporary phase in a "dialectical process" (He Xinquan 2000, 93), for if the static, primary position of morality precluded a recognition of the full plurality of knowledge, its total absence would have devastating consequences for society, which would become like "a lone boat without a compass, tossed in a stormy, limitless sea" (He Xinquan 2000, 95). In the dialectical process that linked the possible acquisition of scientific knowledge with axiological regulation (or moral guidance), the moral Self (*daode lixing*) was thus seen as a "bridge connecting Confucianism with modern democracy"(He Xinquan 2000, 97). For He Xinquan, this is Mou's main contribution to Modern Confucian attempts to develop and modernize the seeds of democracy and science already present within the Chinese intellectual tradition:

> When viewed in terms of developing democracy and science, the dialectical development of the moral Self is, of course, not the only possibility... But when viewed in terms of Confucianism, which has been the dominant factor in determining the value systems in Chinese culture, then Mou Zongsan's theoretical framework of incorporating democracy via the inner dialectical development of Confucianism appears as very significant for the preservation of China's long-running national sovereignty. (He Xinquan 2000, 97–98)

However, Mou Zongsan was primarily a philosopher, and as such, he was the second generation thinker who dedicated the most effort to creating a new, active subject which, in his view, was indispensable to developing any kind of modern science and democracy. His approach here was essentially twofold: on the one hand, seeking to renew the subject based on the fundamental assumptions and tendencies of Confucian philosophy, while at the same time correcting certain deficiencies in the concept of the subject, as found in German classical philosophy. He did this by focusing on three fundamental attributes which constitute indispensable features of this concept, i.e. reason, essential for the development of science,[12] and free will and autonomy, or the two elements that underpin democracy. Mou

122   The Rebirth of the Moral Self

Zongsan summed up his new version of these key ideas as follows:

1. Free autonomous will is the core of acting in accordance with moral consciousness; it is heart-mind (*xin*);

2. It represents the legislation of the Self; hence, it is the structure of reason;

3. While it can be defined as being determined by unconditional laws, it is actually self-aware, which means that it is derived from autonomy. In other words: free, autonomous will is not something passive or involuntary, but functions based on principles established by and for itself. Mencius confirms this when he notes that justice and the structure of reason are something pleasing to human heart-mind;[13]

4. "Decisions" thus derive from a will that is based on this self-defined code, and which marks or emphasizes its own specific features;

5. When speaking of this self-defined code, it is important to note that its maxims cannot be in conflict with moral laws. Therefore, the will is sacred, for it is its own reason;

6. Ideas that have emerged under the influence of feelings cannot be considered as belonging to this free autonomous will, as they imply good and evil in the sense of "two existences with different expressions", while the free autonomous will is pure goodness without evil, i.e. "one center with two functions";[14]

7. Moral laws are synthetic in relation to volition, but analytic in relation to free, autonomous will;

8. Thus, free autonomous will is merely law-giving for self; it commands or determines duties. "Command" means commanding a human being whose duty it is to act in accordance with these laws. Here, commands and duties do not refer to the free autonomous will. The law giving of the free autonomous will for self is the final limit marking the ultimate capacity of the substance of the innate nature (or innate qualities, *xingti*) in human beings. The duties deriving

from it are nothing other than my own share or apportioning.[15] What determines this apportioning is thus the capacity of the substance of innate nature (or innate qualities). (Mou Zongsan 1975, 76, 77)

But our interest here is in the actual features of the democratic system conceived by Mou Zongsan. In Confucianism, the intimate "apportioning" (*fen*) of each individual has always been linked to their social position and thus, as Mou argues, is limited by the capacities (*bu rongyi*) of their moral Self.

This raises the question whether men as beings are thus even more determined by this system, than by the systems of the modern natural sciences? Such an "apportioning" would necessarily have a decisive influence on the existence and possibilities of the "degree" of realization of the moral Self. General possibilities for such a realization had already been offered to each individual by original Confucianism. At the same time, we should bear in mind that these possibilities always only represented an ideal construct which was, most probably, never realized.

Modern Confucians have responded in various ways to these criticisms, based on the epistemological concept of *chengxian*, which denotes the instantaneous emergence of the contents implied in human inwardness, within the sphere of the transient concrete actuality. There was thus no serious or exhaustive effort to define the ways by which this concept of infinite consciousness, which is necessarily conditioned by some kind of continuity, can be formed within the sphere of concrete actuality, which is merely composed of instantaneous forms of existence.

Additional questions as to how and in what way all these modern versions of Confucianism could be connected with the concrete problems that actually affect contemporary Chinese societies have also not been addressed in any significant way by the representatives of this current, which underscores the fact that the Modern Confucian current has also failed to formulate a critical social theory. A similar tendency can also be observed in their views on science, for the theorists of the second generation have yet to offer any complete and coherent theory of science (or scientific method), to correspond with Mou Zongsan's theory of "two kinds of truth" and the two forms of reason.[16] Only such a theory of science would be able to transcend the many individual contradictions and unite them into complementary relations within the structure of reason (*li*). Such a concept of science would no longer be based on exclusion, or formally determined limitations of quantitative methodology and therefore enable human beings to endow their lives with more meaning.

Most of the thinkers of the second generation attach great importance to the modern Confucian concept of meaning (*yiyi*),[17] generally viewed (through its aesthetic, epistemological and axiological connotations) as something which permeates all dimensions of existence, or even as something by which all of these dimensions are defined. In Modern Confucian discourses, this sort of imparting of meaning does not refer solely to the subject but, with respect to the axiological dimensions of Chinese onto-epistemology, also to the subject's intimate connection with fellow human beings who were thus seen as being something more than solely the "Others".

6. The Midwives of Modern Cultures: Reason, Subjectivity and their Philosophical Connotations

The majority of Modern Confucians believed that in the process of its own modernization, China—like all other "non-Western" countries—had to appropriate certain Western conceptual elements, essentially linked to the development of technology and modern socio-political systems, given that modernity as such had begun in the Western world. However, this did not mean that China necessarily had to give up the essence of its own tradition. In their view, classical Confucianism implied several concepts which could be developed so as to meet the social and epistemological requirements of the new era. Confucian philosophy also implied some important notions similar to the Western concepts of reason and subject, which represent the main foundations on which a modern society can be developed. The semantic connotations of these notions of course did not correspond with their Western counterparts, given that in traditional Chinese society they functioned in a completely different social, political and economic context. On the other hand, the majority of the second generation of Modern Confucians were convinced that numerous connotations rooted in the Confucian tradition were precisely those lacking in the Western intellectual tradition. An imaginative synthesis of both traditions could thus lead to a better, socially more justified and morally more mature form of modernity. Based on these assumptions, the Modern Confucians believed that the modernization of their countries did not represent a threat to their own culture but, on the contrary, that this process could offer new opportunities for dialogue and mutual exchange for both cultures.

However, the modernization processes that took place in China in the latter half of the twentieth century were not only linked to the issues of Westernization in a narrow sense, but also—especially in the period of economic liberalization which took place in the last two decades of the twentieth century—to specific features of globalized development.

As in the first attempts to modernize and move beyond the tradition during the period of the May Fourth cultural renewal movement, the intellectual reflection on or ideologization of modernization processes in Modern Confucian discourses also focused primarily on an idealization of the concepts of reason and subjectivity, in terms of individual autonomy (Rošker 2008, 312). In the course of European intellectual history, reason had been generally understood in terms of the self-referentiality of the subject of recognition. In the context of "classical" or "Western type" modernization, subjectivity was thus a fundamental and creative, even "fundamentalist" (Habermas 1998, 199) notion, for it provided the sort of demonstrability and certainty by which all else could be placed in doubt and criticized. At the same time, this self-referential subjectivity also represented a basic structure of reason, and both functions were typical and necessary preconditions of the so-called "new era".

For contemporary Chinese theorists dealing with the problems of modernization, the notion of subjectivity[1] is especially interesting, for it refers to a relation between individual and society which is not rooted exclusively in the suppositions of the European tradition, but also implies elements that can be linked to certain basic concepts found in the leading ideal currents of classical Chinese philosophy. In this context, subjectivity has both a universal and an individualistic meaning, for being based on a mutual respect amongst all members of a social community, it also provides an essential criterion for the assessment of an individual's intrinsic right to personal fulfilment and happiness.

In the process of accepting and reflecting on modernization, most Chinese thinkers accepted the general supposition that the necessary precondition for a "normal" development of this process was the consolidation of a subject situated at the center of a rational perception of reality and which, thanks to its autonomy, was able to actively and creatively generate and change this reality.

Underlying the philosophy of modernization is Reason, which champions subjectivity. The notion of the "subject" was rediscovered in the period from the Renaissance to the Enlightenment, ultimately becoming the focus of all meaning and values. The thinkers of the Enlightenment were convinced that human beings, as subjects and with the indispensable aid of Reason, were able to achieve happiness in this world (Dai Liyong 2008, 12). Modernity was thus understood as the generalized "rationality" or "rationalization" of social interactions.

The Chinese enlightenment, which was rooted not in socialist discourses but in the early French Enlightenment and Anglo-American liberalism, applied the ideology of science or a "spirit of science" (actually of scientism) as a tool for better understanding the Western modernization model and a corresponding restructuring of the world and of Chinese history as such.[2] Certain of its exponents, through philosophical or literary-theoretical discourses, reopened questions of subjectivity that were often connected with individual freedom (Wang Hui 2000, 18). They generally advocated a radical change of social norms, arguing that given that the traditional norms were based upon the suppression of individuals in favor of an unjust social structure, the new norms should be oriented towards the liberation of individual human integrity.

In this context, subjectivity means both individual subjectivity and the subjectivity of human beings as a species, with the former in contraposition to the dictatorial state and its ideology, and the latter to the natural world. This discourse is imbued with the optimism of the eighteenth and nineteenth century European Enlightenment and couched in the binary framework of subjectivity/objectivity (Wang Hui 2000, 19).

While many representatives of this movement were also familiar with recent Euro-American philosophical and social theory, the critique of modernity as such implied in many of these theories never had any following in China. Among "progressive" Chinese theorists, thinkers such as Sartre (Wang Hui 2000, 19) were seen primarily in terms of an autonomous subject who was resisting the power of an authoritarian state.

In this context, the autonomy (in the prevailing "Western" sense, see Rošker 1996, 98)[3] of free individuals was mainly understood as something in antithetical (dichotomous) opposition to the obsolete Confucian tradition. In their early insight into the need for the division of labor,[4] the Confucians generally explained any instrumental activity as rooted in communication and coordination, a conceptualization which enabled them to control social reality through clannish social patterns and mechanisms. In productive activity, the individual enters into a direct relation, first with Nature, in the sense of raw material, and then with the actual products of that labor. In this way, the individual creates the margins for developing their own subjectivity, which is tendentially directed towards autonomy.

Hence, contemporary Chinese thinkers generally embraced a model of modernity or modern society in which the traditional worldviews and constructions, rooted either in religion or in ideologies based upon an immanent metaphysics, were seen as no longer viable or credible. In essence, this meant they could no longer function as generally binding discourses, or offer a meaningful orientation for collective interactions among individuals and their social activities. The concept of subjectivity which emerges from such contexts is the result of the loss of a general normativity, which forces the individual to generate a new normativity for themselves. This self-referential subjectivity is meant to replace the lost power of religion or immanent metaphysical ideologies. The fracture between tradition and modernity is thus always marked by the search for an inherent principle that can replace the stabilizing function of past religions or ideologies.

In Europe, questions related to the "self-justification" of modernity were already treated as serious philosophical problems beginning with Hegel (1970, 398–441). Subjectivity understood as a self-referential structure has, in its function as an omnipresent principle of the "new era", also represented the basic structure of Reason. However, a Reason based upon subjectivity failed to attain—in terms of "self-justification"—a sufficient (or at least satisfactory) level of credibility. In European philosophical discourses dedicated to the problems of modernity, it became clear that Reason was limited by the existing semantic or linguistic framework; thus, when attempting a "totalizing self-critique" (Habermas 1998, 210), it inevitably became entangled in contradictions. In fact, a subject-centric Reason always tends towards an absolute form of purpose or utilitarian rationality (Adorno and Horkheimer 1969, 49). In this paradigm, any liberalization or emancipation of the subject is necessarily linked to the determinations and dynamics of the pragmatic patterns from which it arises. The consequences of these patterns manifest themselves in the mechanisms used and applied by Reason in order to criticize and eliminate various forms of exploitation and oppression, humiliation and alienation and replace them with a rationality which, ostensibly, possesses unlimited credibility (Habermas 1986, 104). Hence, the critique of modernity reveals that its supposed innovativeness is basically nothing more than a kind of automatic *habitus*. Modernity thus has been determined by the illegitimate rule of a totalitarian principle of rationality (which implies certain despotic aspects) and by a one-dimensional and deterministic concept of progress.

In Europe, the recognition of the hopeless situation of modernity and its philosophical reflection has led to various attempts to square the circle. According to Habermas (1986, 197), the philosophy of existence, represented chiefly by Heidegger, and which was tentatively superseded by Derrida's "grammatology", cannot be separated from traditional metaphysics and thus cannot represent its transformation. At the same time, post-modern[5] philosophers tried to replace subjectivity with anonymous ontological-historical processes, which led to a situation in which subjective "activity" was replaced by de-subjectivized (i.e. impersonalized) "events" (Habermas 1986, 210). Philosophical reflection was thereby deprived of any possibility of evaluating history and presence, or of influencing the future. Post-modern thinkers tried to place relativity alongside the absolutistic principle of rationality; but it was precisely this relativity which brought about the dissolution of the image of reality. With the annihilation of the subject, the individual was deprived of their personal responsibility (and vice versa).

Rationality and subjectivity as the core concepts defining modernization were also of immense importance in the Chinese philosophy of the twentieth century, starting with China's entry into the globalization process. While the mainland philosophers Li Zehou and Zhang Dainian tried to deal with these concepts through their own methodological systems, and many other scholars[6] sought to consolidate and redefine the concepts of rationality and subjectivity within the new current of Sinicized Marxism, it was Modern Confucianism which aimed specifically to solve the crisis of the subject—caused by the alienations of modernity—through a synthesis with classical Chinese thought. In this process, they relied mainly on a concept of the subject which was first developed by classical German philosophy and, in particular, by Kant. In fact, according to Modern Confucians, Kant's idea of a subject defined by a rationally conditioned ethics and an autonomous self-responsibility definitely has a greater affinity with the specific features of classical Chinese thought than any other Euro-American current of (pre)modern or Enlightenment philosophy.

In (primarily Western) academic circles, it is the intensional performance of the subject which constitutes its "essential European characteristic". The subject, in terms of its primary function as an "actor", was thus seen as that concept that could not be completely understood in the contextual frameworks of Asian traditions. This lack of understanding meant that the notion "subject" could not appear as a concept within any kind of renewed non-European discourses which followed non-European traditions.

As we shall see, the consolidation of an active subject on the basis of the traditional Chinese idea of the individual as an entity that (at least potentially) possesses a moral Self, is certainly possible. Contrary to what many academics, including numerous sinologists and Chinese scholars, believe, the classical Confucian moral Self is not merely a passive recipient of commands emanating from some higher power, nor a completely determined plaything in the hands of fate (*ming*).[7] Indeed, the exact opposite is true: the ideal Confucian personality (the nobleman, *junzi*) must intervene autonomously and actively in society and influence those around him with the highest degree of self-responsibility. This is one of the basic paradigms of the (self)-realization of the moral Self. This indivisibility of the moral Self from its concrete activities within the social sphere differs radically from prevailing Western political and philosophical theories that are based on the separation of the empirical self and the transcendent subject (examined in detail below). Hence, this holistic special feature of the moral Self is closely related to one of the basic paradigms of Chinese intellectual history, i.e. the paradigm of immanent transcendence, also known as the paradigm of "radical transcendence".

6.1 Some Fundamental Distinctions: The Problem of Immanent Transcendence

As we noted earlier, ontological issues were unavoidable for the second generation of Modern Confucian theorists. Addressing these issues meant reacting constructively to the developmental trends of the theoretical (but also practical) problems of modernization with the aid of certain elementary aspects of traditional Chinese philosophy.

The focus on ontological questions can thus be seen as a specific reaction of traditional Chinese philosophy to modernization. In Modern Confucian interpretations, classical Confucianism saw Heaven (*tian*) as the ultimate noumenon. It represented the elementary entity, creating and changing all that exists. Due to its ontological duality, one of the characteristic features of the classical Chinese intellectual tradition, the Modern Confucian Heaven was simultaneously transcendent and immanent; it endowed human beings with innate qualities (nature, *xing*) that were essentially determined by the elementary Confucian virtue of humanity (*ren*). This was a development of the Mencian understanding of the Self, which was typical of the Neo-Confucian discourses in which Mencius was canonized as a "proper" follower of Confucius. However, in their interpretations of traditional systems, the Modern Confucians went a step further and in their discourses human innate qualities (nature, *xing*) became that potential which not only formed the moral or spiritual Self, but also transcended the individual's empirical and physiological characteristics. By acting in accordance with humanity (*ren*), the individual could be united with Heaven (*tian ren heyi*) and thus comprehend the genuine meaning and value of existence.

The elementary features of the concept of Heaven (*tian*) can help clarify the difference between external (*waizai chaoyuexing*) and internal (or immanent) transcendence (*neizai chaoyuexing*),[8] with the latter being one of the typical features of Chinese philosophy.

> In interpreting traditional Confucian thought (especially the idea of Heavenly Dao or the Dao of Nature), the contemporary New Confucians often made use of the concepts of "transcendence" or

"immanence". They pointed out that the Confucian Dao of Nature, which is "transcendent and immanent", is diametrically opposed to the basic model of Western religions, which are "transcendent and external."[9] (Lee Ming-huei 2001b, 118)

Immanent notions, which are essential to defining Chinese philosophy, are necessary outcomes of the holistic worldview. If there is no separation between two worlds (material/ideal, subjective/objective), it is difficult to define which of the two is more important or absolute. This also explains why transcendent notions, which are generally perceived as transcending one and proceeding into another (usually higher) sphere, are also immanent in most traditional Chinese philosophical discourses. Most scholars count to such immanent transcendent notions the concepts of Heaven (*tian*) and of the Way (*dao*). Mou Zongsan has explained this double ontological nature of the Confucian Heaven in the following way: "The Way of Heaven, as something 'high above', connotes transcendence. When the Way of Heaven is invested in the individual and resides within them in the form of human nature, it is then immanent" (Mou Zongsan 1990, 26).

David Hall and Roger Ames have criticized Mou's notion of immanent transcendence, noting that while he underscores the inseparability of Heaven and humankind and offers an immanent characterization of the concept in question, at the same time he claims that it is transcendent "to the extent that it connotes independence", a definition which, in their view, "seems inappropriate" (Hall and Ames 1987, 205). On the contrary, the notion of transcendence as it has been shaped and generally understood in Western culture, can be defined as follows: "A principle A is transcendent in respect to that B which it serves as principle if the meaning or import of B cannot be fully analyzed and explained without recourse to A, but the reverse is not true" (Hall and Ames 1987, 13).

Their fear is that the application of these notions might lead to still further misunderstandings in the already difficult dialogue between Western and Chinese traditions of thought. They also take Mou to task for his distinctions regarding transcendence and the Decree of Heaven: "To have a sense of the Decree of Heaven, one must first have a sense of transcendence, which is possible only if one accepts the existence of such transcendence". (Mou Zongsan 1990, 21)

Hall and Ames (1987, 205) believe that in such passages, Mou is clearly attempting to attribute a "strict transcendence" to the early Chinese tradition; for them, such attitude seems to be rather problematic. For Lee Ming-huei, however, their criticism is the fruit of a "misunderstanding" (Lee Ming-huei 2002, 204):

> When Modern Confucians apply the concept of "immanent transcendence", they are adhering to the basic premise that "immanence" and "transcendence" are not in logical contradiction. This means that they never apply the concept of "transcendence" in the strict sense understood by Hall and Ames. Their critique is thus clearly based on a misunderstanding.[10] (Lee Ming-huei 2002, 226–7)

Notions, especially if abstract, have different semantic connotations, and in this instance, the term "transcendence" is no exception.[11] In the history of Western philosophy, it has various connotations. The notion of "immanent transcendence" denotes a certain type of transcendence; it certainly does not cover the entire spectrum of the possible semantic connotations of this concept, especially not those linked to "independence" or to the "separation between creator and creation".

Besides, the Modern Confucians have never interpreted these notions in the sense of a "strict transcendence". On the contrary, they have often exposed the difference between "pure" (or "strict") and "immanent" transcendence on the basis of discursive differences between Christianity and Modern Confucianism:

> The theological worldview of Christianity could be defined as "pure transcendence". This means that God has created the world, but is not part of it. Thus, God possesses a transcendent nature which is beyond or outside of the world. This is the actual traditional belief in the Christian tradition... The Chinese tradition instead believes that Dao circulates between heaven and earth. The *Xi Ci* chapter of the *Book of Changes* states "that which is above the form exists as Dao (the Way, the Great principle), and that which is below them exists as a definite thing". But it also affirms that "Dao is the definite thing and vice versa". On the one

hand, Dao is above the forms (i.e. it is metaphysical), and thus not a definite, visible or perceivable thing. Therefore, it is transcendent. On the other, it can only be put into practice through definite things (i.e. through physical forms); thus, it is immanent. This is the form of "immanent transcendence." (Liu Shu-hsien 2005, 14–15)

The notion of Dao, which is one of the core concepts of traditional Chinese philosophy and manifests itself in multiple ways in the category of the Way, is thus a notion of "immanent transcendence" (*neizai chaoyue*). In its oneness and indivisibility it reflects the original cosmic principle, but at the same time it also reflects the smallest atoms of existence, constantly creating through their infinite combinations all existing worlds. Dao is both the elementary, abstract driving force of the universe, and the concrete, intimate path of every human being. Dao is the fundamental source of all existence, and the incorporation of each particular appearance. "In Chinese philosophy, 'Dao' represents the essence of the universe, society and every individual, but also the moral substance implying humanity, justice, rituality, loyalty and similar axiological contents" (Liao Xiaoping 1994, 46).

However, Dao does not constitute an absolute principle, as in the theological idea of Divinity or the ancient Greek idea of substance. Immanent notions are never incorporations of absoluteness, for their nature is conditioned by everything they surpass; they create existence, but are simultaneously an inseparable part of this creation.

The concepts resulting from the immanent worldview are based upon the relativization of all that exists. Therefore, they seldom appear independently or individually. In traditional Chinese philosophy, this essential relativity was expressed through binary categories, composed of binary oppositions. The complementary, mutual interaction of both antipodes was able to express every, even the most complex, area of time and space. For a better understanding of binary concepts and the principle of complementarity, we must first examine their theoretical foundation, which is reflected in the traditional, structurally ordered and, at the same time, comprehensive Chinese worldview.

As it is well known, the traditional Chinese worldview was a holistic one.[12] Traditional Chinese thinkers did not strictly or categorically distinguish between the spheres of matter and idea, nor between any other dualistic connotations resulting from this basic dichotomy.[13] What is much less known or recognized is that this holism was by no means indiscriminate. The traditional Chinese holistic world was not some sort of homogenous unity in which everything was connected to everything else, without boundaries or distinctions. On the contrary, the traditional Chinese worldview was logically ordered based on relatively strict, binary oppositional patterns. On a mental-reflective level, these patterns formed a series of specific Chinese analogies,[14] which provided the basis for the prevailing method of logical thought (Cui and Zhang 2005, 14–24).

Binary categories (*duili fanchou*) are thus one of the fundamental characteristics of traditional Chinese philosophy. They are a kind of duality that seeks to attain the most real (possible) state of actuality through relativity, expressed in terms of the relation between two oppositional notions.[15] As Graham (1989, 286) points out, distinctions were seen in binary terms, and primarily between pairs of opposites (with even figure and colour reduced to square/round and white/black). Having drawn them, and recognized some recurring or persisting pattern (e.g. white, large, square, hard or heavy), we can then detach a stone from other things in the same way we cut out a piece of cloth or chop off a piece of meat. Things were not seen as isolated, each with its own essential and accidental features; instead, distinguishing characteristics were mostly seen as relative.

Of course, binarity as such is not a specific feature of Chinese philosophy, for in its function of differentiation it is basic to human thought. What distinguishes Chinese binary categories from traditional Western dualisms is the principle of complementarity, which forms a basic method for their functioning (Rošker 2012a, 12–13).

In effect, what we have is a structural pattern of binary oppositions, which, however, differs fundamentally from the model of Cartesian dualism. The Cartesian model involves a dialectic between the mutually exclusive, polar opposites of thesis and antithesis, that have been determined by an opposition which is also a contradiction. This contradiction creates a tension, in which the mutual negation of thesis and antithesis forms a synthesis. Instead, the complementary model which was dominant in the Chinese tradition of thought, is based on a non-contradictory opposition between two poles which do not exclude but complement each other, and which are interdependent (Rošker

2012a, 14). Contemporary Chinese scholars generally define this difference as that between two types of dialectical reasoning, in which the Western, Hegelian model tends to look for divisions and contradictions, while the traditional Chinese form of dialectical thought seeks to achieve a unity between these binary oppositions.

In the traditional Chinese complementary model, binary patterns did not produce any separate syntheses that could preserve "positive" elements from their previous state, while eliminating the "negative" ones. Zhuangzi described the relation between the two binary poles of a complementary model as follows:

> Therefore: why do we not preserve truth and abolish falseness? Why do we not preserve order and abolish chaos? If we think in this way, we do not understand the structure of nature, nor the state of being in which everything exists. This would mean preserving earth and abolishing heaven, preserving *yin* and abolishing *yang*. It is quite clear that this would not work. (Zhuangzi 2012, Qiu shui, 5)

But in the Judeo-Christian tradition the dominant pattern was one of "logocentric" binarity which aimed at preserving one anti-pole, while eliminating the other. The post-structural theorist Jacques Derrida, the founder of "Deconstruction", pointed out that we live in an intellectual tradition that tends to preserve the significant at the expense of the signifier, speech at the expense of writing, noumena at the expense of phenomena, Nature at the expense of culture, life at the expense of death and good at the expense of evil (Derrida 1994, 95–6, 1998, 35). As Graham affirms (1992, 65), in reflecting on the more profound implications of this tendency, we can note a certain affinity among a number of apparent oppositions in "Western" culture, given that the majority of Western discourses are based on the idea of a universal causality that tends to eliminate one oppositional pole in order to preserve the other (Rošker 2012a, 142). Such an affinity can be found, for example, between Christian beliefs regarding the immortality of the soul, and the tenets of traditional science (before the discovery of quantum mechanics).[16]

In their article, "Chinese philosophy" for the *Routledge Encyclopedia of Philosophy*, David Hall and Roger Ames (1998, 1–2) list and compare some of the typical chains of binary patterns. They conclude that the dominant Western tradition of thought usually treats one of the poles as being "transcendent", i.e. in a way that allows it to exist independently of its oppositional pair, which instead does not have this possibility (Hall and Ames 1998, 1–2). Graham argues (1992, 65) that reasoning in accordance with such patterns means being incapable of imagining the possibility of creation without a creator, reality without appearances or good without evil.

In their own discourses, Modern Confucians have always emphasized the significance of "immanent transcendence". According to Lee Ming-huei (2001a, 118), this emphasis is explained by the fact that they wished to overcome the widespread prejudice against Chinese philosophy (including among sinologists) prevalent in the Western academic world since Hegel. In his *Vorlesungen über die Geschichte der Philosophie* (1969, 142–3), Hegel described Confucius as an ancient "master" who had disseminated a collection of thoughts on morality without creating any real philosophy. This naturally implies that his work did not contain any transcendental dimensions. This superficial (mis)understanding of ancient Chinese texts continues to hold sway in Western theory not only with respect to Confucius, but in terms of Confucianism in general, and the whole of traditional Chinese thought.

6.2 Transcendental Subject and Empirical Self: The Problem of the Individual and their Subjectivity

The problems of immanence and transcendence, which have been addressed in various ways by Modern Confucian philosophers, inevitably appear in their discourses on the onto-epistemological position of the Self, and the subject. As noted, the central problem of establishing the subject and subjectivity never emerged in Confucian theory, as many still believe, due to the absence of an active subject within traditional Chinese or Confucian intellectual history. As we shall see, Modern Confucians tried to show that the ideological role played in Western modernization by the concept of the autonomous subject, was instead assumed by the moral Self (*daode ziwo*) in Asian modernization processes. Examining this concept in the works of various second generation thinkers, means perforce focusing on their understanding of the relation (or difference) between the transcendental subject and the empirical self (Kupke 2007, 1), which usually manifested itself in the Confucian tradition as the problem of the relation between the "inner sage and the external ruler (*neisheng waiwang*)".

The divide which separates traditional Chinese concepts from those which, to a great extent, formed the intellectual horizon of European modernity, is especially evident in the semantic connotations of the notion "subject", which were necessarily linked to the concept of the individual throughout European intellectual history. Hence, the Modern Confucian concept of the moral Self cannot be properly understood without first identifying the differences between the dominant conception of the individual in both the European and Chinese intellectual traditions.

The concept of the individual is a fundamental and central part of modernity; it separates the modern era from the Middle Ages as surely as the concepts of God, sin and salvation separated the Middle Ages from antiquity, and as the concepts of *polis* and citizen separated antiquity from earlier cosmologies. We must therefore clarify this pivotal aspect of modern (i.e. post-medieval) political and social thought (McCormick 1979, 689).

In European intellectual history, the problem of human individuality became important as a consequence of the decomposition of a fairly integral social order. As McCormick (1979, 689) points out, liberal theories of the subject were usually derived from the individual; the notions of society and politics were established on this basis. In these theories, one rarely encounters the need to construct a relation between the individual and society, in which society is conceived as something more than just a set of physically separated human beings. While within the European historical context such an elementary supposition appears as self-evident, it is nonetheless misguided in both a historical and existential sense. Society is, in fact, of primary importance and should be posited before the individual.

The normal human perception is not of a sovereign self around which society must be configured, but of an imposing social edifice within which the individual must adapt and fit. A historical phenomenon such as the Founding Fathers in America is so rare that it cannot serve as a human prototype or paradigm. Normally, the proper functioning of a highly integrated society will assign each member an identity; an awareness of the autonomous, differentiated, self-determining individual emerges only when the rationale and mystique of that society begins to break down, and when the assignment of identities based on status, heredity and custom is no longer perceived as a functional and legitimate natural process (McCormick 1979, 689).

Traditional Chinese society was a highly integrated social community. As a recent comparative study on the perception of the notion of autonomy has shown (Rošker 2012b), while the awareness of the primary role of society over the individual is still present in contemporary China, the opposite is true for the inhabitants of Central Europe. The notion of the individual in most Western political theories is not that of an "*a priori*" of human existence, but is a very complex conceptual construct deriving from a specific type of social experience, i.e. that of social decomposition. In this sense, individualism is the essence of European modernization. Because the forces of liberal democracy had propagated and stressed the positive meaning of individualism for many decades, it became necessary to invent opposing constructs, such as the completely misguided concept of "collectivism".[17] Such constructs mainly served as expressions of social phenomena and movements to which liberal democracy was opposed. As worshippers of the individual, Western societies portrayed collectivism as regimented and dehumanized masses marching in blind obedience to the ruler, society and the state. But as McCormick (1979, 690) has shown, this image is a caricature and does nothing to clarify the issues in question, but only obfuscates them further. Given that movements like Marxism and even Fascism were also built on a notion of the individual (though not of the liberal-democratic type), and because their indictments of liberalism also tended to include charges of conformism, the monopolization of this label stifles investigation, and leads to the exchange of slogans instead of rigorous analyses (McCormick 1979, 690).

In all ideologies in which it has appeared, the notion of the individual has been elevated to the category of self-evident truths, in what is an obligatory step in the process by which ideologies become self-sufficient (McCormick 1979, 690). However, in the processes of social development, ideologies gradually tend to lose the ability to meet the modified requirements brought about and defined by the transformation of social conditions. Hence, in situations of radical social change, ideologies either collapse and have to be replaced by new, more suitable ideologies, or the central concepts they imply have to be modified to a degree which enables them to function again as the internal "glue" of newly transformed societies. The modernization of European societies began with the collapse of medieval paradigms, which were replaced by a series of ideologies based on the concept of individual. But the era of modernization was not the first time the notion of the individual played a leading role on the stage of European history, for it had already been in forefront in the scattered city-states of ancient Greece. In the modern era, however, its connotations were transformed. The major differences in the semantic connotations of this concept indicate the broad scope of its meaning.

Individuality in ancient Greece (especially in Athens) was a product of the decomposition of earlier social orders which had been based upon religion and the tributary system. The liberal and ancient Greek notions of the individual differ primarily in their understanding of the Self. Polis was nothing more than a community of citizens and the citizens were nothing more than a part of the polis. Their relation was mutual and complementary, similar to the one that developed out of original Confucianism during the Warring states period (Zhan guo 475–221 B.C.), i.e. before the first unification of the Chinese state under the rule of the Qin Dynasty (221–206 B.C.). David Hall and Roger Ames have linked this type of individual with the aforesaid relation between the transcendental subject and the empirical self, or between the "inner" and "outer" self. Hall and Ames expose (1998, 26) that in Confucianism, the self is contextual and represents a shared consciousness of one's social roles and relationships. In this model, one's "inner" and "outer" (*neiwai*) selves are inseparable. This type of individual can be seen as being rooted in something which McCormick (1997, 692) calls the "agonal self". This is a self which implies an element of circularity that is absent from the liberal notion. In such a model, an individual is not an isolated human being worthy of remembrance, who thus seeks to do great deeds in order to bring this objective fact to the attention of others. The self is rather seen as merely a potential, and it is by doing great deeds that one becomes a person worthy of remembrance. There is no separate "I" that does the deeds and speaks the words, there is only a total of deeds and words. A human being is not something which he or she subsequently reveals. He or she is rather what he or she does and becomes so only in the doing.

The arguments based on the belief that the Chinese notion of the Self did not possess any strong "individualistic" connotations are, for the most part, too generalising. As we have seen, the Western notion of an isolated, delimited and completely independent individual is, to a great extent, also a product of modernization ideologies. Thus, when treating or exploring the Chinese notion of the "self-realization" of the Self, we must proceed with due caution, for whoever has been acculturated within the discourses of Western modernity, automatically tends to equate this term with the self-realization of an individual existence.

David Hall and Roger Ames (1998, 25) emphasize that the notion of "individuality" has two different meanings. First, it refers to a particular, uniform, indivisible entity which can, due to a certain feature, be included in a certain class. As an element (or a member) of a certain kind or class, this "individuality" is interchangeable. This concept of individuality underlies the equality of all individuals before the law, the concept of universal human rights, equal access to opportunities, etc. According to Hall and Ames (1998, 25), it is precisely this understanding of the individual which also makes it possible to elaborate notions such as autonomy, equality, free will, etc.[18] This type of Self belongs in the domain of a one-dimensional, empirical self or, to express it in Chinese terms, in the sphere of the "external ruler" (*wai wang*).

But Hall and Ames point out that the notion of individual can also be linked to the notions of uniqueness and singularity which do not possess any connotations of affiliation, or membership in any class. Here, equality is posited on the basis of the parity principle. According to them, it is this sense of "unique individuality" which enables us to understand the traditional Confucian notion of the Self.[19] Some Modern Confucians also emphasize that the uniqueness which underpins it, is already a value in itself:

> Dao is omnipresent and unites everything in itself to an entity. Therefore, we say that the great Dao is unlimited. But, on the other hand, it also contains specific particularities. We have to accept the uniqueness of these particular entities as being true. Every particularity which has been realized bears in itself a

tendency of value. Thus, its significance cannot be denied.[20] (Fang Dongmei 2004c, 259)

However, even this kind of self which possesses a unique individuality is "unique" in a "typical Chinese" (i.e., relational) way, for it constitutes itself by means of the quality of its relations with the external world.[21]

A person becomes recognized, distinguished, or renowned by virtue of a social or communal deference to the quality of their character. Much of the effort in understanding the traditional Confucian conception of the Self has to do with clarifying this distinction. While the definition of the Self as irreducibly social certainly precludes autonomous individuality, it does not rule out the second, less familiar notion of uniqueness expressed in terms of roles and relationships (Fang Dongmei 2004c, 259).

Thus, in exploring the Modern Confucian views on the relation between the transcendent and empirical self, we must bear in mind that in the Chinese tradition to which it belongs, this relation (in contrast with the dualistic model) has always been posited *a priori* within the structures of the different social networks which form the individual identity.

As noted, the transcendent and empirical spheres of performance correspond to the binary antipodes of "inner sage" (*neisheng*) and "external ruler" (*waiwang*). Lee Ming-huei (2001b, 15) states that while most Modern Confucians saw the inner sage as a basis for the concept of the external ruler, the latter was never understood as being merely an extension of the former. Their aim was to establish the subject within the complementary relation between both antipodes. A subject so constituted could thus unite in itself the awareness of the "subject of moral practice" (*daode shijiande zhuti*) in the sphere of spiritual life, the awareness of the "political subject" (*zhengzhi zhuti*) in the field of society, and the awareness of the "cognitive subject" or the "subject of recognition" (*renshi zhuti*) in the realm of epistemology and the natural world. The inner sage thus had to be posited in the complementary relation with a "new external ruler" (*xin waiwang*) who was responsible for the development of science and democracy.

The second generation of Modern Confucians often denoted the traditional binary category of the "inner sage and external ruler" (*neisheng waiwang*) in more contemporary terms. Tang Junyi, for example, defined this category as a contrast between the moral and the empirical self (*daode ziwo, xianshi ziwo*). In his view, the foundation of the moral self, which belongs to the metaphysical sphere (Keli and Li 1995, III/38), is Reason as defined in Neo-Confucian discourses. This moral, spiritual or transcendental self is the antipode of the real self, which he defines as follows:

> The real self is the self which, as an object of reality, is situated or "fixed" within real time and space and is limited by certain conditions of such time and space. It is a self which is posited in a specific framework and which possesses physical (*xing er xia*) nature. (Tang Junyi 1985, 29)

For Tang, whose definition follows the famous Neo-Confucian idealist, Wang Yangming, and his interpretation of the concept of innate knowledge (*liang zhi*), the moral self is the only true self, for the real self has been limited by the finiteness of time and space. Proceeding from the problems of modernization as conditioned by the freedom of the active subject, Tang also engaged in an exhaustive analysis of the external and the internal conditions of individual freedom. In his view, society is the foundation of the empirical self which appears as an individual, limited by determinants of time and space. Hence, individual freedom must always be conditioned by the freedom of the community in which that individual lives. A truly free individual is one who can find the freedom of the moral self exclusively within themselves. Such freedom is always defined by values arising from their cultural identity:

> The foundation of the individual right to be free is the existence and freedom of the social community. But the individual right to be free acquires true meaning and value only through one's inner freedom, which arises from the realization of ideals that have a cultural value. (Tang Junyi 2000, 344)

144 The Rebirth of the Moral Self

In the framework of his "dual ontology", Mou Zongsan (1975, 37–40) saw both types of self in a complementary relation. He believed that Confucianism (and Chinese culture in general) had failed to develop the idea of the real, i.e. the concrete, individual self. One of the effects of this failure was the lack of an epistemological basis for the development of scientific cognition and technology.

> Historically, Confucian theoretical works had always treated intuition as a manifestation of the personality of a sage or a saint, i.e. in terms of the magical effects of wisdom… These effects were always posited within humanity (or mutuality, *ren*), and therefore could not be separated from it, even temporarily, in order to gain "pure recognition". This is why logic and mathematics were never developed in China. (Mou Zongsan in Han and Zhao 1994, 176)

Hence, Mou's ideal moral self is able to consciously negate itself. It can pass from the sphere of infinity to that of finiteness, and vice versa. In this, it resembles the transcendent dynamic of Hegel's absolute spirit:

> Instead of realizing itself in the relation of causality, the infinite has rather fallen apart in it. The infinitive is in itself the connection of the unconnected, it is the simple that becomes an other to itself, which in turn is the other of its self and thereby the first simple. (Hegel 1986b, 68)

In his theory of the self-negation of the moral self, in which it passes from the sphere of transcendent morality into the sphere of concrete (cognitive, political and social) performance, i.e. from the realm of the "inner sage" into the realm of the "external ruler", Mou Zongsan attributed to both forms of the self a corresponding representation of reason. The moral self which is posited within the "detached ontology" (*wuzhide cunyoulun*), thus corresponds to the functional representation of reason (*lixingde yunyong biaoxian*), while its self-negation (*ziwo kanxian*), which manifests itself in the cognitive subject and is posited within the "attached ontology" (*zhide cunyoulun*), corresponds to the constructive representation of reason (*lixingde jiagou biaoxian*).

The inner sage	The external ruler
The detached ontology	The attached ontology
The moral self	The empirical self
The functional representation of reason	The constructive representation of reason

Both phases are thus complementary and the phase in which the moral self passes (self-negation) into the empirical self is therefore only temporary. Like other Modern Confucians, Mou Zongsan conceived of the moral self (i.e. the "inner sage") as the foundation (Lee Ming-huei 2001b, 14) and necessary precondition for any kind of civilized society. At the same time, his empirical self, which is endowed with the "constructive representation of reason", does not contradict morality. The empirical self which manifests itself in a "new external ruler" and represents a necessary precondition for China's modernization, is amoral only in the sense of the absence of a moral valuation of the natural world. This "new external ruler" is focused on "instrumental rationality" (*mudi helixing*) which, in the dialectical development of complementary relations between both phases, always returns to the basic realm of the moral self which acts again in the framework of the "rationality of values" (*jiazhi helixing*).[22]

In his sometimes a bit too idealizing interpretations of Chinese culture, Fang Dongmei proceeds from the holistic worldview in which noumenon is equated with phenomenon, and in which they are both equally permeated by the sphere of values. He exposes (1957, 60–61) that the universe is a place to live in, and not a place to escape from, because it is a realm of value. Thus, for him, human nature is something to rely upon, and not something to dispense with, because it has been proved to be not sinful, but innocent. This holds equally true for the whole universe, which is a coalescing of matter and spirit. It is, in other words, a transformed realm wherein matter and spirit tend to assume a higher form of perfection, which can be called exalted life. Universal life permeates the universe and penetrates everything that exists. In the process of continuous creation, it increases the value of what is already valuable, as well as what is quite indifferent. For Fang Dongmei, the existential aim of life is the realization of the supreme Good, which, however, is not merely to be found in some "other world". Hence, Fang stresses that, from the very start we must learn what is most precious in life by actually living in the real world.

Therefore, in his system, there is no place for any kind of separation within the self. Fang does not accept the concept of the subject and thus fails to see the line dividing its transcendent factors from its empirical ones. He remains loyal to his holistic metaphysical pragmatism:

> Because human beings possess both a rational and a spiritual nature, their experience of the Divine and of human nature is direct and not inferential; it is intimate, not separate, intuitive and not analytical. This direct experience permits Chinese philosophers to posit that the ultimate goodness of human nature is rooted in the divine nature. And while human beings can certainly lose this capacity or potential, this loss is never casual, but is due to the individual straying or deviating from the heavenly way.[22] (Fang Dongmei 1979, 270)

Xu Fuguan tried to illustrate the relation between the concrete individual and their moral self based on certain differences between Chinese and Western cultures. As noted, in his cultural studies he argued that the driving spiritual force of the former was a "sense of concern", while the development of the latter was conditioned by curiosity, the sense of wonder and the desire for control (Huang Chun-chieh 2011, 185–204). The moral spirit of the latter is situated within the scope of cognitive or religious models of morality, while the moral spirit of the Chinese tradition does not pertain to any metaphysical typology. In the Confucian worldview, the concept of a definite empirical self was unnecessary before the tenth century B.C., when there was a radical intellectual shift from religion, in the sense of faith in an external higher force, to moral responsibility, centered within the human self. "Life and the real world could not offer human beings a secure existence. Thus, they did not feel the need to act" (Xu Fuguan 2005, 117).

Only after this shift did individuals, through a moral responsibility rooted in their innate moral virtues, become free and autonomous members of society. But this autonomy remained limited to morality and Xu does not posit the need for a subject which can actively and independently acquire knowledge about the external world. Although Chinese intellectual history has also known explorations of external reality, the fundamental goal of such explorations was always limited to finding new possibilities for developing one's personality (Fang and Li 1989, III/613). Xu Fuguan argues that with this orientation the Chinese tradition offers a method for directly experiencing one's own life, for its development and fulfillment, and for unifying the external and internal worlds. Subject and object are fused in one coherent unity and knowledge merges with morality. Like Tang Junyi, Xu understood Mencian concept *ben xin* as differing completely from the Western concept of moral spirit. It was, in fact, the basis of human morality and the germ of goodness intrinsic to every human being.

> In contrast with the view that human mind was defined only by cognitive potential and could thus not be autonomous, Mencius introduced the concept of a moral self which is the heart-mind of goodness and morality. When this moral consciousness is seated in a person, it will naturally begin to direct their life and guide their desires through moral reason. (Xu Fuguan 2005, 178)

Thus, Xu Fuguan's theory does not make a strict distinction between the external and internal self. The active, autonomous subject which is a precondition of modernization, manifests itself in Xu's work only as a germ of independent social activity which is not aimed at exploring the natural world or developing the natural sciences and technology, but proceeds exclusively from a moral responsibility towards others. Here, we could draw a parallel with the moral and empirical self (or, in Chinese contexts, with the inner sage and external ruler) based on his (complementary) demarcation between the "cultivation of the self" (*xiu ji*) and the "regulation of fellow human beings" (*zhi ren*) (Xu Fuguan 1980a, 48). Thus, Xu did not endow his active empirical self with any possibility for its own development, and it remains confined within the dynamic duality of the traditional Confucian self. As noted by Huang Chun-chieh (2011, 185), both antipodes represent "two sides of the same coin" and are viewed as the beginning and end (or, in terms of the traditional Chinese binary category, the "roots and branches" [*benmo*]) of the

Confucian self. The "regulation of fellow human beings" is therefore necessarily rooted in the "cultivation of the self", and the latter always returns to the former, i.e. to the sphere of social and political performance. Like the two wheels of a rickshaw, the inner sage and external ruler represent two modes of human self (Xu Fuguan 1980a, 48).

As noted, Mou Zongsan was the only second generation theorist who—due to his belief in the need to establish an empirical, free self that could meet the requirements of Asian and Chinese modernization—tried to modify the traditional complementary unity in the relation inner sage/external ruler and formulate it in a dualistic form, defined by a distinction between the moral and empirical self. This approach was consistent with his general belief in the necessity of a Kantian separation between things in themselves and the human perception of them. As we shall see later, he tried to transcend this limit by means of his concept of unlimited heart-mind or intellectual intuition. Similarly, he also tried to introduce the dynamic of complementarity into the dualistic relation which defines the antipodes of the transcendent and empirical self. However, this method raises the question of whether his concept of the self-negation of the subject is truly an elaboration of the traditional complementarity between the inner and outer self, or whether his model merely represents a more sophisticated and structured reproduction of binary categories as applied by other Modern Confucians.

The self-negation of the moral self is seen by Mou as a part of a dialectical process which activates the extensional truth, the empirical self, the cognitive subject and the constructive reason. This "dialectical process", however, is controlled by the free will and moral autonomy that serve as its counterpart and activate intensional truth, the transcendental self, the moral/artistic subject as well as the functional reason. In a framework of Hegelian dialectics, such process cannot be regarded as a classical form of dialectics, for it lacks the necessary tension between two equally important and mutually contradictory counterparts, represented by thesis and its negation, i.e. the anti-thesis.

Hence, Mou Zongsan's model cannot produce any forms of synthesis (that can only be produced by the mutual "Aufhebung" [sublation] of both, thesis and anti-thesis).[23] In Hegel's dialectic, both anti-poles mutually exclude each other; the synthesis, forming the third stage of the dialectical process, is representing a qualitatively different stage, in which the positive (progressive) parts of the two mutually contradictory anti-poles are preserved, whereas the negative ones are removed. Due to the fact that Mou's moral self is infinite, all-embracing and overall, integral or comprehensive, and that it implies the very essence of the goodness in a sense of an onto-hermeneutical (or onto-epistemological) value, it cannot represent a thesis which is to be negated; it can neither represent a "positive" or "progressive" part of a synthesis, in which its certain elements would be removed and only the positive ones would remain.

But since the nature of Hegelian "syntheses" has confronted humanity with too many serious problems, the lack of a synthesis is not necessarily the central point of this critique. The central point is that Mou's concept of the moral self cannot be placed into the framework of hegelian dialectics.

The main inconsistency of Mou's model of self-negation of the moral self can be found in the following problem: If any model of a classical Western "dialectic" (take the one involving matter and idea, for instance), is namely "controlled" by axiological postulates, it cannot further be named "dialectic", but represents a model of mutual contradictions lacking any inner coherence, or, even worse, mutually dissolving themselves.

In Hegel's dialectics, the anti-thesis is a reaction to the thesis, which cannot be actively caused by the thesis as such. In Hegel's model, the anti-thesis is an independent force or entity which represents an external reaction to the thesis. In Mou's understanding, however, the thesis (the moral self) actively negates itself, in order to promote the acting of the empirical self, which is (as visible from the traditional Chinese complementary model of the inner sage and external ruler) forming a part of itself. In short, in the Hegelian model, the thesis is separated from the anti-thesis, which is not the case in Mou's philosophy.

In order to resolve the static nature on which this dialectical model is resting, and to explore further possibilities of creatively uniting spiritual and physical existence, idea and matter, or subject and object, we need a new referential framework. Here, we could consider applying the classical Chinese principle of correlativity or complementarity which could offer a truly dynamic model, possibly surpassing the limitations of classical dialectics. In his theory, however, Mou has not applied a pure form of this traditional Chinese model, but has been at the same time claiming that his model of self-negation of the moral subject was an upgraded model of Hegelian dialectics.

The reason for the main inconsistencies of Mou Zongsan's model of a new subjectivized moral self might lay in the fact that he went too far in accepting deeper levels of Kant's demarcation line between the things in themselves and the things for us. By gifting to the humans intellectual intuition, as Mou's theory suggests, and by allowing this gift to function as an axiological criteria determining (and creating) existence, his theory is namely neither solving Kant's insufficiencies, nor providing a coherent explanation of the "dialectical" process offered by the self-negation of the moral self.

6.3 From the Self-Negation of the Subject to the Modern Form of the Confucian Moral Self

The four theorists who represent the core of the second generation of Modern Confucianism all focused on ethical problems and the metaphysics of morality in their works. With the exception of Fang Dongmei, they were all former disciples of Xiong Shili, who left an indelible trace in their philosophies. For Xiong, the development of the concept of the moral self, in the sense of an innate moral imperative (*xingti*), was one of the key contributions of Neo-Confucian philosophy, and he stressed that this moral self was not a hypothesis, but a reality (Bresciani 2001, 377). All three of his students accepted this basic platform, developing it in different ways in their own discourses. Xu Fuguan explored the development of the idea of the moral self throughout the history of Chinese philosophy, and focused on questions linked to the concrete realization of this abstract concept in the social and political sphere. Mou Zongsan and Tang Junyi instead developed their own philosophical systems based on this concept.

Tang's system grew out of a life-long study of the problems of culture, both Chinese and non, and his final synthesis is a compendium of human achievement in the area of knowledge. Mou instead elaborated his system based on a rigorous logic that split each question "to the final hair". And while both syntheses are majestic and fascinating, Mou's is the most technically accomplished in philosophical terms and the most profound and far-reaching in its conclusions. Indeed, his philosophical system can be seen as the synthesis of a century-long effort by the New Confucian philosophers to build a Confucianism for the future, based on the concept of the inner sage and external ruler.

Although Fang Dongmei was the only member of this group who had not been a student of Xiong Shili, his work is nonetheless linked to this pioneer of the Confucian revival due to a similar insight into the self, based on the Buddhist contradictions and paradoxes revolving around the sustainable self (the awareness of *prajñā*) and the transient awareness of life and death. Like Xiong, Fang also tried to resolve this paradox through of a complementary interaction between substance (*ti*) and function (*yong*). For him, the mind is a sort of "supervisor" that governs the operations of all human properties, capacities and faculties. It is both substance and function. As a substance, it can embrace infinite modes of "thought" that are directed at any conceivable object. Its function instead consists of the ways in which it acts spontaneously upon things (Fang Dongmei 1980b, 103).

For Fang Dongmei, the idea of the subject is something which actually distances men from their humanity. He argued that this idea was closely linked to the development of modern European science, understood as the systematic exploration of an organic and inorganic "nature" completely separated from human beings.

From the outset there was the tendency to emphasize de-anthropomorphism (Fang Dongmei 1983, 20–25). The distinction between primary and secondary qualities tends to exclude human beings from their real nature. Science pursues pure objectivity while man, in the view of modern psychology and epistemology up to the mid-nineteenth century, is essentially subjectivity (Fang Dongmei 1978, 223–5).

Subjectivity is thus something which is diametrically opposed to and in contradiction with pure objectivity, which science uses to analyze abstraction, record the existent based on quantitative criteria and reduce the multiple dimensions of phenomena to formulas for different identities (Fang Dongmei 1979, 258–60). For Fang, this methodology was essentially the negation of men as natural beings situated within the interwoven organic structures that constitute the universe, as well as in time and space.

With respect to the infinity of individual human characteristics, all these innate differences seek a harmonious fusion in the unity of an infinite multiplicity within the great Dao. Once they are in Dao, they can no longer get lost in the infinite emptiness, or in the trivial solitude of separateness or some apparent form of equality or equivalence (Fang Dongmei 2004b, 261).

Fang does not refer to the subject, but to the "subjective spirit" (*zhuti jingshen*) which is an inseparable part of the ontologization of "life". In his philosophy, the "objective world" (*keguan shijie*) is necessarily joined by means of a "continuous organic creativity of the clear spirit" (*shengming shengshengbuxide chuangzaoli*) to the "subjective spirit of humanity" (*zhutide renlei jingshen*).

The subjective spirit in this sphere of life first transforms itself—through objectivization—into the objective spirit, and then ontologizes itself into a transcendent spirit. Only through self-realization can the individual preserve the organic bond with all that exists and be incorporated into the process of continuous organic creativity, which forms the basis of life. Thus, Fang conludes (1981, 23–28) that between the two paths of self-abnegation and self-affirmation, the Chinese tradition stresses a third way, that of self-development and self-realization.

This process of self-development and self-realization is, of course, closely linked to the inner spiritual cultivation of individuals. We think of the individual in terms of observed actualities and idealized possibilities. From actuality to possibility, there is a complex process of self-development. According to Fang (1981, 27), this self-development can be achieved through self-cultivation and a full range of self-realization.

However, the awareness of the individual's unity with all that exists which results from this process of self-realization, is not metaphysical in the sense of an abstract separation from the actual reality. The concrete values of human life do not belong either to the sphere of idealized imagination, nor to a transcendental paradise, for if they did, it would deprive them of any real value, as it would not be possible to realize them in the real world. At the same time, they cannot remain enclosed within the inner world of the individual, otherwise that person would remain trapped in a subjective egocentrism which cannot benefit any human community. The only sphere in which the individual can realize and fulfill these values and in which they can transcend the narrow limits of their own personal interests, is the state. For Fang, the state represents the only possible form of extended existence, which guarantees the greatest possible happiness for the greatest possible number of people. In order to reach this goal and to liberate ourselves from self-bondage, social constraint and enslavement, we must overcome the many difficulties that stand in our way through effort, courage, perseverance and sagacity. Li Chengyang (2002, 278) exposes that, in this context, Fang laid stress upon the fact that we are "real beings", bound by the limitations and imperfections of the "real world". This is why we continuously have to seek to remedy numerous—internal and external—imperfections that hinder us in achieving this goal. If we do all this, we can escape from the fatality below and behold the light of day in perfect freedom and happiness (Li Chengyang 2002, 278).

While Fang Dongmei refused the notion of the subject as useless for his purposes, the other three members of this group tried to find a concept within their own tradition that could serve as an onto-axiological bridge for a Chinese model of modernization. Ultimately, this led to them all elaborating somewhat different interpretations of the traditional Confucian moral self.

Tang Junyi equated this notion with the Confucian "original heart-mind" (*ben xin*), arguing that the key feature of the moral self was its freedom, in the sense of the ability to overcome itself. He argued that the moral life requires us to be self-consciously self-governing. For him, this is also the reason why we must take full responsibility for ourselves and believe that we are free, for "only a free and self-governing moral activity is essentially the activity of transcending one's actual self" (Chan 2002, 306). In ontological terms, the moral self also represents the spiritual reality. Hence, Tang Junyi saw it as the common source of any human activity, whether physical, psychological, or spiritual. These activities include the most basic human impulses, such as the instinct for self-preservation, which Tang defines as "a call of human beings for future life". Ultimately, all human activities are of a spiritual nature (Tang Junyi 1985, 142). He thus refers to Mencius' thesis on the innate goodness of human nature[24] as a necessary precondition for human refinement. Moral evil is rooted in the limitations of the moral self which, in itself, always has the ability to surpass such limitations (Lee Ming-huei 2001a, 60). Because of this ability, human beings can transcend their empirical (or actual) selves (Chan 2002, 306). Tang thus distinguished between a real and moral self (Chan 2002, 306), affirming the truth of the latter.

> The only common essence of moral knowledge and the moral heart-mind is the surpassing of the real self... People often say that diligence and thrift are forms of moral behavior. But what is diligence? It is the constant application of our actual strength. And what does thrift mean? It means controlling our momentary desires. Both are ways of surpassing the actual self. (Tang Junyi 1985, 54–55)

The real or actual self, which must thus be surpassed, is trapped in real time and space (Tang Junyi 1985, 29). All that exists in time is transitory and therefore illusory, while all that exists in space is limited and thus cannot be either universal or true. Hence, the real or actual self is not true either. The moral self, however, which is not limited by time and space, is permanent and true, and thus represents the true self of every human being.

Therefore, the moral self which manifests itself in the substance of heart-mind (*xinde benti*) is the universal, metaphysical reality (Chan 2002, 306) possessed by every human being.

> I believe that the substance of my heart-mind is simultaneously also the substance of the heart-minds of all people, because the heart-mind represents the highest goodness. It manifests itself in my moral behavior and moves my actual self to surpass itself. It sees my fellow human beings as myself, and thus manifests itself as the substance of heart-mind which is common to myself and others. (Tang Junyi 1985, 109)

Although in Tang's work the notions of soul (*xinling*) and spirit (*jingshen*) are often interchangeable, he defines the former notion as subjective, while the latter is objective, for it represents an objectivization of the former. In describing their mutual relation, Tang applied the classical binary category of *ti* and *yong* (substance and function) in a new way (Tang Junyi 1989a, 188).

In his work *The Existence of Life and the Horizon of the Soul* (*Shengming cunzai yu xinling shijie*), he suggests that in its different developmental phases, the human soul is confronted with different horizons (Lee Ming-huei 2001a, 63). He conceived of a dialectical scheme of the soul which proceeds from the objective to the subjective sphere, until it reaches the absolute horizon where it transcends the distinction between subject and object. Below each horizon, Tang postulated three partial horizons that are structured in accordance with three aspects, i.e. substance (*ti*), attribute (*xiang*), and function (*yong*).

On the "objective" level, the soul functions as a subject of recognition: on the first level, perceiving objects in the external world as individual, particular things or issues, on the next level as universalities, and only on the highest level of development being able to see them within complex causal relations. The "subjective" level is linked to the self-awareness or self-reference of the soul. The partial horizons that compose this subjectivity are determined by feelings, abstract meanings and moral worldviews.[25]

Only after the human soul reaches the highest (absolute) level, can it gain access to the horizon of religion in the broadest sense. The three partial horizons that compose this level are, first, the sphere of monotheism, which represents the human desire for an anthropomorphic God;[26] second, emptiness which embraces both material as well as ideal objects,[27] and third, the "highest" partial horizon where the soul can finally merge with the creative power of heaven (*tian*), which can be realized in the empirical world through human moral performances.

The notion of spirit is also of paramount importance in Tang's philosophy of culture, for the entire category of culture, which he denoted as "the world of human culture" (*renwen shijie*) is, in essence, a product of the human spirit.[28]

Tang conceived of the world as being composed of nine horizons (*jing*), i.e. the horizons of scientific knowledge, technology, art, literature, economy, law and politics, morality, religion and education (Lee Ming-huei 2001a, 63). The moral self is always posited in a certain relation to one or more horizons of the world of human culture. In contrast to naturalistic, materialistic and utilitarian conceptualizations of culture, Tang argued that all human cultural activities are subordinated to the moral, spiritual or transcendent self, for they always appear as its manifestations (Tang Junyi 1985, 139). Included here is the state, which is rooted in the inner need (common to all men) of the reasonable self for its own objectivization (Tang Junyi 1985, 215). The best possible objectivization of the reasonable self is (Western) democracy, which Tang believed was fairly capable[29] of controlling the individual desire for power.

Mou Zongsan also proceeds from a concept of the subject which is rooted in the moral self. The moral self manifests itself through the innate moral substance (*xingti*), which unites in itself everything found in Kant's concept of practical reason, including free will. Moral substance is rooted in original heart-mind (*ben xin*), which manifests itself as a phenomenal form of infinite heart-mind (*wuxiande zhixin*) and is an elaboration of the Neo-Confucian concept of innate knowledge (*liangzhi*). This elaboration is the basis of moral performance; it is transcendent and infinitely universal. As a form of infinite heart-mind, it is a precondition for the actual realization of the categorical imperative which is also infinite. Mou's understanding of free will as a constitutive element of the moral subject is thus rooted in the view that this will represents the basic reason for any action. In this respect, it is the equivalent of Divine consciousness and thus absolute and infinite. Mou agrees with Kant's premise that the nature or essence of morality lies in the autonomy of the will and the moral subject. But he argues that the philosophical meaning of this postulate cannot be fully developed within the framework of Kant's ethics, which presupposes a dualistic division between rationality and feelings within the acting subject. This division means that the moral subject (or free will) can, at best, act as the "principium dijudicationis",[30] and not as the "principium executionis"[31] (Lee Ming-huei 2001a, 72). Free will, however, cannot merely be an object of faith: "God and the soul can both be grounded on human faith, but free will cannot be rooted merely in faith. Kant failed to treat faith in terms of freedom; he saw it merely as a postulate, and not as an object of recognition" (Mou Zongsan 1975, 38).

Kant's subject is thus incapable of self-realization; being unable to set laws for itself, its autonomy is purely formal. For Mou, Kant's metaphysics remain trapped in a "metaphysics of rituality". Thus, it can only be regarded as a "metaphysics of morals (*daode di xingshangxue*)" and cannot be considered a "moral metaphysics (*daodede xing shang xue*)". In fact, the former is only a metaphysical justification of morality, while the latter (i.e. his own moral metaphysics) represents a "transcendental" metaphysics grounded upon human moral heart-mind. Mou Zongsan finds a prototype of a "moral metaphysics" in Confucian philosophy (Mou Zongsan 1975, 38), specifically in Mencian concept of *xin*,[32] which he considers to be the foundation of the moral self. Mou's analysis of the Gaozi chapter confirms that, through his principle of the inherent morality (*renyi neizai*) possessed by the moral subject, Mencius attributes autonomy to that subject. Within the framework of Confucian philosophy, the Mencian moral subject was transformed into the concept of innate knowledge (*liangzhi*), understood as a moral compass intrinsic to every individual. Based on this premise, the idealistic philosopher Wang Yang-ming (1472–1529) proposed two theses, (Mou Zongsan 1975, 100), i.e. the thesis of the unity of subject and the structural principle (*xin ji li*) and the thesis of the unity of knowledge and action (*zhi xing heyi*).[33] While the first thesis posits that the concept of innate knowledge, in its function of the moral subject, represents the ultimate and highest instance of moral law, the second confirms that innate knowledge is not merely a "principium dijudicationis", but also the "principium executionis" of moral goodness.

Here, Mou Zongsan confirms that traditional Chinese philosophy is much more suitable for the theoretical elaboration of a truly autonomous subject than modern Western philosophy which, in essential terms, is incapable of establishing the moral self. Indeed, Mou points out that Confucianism has, in the course of its development from the *Book of Changes* or the discourses of Confucius and Mencius, to the mature moral philosophy formulated within the framework of the neo-Confucianism of the Song and Ming Dynasties, offered a more or less unified discourse in which the substance of heart-mind (*xinti*) provides the basis (but is also the result) for a conscious moral practice. This constitutes the conceptual core which—through the unity of the cosmic and moral order—makes it possible to elaborate an ontology that unifies the substance of heart-mind with the substance of the innate qualities (or nature) of human beings. Since Western philosophy failed to formulate and establish the latter concept (i.e. *xingti*), it was also incapable of establishing a unity of morality and religion, or of morality and metaphysics (Han and Zhao 1994, 132). Mou stresses the importance of the cultivation of personality and, like Xu Fuguan, uses the concept *gongfu* to illustrate this point, although he is certainly more famous for his ambitious metaphysical speculation than for the sophistication of his self-cultivation theory (Billioud 2012, 197). However, it is still evident throughout his works that *gongfu* is fundamental for him. What is at stake in Mou's restoration of a moral metaphysics is nothing less than the possibility of sagehood. On the other hand, concepts such as autonomy, detached ontology and intellectual intuition were ways of articulating a possible dialogue with the West.

However, due to the specific economic and political factors that determined traditional Chinese culture, the traditional Chinese concept of moral Self could not provide (or, at least, formulate) possibilities for gaining "objective" knowledge (i.e. knowledge not necessarily linked to morality) and exploring "natural" phenomena. For Mou Zongsan, this was the key ideological factor that explained why traditional Chinese culture did not develop discourses of science and democracy. He therefore argued that the traditional Confucian moral Self should (temporarily) negate itself (*zwi kanxian*), in order to make it possible for these discourses to develop:

> This is about a shift from a dynamic moral reason which creates virtues. It could be said that this is a self-negation of the subject. Through such self-negation, the dynamic becomes static, non-duality becomes duality and the subject shifts from the realm of concrete practice directly into the realm of understanding. The form of reason that is established in this shift is pragmatic and its inner nature has nothing to do with morality. The representation of this reason is constructive; hence, this representation, as such, as well as its products (i.e. knowledge) have nothing to do with morality. Here, we can confirm that both pragmatic reason, as well as the results of its activities are amoral (in the sense of neither contradicting nor surpassing morality). (Mou Zongsan in Han Zhao 1994, 176)

It is very important that the Self makes this shift in a fully conscious manner, for it is both a shift from the sphere of detachment to one of attachment, and one which is necessary for establishing the cognitive subject (*renshi zhuti*) as a basis of science and democracy, and thus also of "modernization" (Mou Zongsan 1995, 452).

Xu Fuguan notes that the moral Self—at least in terms of its basic characteristics—was already present in the early Zhou Dynasty (tenth century B.C.). In his work entitled *The History of Human Nature Theories in China (Zhongguo renxing lun shi)*, he argues that while religion is a state of mind in which human subjectivity dissolves in a total dedication to God, the Chinese already worshipped the spirit of humanity in the period of the early Zhou Dynasty. This spirit was focused on subjectivity; its bodily desires were incorporated into its moral responsibility and they thus manifested themselves in rationality and autonomy (Xu Fuguan 2005, 34). As Ni Peimin (2002, 285) points out, Xu here reveals the importance of a mature self-responsibility, claiming that human beings were no longer merely passive recipients of external imperatives. Heaven manifested itself in one's nature, and the requirements of Heaven became the requirements of the nature of the subject itself.

He believed that through Confucianism, the ideological foundations of self-responsibility became a central feature of classical Chinese culture. A result of this primary motivation was the formulation of two closely linked, ideal paradigms defining the basic lineaments of the Self. It was thus not limited to autonomous self-responsibility, but also included active and intensional performances. The former manifested itself in the principle of self-cultivation, and the latter in the principle of influencing the external world through internalized virtues. Both paradigms are closely connected with the actual reality and with concrete values, and are not focused on a theoretical interest in acquiring objective knowledge about the natural world (Ni 2002, 285).

Xu argues that the insight into the need to find solutions to (external) problems within the self-led Chinese thinkers to explore and cultivate that part of human "innerness" which "rules the Self", i.e. heart-mind (*xin*), which includes both feelings and reason (Ni 2002, 285). The innate moral basis which constitutes this awareness and which manifests itself externally (i.e. in the cultural sphere, where it functions as an inner binding for human societies) in the principle of rituality (*li*), is the virtue of humanity or mutuality (*ren*). This virtue represents an original state of mind, comprising both the constant striving for self-completion and the unconditional fulfillment of one's duties towards others. In actual life, both principles are posited in a mutually complementary relation. According to Xu, Confucius shifted the principles and rules which regulate the external social world and manifest themselves in the respectful and responsible performance of rituals, into human inwardness, thereby creating an "inner world of moral nature" (Ni 2002, 285), in the sense of a morality which represents the source and foundation of all the main human values. For Xu Fuguan, this crucial shift constitutes the greatest contribution of original Confucianism to Chinese culture. Once individuals are "endowed" with an inner world, they need no longer strive for a physical domination over the external world in order to be free, for freedom and autonomy are now accessible to the subject through self-cultivation and mature responsibility.

In contrast to such a view, Plato's world of ideas and Hegel's world of absolute spirit are products of speculation, whereas the theologian's Heaven is a conjecture of faith (Ni 2002, 284–5). None of them have anything to do with this internal world of humanity. The access to this inner world is preconditioned by deep reflection and cultivation. What can truly be experienced, is the actual world in which we are living. Hence, Xu Fuguan concludes that the modernized concept of the Confucian Self is perfectly suited to providing an ideal basis and inner support for modern individuals:

> Only after the emergence of the idea of a "Self defined by nature" enabled the human spirit to root itself in actuality did people stop being merely "transient" creatures floating to and fro. We find a similar situation in the contemporary world, for only after the emergence of the idea of "naturally given rights" can human rights become securely rooted in politics. (Xu Fuguan 2005, 118)

Xu's idea of the Self is thus grounded in the unity of external and internal nature. This idea is based upon a specific concept of natural law, which in truly democratic countries is reflected in both the intimate inwardness of individuals, and in the laws of the state.

The Modern Confucian principle of subjectivity is thus founded on a basis similar to Habermas' concept of personality as being both "the source and ultimate instance" (Habermas 1998, 199) of its self-identification. Here, the subject does not follow any external dictates, but is truly "autonomous" in the original sense of the word (Rošker 2012b, 27). As Heiner Roetz (2008, 376) points out, this means that, formally speaking, modernity is a secular project, in which religious faith is the result of a personal decision. Furthermore, as opposed to the functioning of religions in the past, modern societies, especially in the context of a growing pluralism, are no longer able to define the identities of their members through specific cultural contents ("Leitkultur", Roetz 2008, 376). In modernity, the subject represents the basic institution of society (Roetz 2008, 376). Like most of the second generation of Modern Confucians, Heiner Roetz also sees democracy as the only possibility for realizing such a concept of Self. He exposes that this is the only form of government in which every member of the polity can, in principle, understand themselves as a co-author of society and a co-creator of change. Hence, a new cohesion to compensate for the weakening of traditional ties can be produced. It is difficult to see how democratic institutions can be legitimized if not by the principle of subjectivity, which gives everyone a voice in matters and decisions that affect them. However, it is likewise difficult to envision a future alternative for China that could bypass the corresponding institutional changes (Roetz 2008, 376). Even the neo-classical principle of (inter) subjectivity, which leaves personal identity intact but avoids isolating the individual by allowing them to avoid the pressures of collective considerations, is not necessarily in contradiction with the Modern Confucian reinterpretations of the subject. On the contrary, it comprises a number of crucial topics that offer common ground for a fruitful encounter. Roetz also draws attention to the fact, that the notion of "inner transcendence", even if formulated in ontological terms within Confucian literature and in post-ontological terms within the communication paradigm of linguistic philosophy, still means, in both cases, "that the most generalized level of universality (Heaven) is rooted in concrete and specific acts in the everyday lives of human beings", rather than in some realm which lies "beyond" (Roetz 2008, 376).

6.4 Reason and Intuition

Most Modern Confucians accept the traditional Chinese tenet that the moral cultivation of the Self is a precondition for comprehensive knowledge. A corollary of this premise is that human perception is not only rational, but also irrational, in the sense of also being determined by will or intention, desires and feelings.

> While Western epistemology tends to focus on the rational aspect, Chinese philosophy stresses the irrational factors in cognitive activities. In particular, the "stillness" in the expression "vacancy, singleness and thus stillness" describes a kind of human mindset, a requirement for the emotional cultivation of a cognitive subject… Singleness and deep speculation are a prerequisite for making the leap from perceptual to rational cognition, and for developing intuition (immediate enlightenment), a point which was elaborated fully by the Neo-Confucians of the Song and Ming dynasties. (Xu and Huang 2008, 399)

Like their teacher Xiong Shili, most second generation theorists assumed that the same border which divided reason from intuition, also divided science from philosophy. They were not opposed to science, but scientism, arguing that science, which aims at the recognition of objects in the external natural world and applies an exclusively rational and analytical methodology, would never be able to solve questions connected to the meaning of life, and therefore would never be able to influence an individual's worldview. While science explores fact, philosophy investigates meaning and values. The divide between reason and intuition did not merely separate science and philosophy (or natural sciences and the humanities), but also the sphere of phenomena from the sphere of values.

Traditional Chinese epistemology was founded primarily on the method of introspection and the intuitive perception of reality.[34] In the Neo-Confucianism of the Song (960–1279) and Ming (1368–1644) Dynasties (upon which the majority of Modern Confucian discourses are based), there were two schools: the first was "realistic", and was known as the School of the Structure (*Li xue*) or the School of Reason (*Xingli xue*). Greatly influenced by the teachings of the most important medieval Chinese philosopher, Zhu Xi, its epistemology emphasized realistic modes for the perception of reality, and it introduced a new methodology suited to this form of recognition called "exploring objects" (*ge wu*). The second school, which instead advocated more solipsistic and intuitive methods for the recognition of reality, was known as the School of Heart-Mind or the School of Consciousness (*Xin xue*), and was led by the most important "idealistic"[35] philosopher of the Ming Dynasty, Wang Yangming.[36] Most Modern Confucian philosophers were more influenced by this second school than by the more realistic Zhu Xi's philosophy, and they have derived their concept of reason from the German philosophy,[37] generally occupies an important position in their discourses. In any case, in both schools the intuitive recognition of reality was closely linked to the concept of innate knowledge (*liangzhi*), which represents the core of the moral nature of any individual.

Given that the concept of reason represents one of the ideal bases of modernization, and that notwithstanding their opposition to scientism most Modern Confucians advocated (or stressed) the significance of science and technology for the further development of Chinese society, the question of the sinization of this term became a fundamental question for these philosophers. Essentially, this meant trying to find a synthesis between the traditional Confucian concept of intuitive recognition and the mental foundations of that part of the human cognitive apparatus which is instead grounded in rationality and logical inferences. Hence, any such inquiry had to begin with a detailed exploration of the notions of reason and intuition, as well as their mutual relations. One of the leading members of the first generation of Modern Confucianism, Liang Shuming, had already dealt extensively with the notion of intuition, which he denoted with the term *zhijue*.

Etymological studies have shown (An 1997, 337) that this term does not appear in the classical works of Confucianism. It came to China only as a modern translation of the Western term "intuition", which was closely connected with connotations arising from Bergson's vitalism.[38] The term *lixing*,[39] which denotes "reason", also entered Chinese discourses as the translation of the Western notion, at about the same time. However, in Neo-Confucian philosophy we can encounter very similar notions (e.g. Zhu Xi's term *xingli*). The relation between rational and intuitive methods of cognition was studied even earlier by numerous traditional philosophers, though these concepts were denoted differently. As one of the first modern Chinese theorists, Liang Shuming published an essay[40] in 1921, in which he compared Bergson's philosophy with the Neo-Buddhist theory of pure consciousness (*weishi lun*) and attempted to clarify the relation between reason and intuition (Liang Shuming 1924, 97–102). Later that same year, Liang published his chief philosophical work *The Cultures of East and West and Their Philosophies* (*Dong xi wenhua ji qi zhexue*), in which he systematically explained his concept of intuition (*zhijue*), distinguishing it clearly from reason. Liang not only argued that these two concepts are in mutual contradiction, but also claimed that they have to a great extent defined the difference between Western and Chinese culture, with Western theories generally implying reason, while the latter were based on intuition. Although later in his career he distanced himself from the concept *zhijue*, which does not appear in any of his works published after 1934 (An 1997, 338), it is still important to note that in his rigorous, even contradictory separation of these two concepts, he differed from the majority of Modern Confucians who, by means of exhaustive explorations of the Confucian philosophical tradition, tried to demonstrate the complementary nature of these two cognitive methods. Such an understanding of their mutual relation is also alien to most Western thinkers, even if the concept of reason or rationality has often been equated with its antipode, intuition (Fricker 1995, 181). However, as Thomas Kuhn has demonstrated in his *Structure of Scientific Revolutions* (1962), the concept of intuition is actually at the heart of rational exploration, as the crucial catalyst of theoretical shifts in science.

If these arguments are sound, we ought to abandon any idea that reason and intuition are opposed, or even wholly discrete "ways of knowing", and recognize instead their essential co-operation. Of course, there continue to be legitimate uses for a narrow or technical conception of reason, such as in routine logical operations. But it is a mistake to take such a technical conception as a general model of reason *per se*. (Fricker 1995, 181)

However, most Modern Confucians have followed Liang Shuming's assumptions. Already Carsun Chang (Zhang Junmai), another important theorist of the first generation, in his *Reason and Intuition in Chinese Philosophy* published in 1954, argued that the rational method of recognizing the external world and obtaining knowledge was in the forefront of Confucian thought. Citing Confucius' famous dictum: "Learning without reasoning is useless, but reasoning without learning is perilous" (Confucius 2012a, Wei zheng 15) he interpreted this as an encouragement to think with the aid of reason:

> If one has no data to work with, and merely plays with the phantasms of one's imagination, thought will be unreliable or adventurous. If one collects a great deal of data in a scattered, piecemeal or unrelated fashion, no principle will run like a thread through the congeries to organize them into a system. One may know much but be unable to reach a goal or establish an ideal pattern of life. (Chang 1954, 99)

Mencius, whose philosophy provided a basic template for new interpretations of original Confucianism for neo- and Modern Confucian philosophers alike, argued that both the structural principle li^{41} and justice yi (as fundamental symbols of morality) are inner attributes of all human beings.

> Therefore I say: men's mouths are similar in having the same tastes; their ears are similar in enjoying the same sounds; their eyes are similar in recognizing the same beauty—why shall their minds alone be without such similarity? What, then, is the similarity of their minds? I say, it is to be found in the principles of our nature, and in the determinations of justice… Hence, the principles of our nature and the determinations of justice please my mind, just as the flesh of grass and grain-fed animals please my mouth. (Mencius 2012, Gaozi 7)

This understanding is grounded in the fusion of rational and moral elements within human heart-mind. As opposed to Liang Shuming, Chang claimed that this view of the unity of reason and morality reflects a fundamental and general equality between the prevailing currents of Western and Chinese philosophies:

This is also what Mencius meant by "determinations of righteousness", or reason. In the eyes of the Oriental, theoretical principles and principles of moral evaluation provide the foundations for the whole structure of civilization. The fundamental nature of Eastern and Western philosophy thus agree. (Chang 1954, 100)

Based on this conviction, in the same essay[42] he describes the development and specific connotations of reason and intuition within traditional Chinese philosophy, stressing that Chinese scholars have always devoted considerable attention to moral values and have thus focused upon the transcendent level which manifests itself in the concept xing (innate qualities, "human nature"). They joined the term *xing* and *li* because they believed that the latter necessarily formed part of human nature (Chang 1954, 101). For Chang, the question of the relation between these two concepts in Chinese philosophy is similar to the problem of the relation between universality and particularity in Western thought. He also stated that all the most influential philosophical schools in the Chinese tradition were based upon rational grounds (Chang 1954, 102), and that they all shared the following postulates:

1. Truth on a purely intuitive basis, not embedded in knowledge and logical thinking, cannot be truth. There must be an intellectual foundation without which intuition is blind. This is the intellectualistic aspect.

2. Behind intuition there is also conviction and will which directs human effort. This is the voluntaristic aspect.

3. Intuitive truth arises from the depths of the heart and from an intense love of the cause in which one believes. This is the affective aspect (Chang 1954, 111).

Hence, recognition obtained from intuitive perception is deeply rooted in cognition, human will and feelings. It thus represents a synthesis on a high epistemological level. Chang stressed that this synthesis cannot be created by study alone, where reason and intuition appear in a mutually contradictory relation, but only on the basis of much broader platforms (Chang 1954, 111).

This belief found many of the second generation Confucians in substantial agreement. However, Fang Dongmei and Xu Fuguan devoted much less attention to elaborating and modernizing traditional concepts of rationality, as their primary focus was on other aspects of philosophy and intellectual history.

In his arguments, Xu appropriated the traditional Mencian concept of moral reason (*daode lixing*) that served as a basic principle for the regulation and guidance of human life and desires within the moral heart-mind, which manifests itself as an awareness of the good and ethical within the moral Self (*benxin*) (Xu Fuguan 2005, 178). Xu's epistemological discourses are based on the premise that this awareness is innate to all human beings.[43] Hence, the realization of moral action is preconditioned by the individual recognition (or awareness) that everything innate derives from the Heavenly Mandate (*tian ming*). According to Xu, this concept belongs to notions that were originally in the sphere of external moral codes and which were subsequently transformed by Confucius into notions that also determined human inwardness. Xu Fuguan points out that moral ideas before the rise of original Confucianism were limited to prescriptions of proper and suitable behaviour. They were thus integrated exclusively into the relations of the objective world and were unable the aid the individual gaining awareness or opening their inner world. Only after Confucius could these norms also embrace the world of inwardness. In the framework of the Confucian teachings, this unity enabled the individual to pursue a better, more complete existence. All this led to the elaboration of the Chinese moral spirit which is both immanent and transcendent. In Xu's view, this unification was based upon the method of internalizing traditional religious concepts which were transformed and changed from abstract external ideas into symbols denoting various existential forms of the inner moral substance. Unfortunately, Xu does not offer a more detailed description of the concrete epistemology underlying such a unification, and never describes in detail the methods or procedures that could lead individuals to make this identification. Thus, it remains unclear whether they merely discover the identification through introspective experience or are more involved in the identification of the two. Xu often used the word *chengxian* ("emerge") to describe the presence of *ren*, Confucius' mind, and he used *faxian* ("discovery") for Confucius' realization of its presence as the Decree of Heaven. On the other hand, however, he also often suggests that this identification was also a positive decision and act, as the citation from *The Doctrine of the Mean*, "select the good and adhere to it", indicates. Ni Peimin (2002, 287) comments that a profound question is hidden behind this ambiguity—namely the question of the relation between "is" and "ought".

In this context, Xu Fuguan introduced[44] a new method of recognition which he called *tiren* (bodily recognition) and *tizhi* (knowledge obtained through the body). This method is not based on intuition in the usual sense, nor on rational reasoning about logical relations between premises and inferences. Instead, *tiren* is a retrospective and active process in which "the subject discovers moral subjectivity in the pseudo-subjectivity of human desires and affirms and develops it". Here the word *ren* ("recognition") means both realization and recognition. One reveals one's own moral nature through "overcoming the self" and "reducing sensual desires". By freeing oneself from these constraints, the subject lets the original mind emerge (Ni 2002, 287).

In this process of recognition, knowledge and action (*zhixing heyi*), as well as objectivity and subjectivity merge into a coherent whole. If the subject of recognition wants to gain objective knowledge, it must "immerse" (Ni 2002, 292) itself in the object of recognition, that is, in all that can be recognized in that object. Further, the very act of simultaneous recognition implies its realization in practice. Another important aspect of this process is the concept *gongfu*, which includes both the subject's capacity for recognition, as well as their active efforts to obtain recognition or knowledge. Only by applying *gongfu* can one obtain insight into their transcendental moral Self which is outside *gongfu*. A recognition or an insight which has been acquired in this way must be internalized by the subject and integrated into their physical body, as well as their rational dispositions. Only in this way can a given insight become part of an individual's knowledge. In this case, the separation between knowledge and the subject of recognition can be cancelled completely and the incorporation of what has been recognized become a precondition for its actual and complete recognition. However, Ni Peimin criticizes Xu Fuguan on this point, exposing that Xu's articulation of the notion of embodiment appears as unsatisfactory, because the notion of embodiment itself has to be embodied for it to be fully understood and appreciated (Ni 2002, 292).

In any case, the idea of "bodily recognition" is quite interesting in philosophical terms, though it was never fully elaborated by Xu Fuguan, which perhaps explains why it was often the object of further inquiries later on by contemporary Chinese theorists.[45]

For Fang Dongmei, reason was rooted in the rational structure (*li*) of the universe which, however, is also defined by feelings (*qing*). His basic supposition was that both elements formed a correlative and complementary binary category that arose from the ultimate pole (*taiji*). Within the onto-epistemological wholeness which is characteristic for the classical Chinese tradition, this category provides both the basis of philosophical thought and the foundation of existence as such.

In Fang's interpretation, *li* is the absolute (highest) expression of objective phenomena, while *qing* represents the fundamental feature of subjectivity. Because his concept of "life" includes both notions, it clearly implies the sense of transcending the separation between subject and object (Fang and Li 1989, III/894). In his *Three Kinds of Philosophical Wisdom* (*Zhexue san hui*), Fang Dongmei also unites the notions *li* and *qing* into an epistemological concept of "sensuous reason (*qingli*)". In its fusion of feelings and rationality, this concept provides a fundamental and original core, or basis of recognition, and can thus be seen as a "seed of wisdom" (*zhihui chongzi*) (Ni 2002, 292).

Hence, for Fang Dongmei, the concepts *qing* and *li* represent a complementary wholeness in which both elements are in a complementary and correlative relation:

> *Qingli* belongs to the original symbolic images within the system of philosophical terminology. *Qing* arises in connection with *li* and the existence of the latter is again dependent on the former. In their magical interaction they circulate around each other and are thus each other's original cause. The realm of their coexistence can be recognized by intuition, but this is difficult to express or explain. (Fang Dongmei 2007, 2)

Because *qingli* implies both reason and feelings, it can only be recognized through the intuitive, and not the rational or analytical method. This epistemological dimension of *qingli* is therefore reflected not only in the field of perception, but also in the field of interpretation, for it is a concept that cannot be expressed, since it surpasses all semantic distinctions that define the concrete reality of human life:

> The *qingli* sphere is both distant and near, deep and superficial, open and concealed. There is nothing which can be seen beyond it, and the structure of its inwardness can only be defined by our hearing and vision, and the cultivation of our personality. (Fang Dongmei 2007, 2)

And yet human beings need both *qing* and *li* for their existence and life: "Human life is conditioned by *qing* and human existence by *li*" (Fang Dongmei 2007, 2).

For Fang, reason as such (i.e. when separated from feelings) represents the third of six levels of personal development. This level corresponds to the human mastery of the natural world and manifests itself in the culture of science. While Fang acknowledges the importance of this aspect of human development, he argues that humanity must pursue the even higher spheres of art (beauty), morality (goodness) and perfection (harmony), i.e. the spheres to which human beings cannot gain access without possessing intuitive (moral) knowledge.

Like all Modern Confucians, Tang Junyi also proceeded from the notion of immanent transcendence and defined it based on his interpretations of the Neo-Confucian school of mind (*xin xue*).[46] His epistemology is therefore closely related to his ontology, for he saw the world as a metaphysical reality that is immanent to all that exists in the universe, while also possessing moral qualities (Chan 2002, 306). In this context, the central Confucian virtue of humanity or mutuality (*ren*) is already part of the cosmic structure, while its recognition, or its simultaneous incorporation and internalization, manifests itself in the moral performance of individuals.

Heart-mind (*xin*) as a necessary and constitutional part of the moral Self is the key component in the recognition process. This process is constituted through its function of "sensual compatibility" (*gantong*) which relies on feelings, reason and human will. The fusion of these three factors is conditioned by "proper perception", which must proceed in accordance with the all-embracing, rational structural principle (*li*). When recognizing other human beings, this sensual compatibility must also be based on empathy.

But recognition on the basis of sensual compatibility is also a precondition for the transition between various horizons (*jing*), or for the development from a lower to a higher horizon. The concept of horizon as such is thus not only ontological and axiological, but also epistemological, for *jing* is originally a Buddhist concept which denotes an object towards which the mind is directed and implies a unification of subjective understanding and the objective situation. According to Sin yee Chan (2002, 308), it can therefore be compared to the Kantian view of perception, by which perception is also a product of the mind's unification of sensory data by means of categories supplied by the mind itself.

Tang Junyi's treatment of reason is inseparable from the concept of the moral Self, as developed by the School of Mind.

> I believe reason (*lixing*) is the innate nature (*xing*) which can manifest and follow the structural principles (*li*), and is thus a unity of both. Chinese Confucianism has denoted it with the term *xingli*. It is human essence or substance which causes the emergence of the human moral, spiritual and transcendent Self. (Tang Junyi 1986, 254)

For Tang, reason thus also underpins the moral Self, which he denotes as a "transcendent rational Self" (*chaoyuede lixing ziwo*, Tang Junyi 1986, 254). As we explained in the previous chapter, Tang understands human moral life as something that requires conscious control over oneself and which is common to all human beings. At the level of epistemology, this Mencian universality of human morality manifests itself not only in the cognitive capacity of reason, but also in the empirical recognition of the world through the senses.

> In terms of the actual world, it is obvious that every function of human heart-mind is connected with my body. Thus, I can recognize all that exists through my perceptions. In perceiving my own body and the bodies of others through my sense organs, they all appear as equal parts of everything that exists. My sensory

> perceptions are universal with respect to the bodies of others, as well as my own body. But with respect to my own body I can also perceive manifestations of the transcendent substance of heart-mind. Thus, we can suppose that the bodies of other people are likewise able to perceive this transcendent substance of heart-mind. This conclusion involves two aspects: first, my bodily recognition, performed by myself as a human being (existing) in the actual world, and second, the faith in (the existence) of the transcendent substance of heart-mind. (Tang Junyi 1985, 110)

However, it is important to note that Tang is not speaking of inter-subjectivity, i.e. he did not postulate the existence of some common spirit or consciousness in the sense of all people having the same goals or intentions, but instead is positing a transcendent spirit of the individual which unites itself with others through this process of transcendence (Chan 2002, 313). Such transcendence is possible because human heart-mind forms a unity with the universe.

Tang's epistemology implies both a theory of knowledge and a theory of wisdom. In both cases, reason and intuition are mutually interconnected. Based on this mutual interconnection and influence amongst the different segments and mechanisms of heart-mind, and with the application of analytical philosophy, Tang formulated an interesting and innovative hypothesis regarding the creativity of wisdom (*zhihuide chuangzaoxing*). What he calls knowledge (*zhishi*) includes concepts or ideas, inferences, logical cognitive laws and empirical intuition. "Wisdom" is instead a "miraculous creativity" (*shenmiaode chuangzaoxing*), i.e. a kind of intuitive thought which is neither completely empirical, nor wholly rational. It is a kind of reasoning which can apply previously acquired knowledge, but only based on prior independent decisions for such application. Hence, knowledge is both surpassed and integrated. Morality plays a central role in both theories, for it represents the foundation of the Self and thus of heart-mind.

In his search for an interpretation of the semantic scopes of rationality, intuition, perception, recognition, reasoning and morality that could serve as the basis for a new Chinese concept of reason to meet the requirements of the modern era, Tang ultimately proved incapable of formulating a consistent and coherent theory of traditional

Chinese reason. His discourses on these issues contain a number of logical inconsistencies, which have been identified by contemporary students and interpreters of his philosophy. Han Qiang and Zhao Guanghui (1994, 57), for example, point out his failure to establish a clear succession between empirical intuition, judgments or inferences and rational intuition. In speaking of the creativity of wisdom which both applies and surpasses knowledge, Tang argues that rational intuition is able to "penetrate" directly patterns established on the basis of synthesizing premises, and thus arrive at valid conclusions. This, of course, would mean that rational intuition is above logical reason. But at the same time, Tang claims that pure rational intuition can only lead to knowledge and not wisdom, for this kind of intuition is capable only of non-inferential reasoning. His concept of "miraculous creative wisdom" has likewise never been fully analyzed or elaborated. All that can be said of this concept is that it is based on moral heart-mind, understood as a necessary part of the human Self, and that it functions instantly and unconsciously.

Tang's model of the unity of individual heart-minds is also problematic, for this underpins his concept of infinite heart-mind as being equated with the universe. However, Sin yee Chan (2002, 315) argues that the fusion of no matter how many heart-minds would not automatically produce infinite heart-mind:

> Even idealists like Berkeley tried to maintain a distinction between a mere idea and a real existence. Berkeley affirms that a mere idea is less vivid than a real existence and maintains less coherent causal relations with other ideas, but Tang's idealism seems to overlook this distinction. Based on his line of reasoning, we should say that our bodies are all in our perceptions and are, therefore, all united. But this claim is absurd. (Chan 2002, 315)

Mou Zongsan tried to define the position of reason within traditional Chinese thought by comparing Western and Chinese culture, arguing that they were based on different representational forms of human reason. He called the Chinese form "functional or intensive" (*lixingzhi yunyong biaoxian*) and the Western "constructive or extensive" (*lixingzhi jiagou biaoxian*) (Mou Zongsan 1995, 544–53).[47] This distinction could be compared with the Kantian differentiation between practical and theoretical reason. "The 'reason' which appears in functional representation is a practical one. It is not abstract, but concrete, connected to actual life. This reason can thus be equated with morality within the personality" (Mou Zongsan 1995, 544–5).

However, Mou endows functional reason with intellectual intuition (*zhide zhijue*),[48] as a potential not recognized by the German philosopher.[49]

> Kant only managed to fully and coherently develop transcendental philosophy (i.e. the ontology of the phenomenal sphere) together with immanent metaphysics. But he could not develop transcendental metaphysics, for he denied human beings the possibility of possessing intellectual intuition. (Mou Zongsan 1975, 37)

Mou argued that Kant's refusal to consider intellectual intuition had far-reaching implications, for without the integration of this concept into his epistemology, Kant's entire construct of the autonomous subject would collapse, while the metaphysical construct of the world and of human existence also rests on very fragile foundations. The same was true for Eastern thought, for without this concept traditional Chinese philosophy would likewise be deprived of its ideal foundation. The concept of human intellectual intuition thus occupies the center of Mou's philosophy. As Sébastien Billioud (2012, 70) writes, this concept underpins both his interpretation of Chinese philosophy, and his critique and superseding of Kant's thought:

> If we do not recognize that human beings in their limited existence possess the possibility of intellectual intuition then, given Kant's interpretation of the significance and function of such intuition, all of Chinese philosophy is impossible. And not only: for Kant's entire moral philosophy would also become an empty discourse. But there is no way I can resign myself to this fact. Thus, by means of the Chinese philosophical tradition, we must establish the conditions for the possibility of human intellectual intuition. (Mou Zongsan 1971, Foreword/2)

For Mou, "constructive representation" is an ideal model based on the opposition of subject and object which manifests itself in mathematics, logic, science and in political democracy. "Functional representation" is instead based on the absence of this opposition and manifests itself primarily in moral and religious acting (Lee Ming-huei 2001a, 67). For Mou (1995, 549), the former prevailed in Western, and the latter in Chinese culture.

This was also the main reason why the Chinese tradition had been unable to develop any potential for modern forms of democracy and science, and instead had developed an extraordinarily accomplished system of morality and ethics.

In conclusion, the contributions of constructive representation appear primarily in the areas of science and democratic politics. These issues have been upsetting Chinese intellectuals for several decades now. How is it that China could not develop science and democratic politics? The answer lies in the fact that it did not sufficiently develop the constructive representation of reason. Chinese culture is based on the functional representation of reason (Mou Zongsan 1995, 549).

For Mou, this implied two main conclusions: first, if Chinese society wished to go forward on the path of modernization within the framework of its own tradition, and if it thus wanted to integrate elements necessary for the development of democracy and science, it had to transform itself by appropriating the specific models of thought required for such development. Secondly, if China did not want to become a spiritual colony, it had to elaborate those concepts within its own intellectual tradition that had a potential for developing such models. This meant that the Neo-Confucian "absolute moral subject" (*liangzhi*, i.e. innate knowledge) which had traditionally functioned in the framework of the functional representation of reason, had to stop negating itself (during the developmental phase) and incorporate itself into the ideal mode of the (mutually exclusive) opposition between subject and object. In terms of a comprehensive development, this phase was only temporary: the absolute moral subject had only a transitory recourse to it, without losing its Self. Lee Ming-huei (2001a, 68) emphasizes that while Chinese culture had to be transformed during this process, it could still preserve its original nature. Here, we can once again observe a new application of the (typical) Chinese traditional binary category of "substance" (*ti*) and "function" (*yong*).⁵⁰

Mou's concept of intellectual intuition is also significant as an axiological elaboration of the Western concept of rationality.

Mou's second line of reasoning in favor of human intellectual intuition is based on Kant's distinction between *phenomena* and *noumena*. Mou argues that in order to make this distinction, Kant had to admit human intellectual intuition (Lee Ming-huei 2001a, 68). For him, intellectual intuition is a direct form of reason or intellect. "Intellectual intuition is rational and not only related to feelings or sensations. Such reason, however, is direct and not distinctive, or logical" (Mou Zongsan in Lee Ming-huei 2001a, 170).

Hence, as opposed to perception based on sensation, empirical recognition or logical rationality, intellectual intuition is a "higher" or more complex form of reason. It thus implies a basic method of acquiring knowledge regarding the sphere of meanings and values (Mou Zongsan 1971, 19).

Intellectual intuition cannot be equated with sensation, because the latter refers to objects of the external world. Thus, it is merely a passive receptor. Intellectual intuition, however, refers to no particular object and thus does not imply any distinctions between the subject and object of recognition. In itself, it is the activity of the substance of heart-mind. It is a reflection of itself (Mou Zongsan 1971, 19).

According to Mou, these methods of perception had been developed in all three of the main philosophical schools of the Chinese intellectual tradition. In Confucianism, it was called "foundation of moral heart-mind" or the "moral Self" (*daode benxin*), the Daoists instead called it "heart-mind of the Way" (*dao xin*) and the Buddhists "true eternal heart-mind" (*zhengchang xin*).

In *Appearance and Things in Themselves* (*Xianxiang yu wu zishen*) he tried, through a reinterpretation of Confucian tradition, to explain the concept of things in themselves not only as an epistemological, but also as an axiological notion.

> For Confucians, the metaphysical noumenon (substance) was derived directly from moral heart-mind... Through moral heart-mind, we have direct access to the manifestation of our inner

moral substance. We establish our Self by means of our confrontation with this manifestation of substance, which is both moral and metaphysical. Thus, it can also preserve the significance of its moral value in its permeating of all things and objects (behavioral, as well as ontological). In this framework, all things and objects are "in themselves". Here, the notion of "being in itself" has moral and axiological connotations. (Mou Zongsan 1975, 435–6)

Mou Zongsan argued that a purely epistemological understanding of this notion was insufficient to prove Kant's transcendental differentiation between appearance and things in themselves, for in Kant's system the latter always remained beyond the reach of human perception. In order to solve this problem, Mou advanced the thesis that, while humans are finite, they nevertheless have access to infinity. And this access is made possible by intellectual intuition (*zhide zhijue*).

Ideas emerge only in the beginning, before the appearance of the original Self.[51] At this stage, the original Self is still concealed and is transformed into the heart-mind of recognition. During this phase, all activities of heart-mind are carried out only at the level of innate perceptive abilities. However, due to its inner powers of vibration, the original Self must eventually reveal itself. Precisely because intellectual intuition is possible, it must reveal itself in a moment of perfection and in all its splendor. At this point, changeable ideas return into heart-mind and what appears is the "meaning without meaning", which is also possible and accessible. The "Holy will" is precisely this "unintentional sense". Human beings are thus both finite and infinite. (Mou Zongsan 1975, 79)

Hence, thanks to intellectual intuition, the "thing in itself" no longer belongs to some eternally unattainable "world beyond", but to an axiological sphere which can appear to us directly through our awareness of freedom. Mou insisted that Kant's notion of noumena had to be an "axiological concept in a very strong sense" (Mou Zongsan 1975, 8), for the transcendental distinction between this concept and the concept of phenomena could be understood only on this basis (Tang Refeng 2002, 334). In other words, noumena definitely do not belong to "original phenomena", but neither are they an objective fact which can be approached indefinitely without ever reaching it. Noumena are something which cannot be approached at the level of sensation, nor at the level of rational understanding. Hence, they necessarily constitute a transcendental concept (Tang Refeng 2002, 334).

However, as opposed to Fichte, when ascribing intellectual intuition to human beings, Mou did not wish to annihilate Kant's system, but instead wanted to develop and justify it. For Mou Zongsan, Kant's distinction was philosophically necessary; it only needed to be reinterpreted. Mou's thesis on the possibility of accessing "things in themselves" is compatible with Kant's circumscribing of recognition to the level of phenomena (Lee Ming-huei 2001a, 70), given that intellectual intuition is not a kind of recognition, but a comprehension of values. Tang Refeng argues (2002, 334) that Mou's intellectual intuition (or, in Tang's translation, intellectual intuition) was crucial for his entire system of moral metaphysics. For Mou Zongsan, moral metaphysics constitutes a discourse which refers to the existence of all beings possessing the moral substance, which manifests itself in moral heart-mind. Hence, moral substance is both infinite heart-mind and metaphysical. Infinite heart-mind includes both the moral substance which gives human beings access to morality (Tang Refeng 2002, 334), and the metaphysical substance that enables them to exist in the sphere of the noumena.

A moral Self endowed with this kind of infinite heart-mind of intellectual intuition, represents one of the possible Modern Confucian responses to the global questions of the present time. These questions are linked to the dilemmas of the modern subject who is trapped within the complex technologies of the profit-seeking natural world and has thus forgotten the ethical dimensions which define its humanity.

6.5 The Unemployed God

In the introduction to his work, *On Summum bonum* (*Yuan shan lun*), Mou Zongsan had already emphasized the value and contributions of the practical philosophy which define the Confucian system of ideas.

Confucian pragmatics were primarily directed towards "real life" and thus saw no need escape into "supernatural" worlds. Fang Dongmei proceeded from this same position, pointing out that in the Chinese tradition the universe is a place designed for life and not a sphere to be surpassed or negated (Fang Dongmei 1980b, 99). Fang's critique of the Western God (but also the Buddhist concept of Nirvana) is grounded on the problem of alienation as a consequence of the modern splitting of knowledge—and especially the knowledge of strictly limited scientific disciplines—from the dolorous confines separating modern individuals from their dignity (i.e. their divine nature), thereby isolating them from the ontological sphere of creative creativity. Mou Zongsan also criticized the very concept of God, due to God's inability to unite goodness and happiness.

While Chinese philosophy was neither quite capable of "solving" this problem, in *On Summum Bonum* Mou at least illustrated the problematic nature of the European, and especially Kantian philosophical tradition in this regard. The problem of uniting happiness and goodness can only be resolved within a holistic philosophy that does not impose any artificial division between the Self, time and space. Precisely because Chinese philosophy never implied the need for attaining transcendence or some "Kingdom of God", it could focus its discourses on the refinement of the subject in the world in which it was embedded, within the actuality of here and now. In short, the *Summum bonum* can only be realized in the here and now. The need for a transcendent God condemns this realization to failure in advance (Liu Shu-hsien 2003, 485). Furthermore, the moral Self which manifests itself through its innate moral substance (*xingti*) unites in itself all three essential postulates of Kant's practical reason, i.e. free will, the immortality of the soul and the existence of God. As we have already seen in the introduction to Mou Zongsan's philosophy, all three postulates are infinite and absolute, and because the coexistence of different infinite and absolute entities is impossible, any separation of them is necessarily artificial. Mou thus concluded that the moral Self, or the original heart-mind on which it was grounded, offered the only possible basis for a unity of goodness and happiness.[52]

In Mou's system, the idea of God as formulated in Kant's philosophy is completely redundant and even disturbing. In fact, the

Chinese theorist believed that Kant should have eliminated God from his theory.

Morality, even of a kind which is grounded on the autonomy of a higher (infinite) heart-mind, i.e. on a basis which far surpasses the simple pragmatism of interpersonal life, does not require any higher force beyond this *a priori* reflexive awareness. In this way, the European God became unemployed. If we stipulate (as Kant did) the creation of the unique and unrepeatable world in which we live on a static and immutable line of time and space, then this world which has been "created" by God cannot be changed or improved, in contrast to a human being who—as a subject—possesses the possibility and urgent need for moral development.

Mou argued that this inconsistency in Kant's philosophy was due to the possibility of intellectual intuition being attributed only to God, and to divine consciousness or divine recognition (*shende zhixing*, Mou Zongsan 1971, 51).

According to Kant, due to their limited perceptive potential, human beings cannot gain access to this kind of reason. For Mou, this "theoretical inconsistency" was fraught with far-reaching consequences, for if intellectual intuition was indeed limited to the domain of God, and if human beings were *a priori* completely separated from it, then Kant's entire theoretical system was logically inconsistent and could not be validated.

If human consciousness were not infinite in this sense, then it could not be connected to the moral imperative, which is also infinite. Hence, the categorical imperative could not figure as the basis of morality (Tang Refeng 2002, 333). This meant that, in its essence, human consciousness had to be equal to divine consciousness, a supposition, which reflected the Neo-Confucian tradition of Modern Confucianism, which was rooted in the Mencian view on the *a priori* goodness of innate human qualities or "human nature". Mou's interpretation is thus based on the view that freedom is a cause and not an effect (Tang Refeng 2002, 333); hence, it can limit other principles, but it cannot be limited by them. Because the divine consciousness is the cause of everything, free will (or infinite heart-mind) has to be a part of God or the Divine and is thus absolute and infinite. Mou's second argument for his thesis, which is rooted in his interpretation of Kant's relation between things in themselves and things for us (noumena and phenomena), i.e. the function of the cognitive subject (or the subject of recognition), has already been discussed in previous chapters.

Despite declining God in the sense of a higher force separated from men, Mou viewed Confucianism as a kind of atheistic religion, and tried to refute the widespread prejudice that Confucianism was, in essence, only a code of regulations prescribing proper moral behavior. While this code certainly implied elements of "primitive" religion which were rooted in superstition and the worship of idols, it did not possess any inner spiritual foundation (Han and Zhao 1994, 165). Mou instead argued that:

> This mistaken view was a result of the influence of Western missionaries and state missions, who saw only the external forms of life of the common Chinese people. They never understood, therefore, that at its spiritual core the Chinese moral ethic also implies religious feelings. Confucian transcendent religious feelings must not be confused with superstition, which is widespread among the common people. (Mou Zongsan in Han and Zhao 1994, 165)

In formal terms, while Confucianism does not include any religious ceremonies, it still acknowledges the idea of a creator. This creator manifests itself in the Way of Heaven/Nature (*tian dao*), which is essentially pure creativity, similar to the theological God. Where they differ is in the fact that Confucian creativity is not personalized. However, Confucianism still acknowledges the idea of creation or creativity. The Chinese had anthropomorphic deities in the periods of Shang (Yin) and Zhou Dynasties, but Confucius and Mencius transformed this anthropomorphic form of heaven (*tian*) into the concept of the Heavenly Mandate (*tian ming*), which was a moral or ideal concept. The Confucians were thus not interested in the personification of the Way of Heaven, nor in its transformation into an external, anthropomorphic God. Rather than seeking to establish a symbolic form of creativity, they were looking for methods for its internalization by the individual (Han and Zhao 1994, 165).

Mou also argued that, given that an anthropomorphic God is an ideal construct, it must be illusory:

> The reason for God's ability to create nature is his infinite consciousness. Hence, it is precisely this attribute which is responsible for existence; while existence also necessarily implies (or includes) infinite consciousness. But infinite consciousness is not necessarily conditioned by individual (or particular) existence. Thus, the anthropomorphization of infinite consciousness (and its transformation) into individual existence is merely a projection of human consciousness and, as such, is necessarily illusory. (Mou Zongsan 1975, 243)

For most Modern Confucians, ethical systems based on religion actually belonged to earlier phases of social development, when most individuals were still unable to establish their inner strength and autonomy, in order to endure the transience of life and accept their lack of control over the (external) world. God as a manifestation of a higher, incomprehensible and uncontrollable power that can cause destruction or salvation appears as a consolatory notion, and merely the inverted projection of the individual's actual state of impotence and their inability to deal with facts that enable, determine and limit their existence. The need for religion is childlike, in the sense that it betrays a child's inability to free itself from the care and prohibitions of its parents. In an ethics based upon the idea of God, the subject cannot be autonomous in the sense of a truly internalized (or innate) ability to assume ethical responsibility for its actions. As Mou Zongsan explains:

> Existence is perfect and cannot be controlled by us. Likewise, human beings cannot create existence. Even so, the supposition that "infinite existence" is responsible for existence, is not necessarily wrong. The problem arises with the personalization of infinite existence and its transformation into individual existence. (Mou Zongsan 1985, 243)

Tang Junyi's system of horizons and values grows out of similar views. When the human soul or spirit reaches the highest level of development and enters into the domain of the "absolute" horizon where it is confronted with religious values, its further development entails passing through three partial horizons which are defined by three corresponding levels of values. Since Tang's understanding of the Christian idea of God was very shallow and superficial, it is by no means accidental that God as an anthropomorphic higher force appears only at the lowest level of these partial horizons, and manifests itself as a product of the human desire for a unique divinity, similar to men. Christianity and Judaism correspond to this "primitive" level. The next level which is connected to higher values, is the level of the emptiness of all physical and ideal worlds, which corresponds to Buddhism. Only with the highest partial horizon does the individual gain access to the absolute sphere, where reality and values are united within the same entity. As noted,[53] this is the sphere where the creative potential of heaven (*tian*) is realized through human moral performance. As Lee Ming-huei (2001a, 63) points out, at this level the human soul has already surpassed both the longing for a "transcendent" God, and the phase of negating the reality of the world.

Sin yee Chan (2002, 310) summarizes the nine horizons as follows:

a) Individuals (things or persons),

b) Classes to which individuals belong,

c) Cause–effect relations among individuals,

d) Mutual perceptions by subjective minds,

e) Concepts and pure meaning,

f) Practising morality,

g) Union with a single deity,

h) Realizing the illusory nature of the world and self, and

i) Fulfilling human nature which is the embodiment of Heavenly Virtue.

Tang sees Confucianism as an archetype of the highest horizon, for it is based upon the unity of men and nature. Like his teacher Xiong Shili, he saw Confucianism as a "religion without religious forms" (Lee Ming-huei 2001a, 64), given that its eithical worldview cannot be divided from religion. In this worldview, every moral performance implies elements of transcendence (Chan 2002, 307): on the transcendental level, because they connect one with the general and universal aspects of human virtues, on a spiritual level, because they simultaneously connect the individual with all advanced personalities who act within the framework of these virtues.

Tang Junyi's view of Confucianism thus resembles Mou Zongsan's idea of a sort of godless religion. Underpinning this view is the supposition that ethics and religion are necessarily interconnected and cannot be separated. As Sin yee Chan (2002, 324) points out, we have to acknowledge that even if Tang is wrong and ethics can be separated from religion, his philosophy can still help us to understand Confucianism from another perspective, not merely as an ethical theory, but as a religion. Such a religion is free from institutionalization and focuses on a direct connection between the individual and the cosmos. Hence, the Confucian religious aspects perhaps imply a special appeal and relevance to our modern societies.

Xu Fuguan noted that the emergence of different ethical concepts in Chinese and Western cultures can be explained by their different ideological reactions to similar conditions of social transition.

According to Xu Fuguan's analyses, all cultures find their earliest source in religion, and originate in the worship of God or gods. The specific feature of Chinese culture was that it soon descended, in a series of gradual transitions, from heaven to the world of men, and the real life and behavior of human beings. During the Zhou Dynasty (1066–256 B.C.), the preoccupation with earthly matters, had started: the spirit of self-consciousness was beginning to work and they had developed a clear will and purpose (see Bresciani 2001, 338). They were thus moving progressively from the realm of religion to the realm of ethics. Hence, from this very early stage, the Chinese have been liberated from metaphysical concerns. In contrast to the ancient Greeks, who at the same critical stage in their history moved from religion to metaphysics, they moved from religion to innate ethics.

The moral Self, as essentially interpreted by all second generation Modern Confucians, was established as an ideal core of individual perception and possible identification in a period of conflicting local cultures. For them, its emergence was conditioned by the fact that all of the "feudal" states in the Zhou Dynasty were rooted in diverse traditions that had formed different religious ideas. Just as ancient Greek culture is generally considered the "cradle of European culture", so too the period of the Zhou Dynasty is seen as the "cradle of (Han) Chinese culture" by official Chinese historiography.[54]

In this framework, the Zhou society resulted from the merging of two different types of culture: an agrarian system typical of the defeated Shang (or Yin) Dynasty (1600–1066 B.C.), and the hunting and gathering culture of the nomadic conquerors, i.e. the ancestors of the Zhou Dynasty.[55] This theory is supported by the *Shi Ji* (*Historical Notes*), according to which in spite of the fact that the mythological founding ancestor of the Zhou Dynasty, Ho Ji, was credited with greatly improving Xia (2100–1600 B.C.) agriculture, his son Buzhu abandoned agriculture entirely, living a nomadic life in the manner of their *rong* and *di* "barbarian" neighbors (see *Shi ji* 2014, Zhou benji, 3). Among the consequences of this encounter was the mixing of agrarian and nomadic religions. Xu Fuguan showed that the Zhou society could, in many ways, be seen as a continuation of the Shang culture (Xu Fuguan 1987, 649).

One of the elements appropriated by the Zhou from the Shang Dynasty, was the cult of ancestors (Xu Fuguan 1987, 649). Given that the religious ideas of the Shang Dynasty centered on fertility worship, while its economic system was based upon the cooperation and division of labor within family clans, the cult of ancestors as a ritualized worship which united both aspects, gradually became the common thread which can be traced throughout Chinese history.

In Western Sinology, the cult of ancestors is still commonly thought to be a religion, for it is rooted in a faith in the afterlife and the propitiation and search for protection from the ancestral spirits by the living members of the family clan. But since Confucius was an agnostic,[56] his emphasis on the importance of the ancestor cult cannot be confused with a religious ritual, but must be understood as a moral one. This aspect was underscored by Xu Fuguan, in the context of his research into the ideologies of the pre-Qin period.

> With respect to the worship of spirits and deities, while Confucius could not rationally prove that they existed, he could neither prove that they did not exist. Thus, he transformed this ritual into

186   The Rebirth of the Moral Self

> a form of respectful ancestor worship, in which the living could manifest the virtues of respect, humanity and love. This form of worship, which began with Confucius and was further developed after him, is in no way a religious activity, for what it implies is a purification and elevation of the self-centered perception of individuals. (Xu Fuguan 1995, 614)

This cult provided the basis for the first Han-Chinese ethical codex, as well as the religious ideas of this cultural community. Its basic belief is that the human body contains two souls: the first is animalistic and dies soon after the death of the body, while the second, the so-called "soul of human personality" can move about freely and continue to exist as long as there are living people who remember and feed it. The family clan which respected its deceased ancestors guaranteed itself their protection and assistance. The new ideologies thus merged the cult of Heaven with the family system, such that the ruler became the "Son of Heaven" (*tian zi*), thereby legitimizing the quest for absolute power, while also accomodating the original nomadic Zhou culture.

While in the Shang/Yin period, the people's faith in God or the highest ruler (*Shang di*) did not imply any ethical elements, in the period of the Zhou Dynasty this belief was related to morality. In historical terms, the linking of Heaven with virtue not only resolved the problem of justifying and legitimizing the political power of the early Zhou, but also accelerated the development of the original Chinese religion by raising it from a natural to a moral religion. In its role as the highest anthropomorphic deity, *Tian* was not only the creator of humanity, but also its highest judge, who meted out praise and punishment as recompense for moral or immoral behavior. However, according to Yang Zebo (2007, 2), due to the inefficiency, corruption and nepotism of the ruling class, this moral-religious consciousness gradually declined, reaching its low ebb at the end of the eighth century B.C., during the transition from the Western to the Eastern Zhou Dynasty. As confirmed by several passages in the *Book of Songs* (*Shi jing*), by this time the deity was the object of much anger (*tian yuan*) and doubt (*yi tian*).[57]

As Xu Fuguan has shown, the authority of the heavenly mandate (*tian ming*) was already much weakened by the time of the ruler You[58] of the Zhou Dynasty. The traditional religious concepts which were rooted in the early Zhou Dynasty had almost completely disintegrated. This period marks an extraordinarily important historical and cultural shift, in which Chinese society entered what Karl Jaspers has called "the axial period" (see Jaspers 2003, 98). In fact, as opposed to most other civilizations, China did not develop a theology, but separated itself from it[59] (Yang Zebo 2007, 3).

As Chen Lai (1996, 4) points out, instead of people recognizing their own limitations and turning towards some transcendent, infinite entity or monotheistic religion, they recognized the limitations of deities and oriented themselves towards the real world and the ordering of society and interpersonal relations. Thus, instead of a "breakthrough to transcendence", in China there was a "breakthrough to humanity" (Xu Fuguan 1987, 659). While other civilizations were moving towards "more developed" religions during this same period, China turned towards a pragmatic search for an ideal social order.

By not taking these specific historical circumstances into account, Western scholars have always assumed that the main Chinese religion in the late Zhou period (primarily Confucius) was a primitive form of religious faith. Hegel, for example, in his description of this religion (1996b, 320), concluded that the concept *tian* only referred to the concrete social reality, and that ancient Chinese thinkers (with Confucius at the fore) had thus been unable to gain an insight into the idea of transcendence.

Modern Confucians developed their views on the original Confucian teachings and the ethics they implied based on immanent transcendence. The creative transformation of religion into morality thus also served as the foundation of the new Modern Confucian concept of subjectivity. The second generation thinkers followed the basic supposition that in the aforesaid historical process of social transformation in China, the idea of Heaven (*tian*) was transformed from an anthropomorphic higher force into something which determined the inner reality of every human being (Fang and Li 1995, III/608). As Fang Dongmei (2004b, 99) puts it: "At first, this culture was formed on the basis of a religious spirit, but it was then transformed into a culture with a highly developed ethics. This ethics was appropriated and properly ordered by Confucius".

Xu Fuguan conjectured that original Confucianism attempted to establish a basis for moral decisions in the idea of a subjective righteousness which was intended to serve as a fundamental criterion and thus replace the former fear of spirits.[60] Xu argues that this transformation represents a higher level of spiritual development than that found in monotheistic religions, which are based upon the idea of an (external) God. In his view, in China this transformation led to a humanism based on a high level of "self-awareness" (*zijuexing*):

> All human cultures begin with religion. China was no exception in this sense. But all cultures also form a kind of clear and reasonable idea which influences the development of human behavior; that is, they must develop a certain level of human self-awareness. Primitive religions are, instead, mostly defined by a simple belief in miraculous supernatural forces, which derive from a sense of dread at the destruction that can be caused by heaven. Such religions are not based on any kind of self-awareness. Highly developed religions differ according to the societies and historical periods in which they arose. If we observe the preserved bronze vessels from the Yin period, it is clear that Chinese culture was already highly developed at that time, and that it had a long history behind it. However, if we examine the inscriptions on bones and turtle shells from that same period, we find that spiritual life was still rather primitive, and that their religion belonged to primitive forms of religious faith. People still believed their lives were completely dependent upon various deities, the most important of which were the spirits of ancestors and the highest ruler, Shang di. In the Zhou period, a spirit of self-awareness was incorporated into traditional religious life. In this sense, a culture previously rooted in material achievements was raised to the sphere of ideas. And this contributed to founding the humanistic spirit of Chinese morality. (Xu Fuguan 2005, 15–16)

Like most other second generation thinkers, Xu Fuguan was convinced that this transformation from a "primitive" natural religion into a system of pragmatic ethics was the Zhou Dynasty's greatest contribution to the development of Chinese culture. Xu points out that, while during the Zhou period the people still worshipped and offered sacrifices to various deities from previous natural religions, this no longer occurred within the context of official state religions that could have fulfilled the function of preserving or justifying political power. In the Zhou period, this function had gradually been supplanted by the idea of the "Heavenly Mandate" or "The decree of Heaven" (*tian ming*). The values criteria of this new idea were defined by the reasonableness or unreasonableness of human performances (Xu Fuguan 2005, 24). The most important innovation here was that the idea of the Heavenly Mandate was no longer an ideology intended to protect a real ruler and his real interests. Instead, the ruler always had to be chosen among those who could prove themselves most worthy of this position through their reasonable, responsible and righteous actions. The concept of the Heavenly Mandate was thus no longer something remote, incomprehensible and miraculous, as with the previous ideology of spirits and deities, but a concept which was both sacred and yet completely human and comprehensible. It could therefore guarantee a reasonable structure of society and politics, and enable individuals to attain a fair degree of independence (Xu Fuguan 2005, 24).

Xu Fuguan has explored this process of the formation of morality and the internalizing of the spirit of humanity in great detail. He believed that Confucius was the figure who most influenced this transformation of primitive belief (Xu Fuguan 1995b, 613). Of course, even before Confucius there were various germs of moral ideas in China, which served both as generally accepted behavioral criteria and as a legitimization of affiliation to a given social class. But the gradual process of the "humanization of heaven" and the discovery of its humanistic dimension (*tiande renwenhua*) did not begin before the Spring and Autumn period (770–476 B.C.). By that time, the ideas of reverence (*jing*)[61] and rituality (*li*) had become fairly important as central manifestations of the socialization of morality. Previously, moral ideas had merely represented sets of axiological meanings which served as criteria for the good and reasonable in the ordering of society and interpersonal relations. Moral ideas were thus something external; in Confucianism they instead acquired a new dimension and became part of a completely different discourse:[62]

> Before Confucius... moral and ethical ideas manifested themselves merely in the form of external knowledge and behavior.

They were woven into relations in the objective world and were not understood as something that could be consciously applied to open up the inner world of humanism. Only through Confucius' creative reform was this humanism of the objective world transformed into a world of inner humanism. Individuals were thereby endowed with the possibility of striving for self-improvement (completion) and a spirit of Chinese morality was formed. (Xu Fuguan 1995b, 614)

Xu Fuguan explains that the philosophical reforms enacted by Confucius manifested themselves in two significant ways:

1. in the reform of the worship of traditional spirits and deities, which was transformed into symbolic ancestor worship by Confucius and

2. in the internalizing of traditional religious concepts, such as Heaven/Nature (*tian*), the Heavenly Mandate (*tian ming*) and the Way of Heaven/Nature (*tian dao*); these concepts were also transformed from abstract external ideas into symbols denoting various forms or states of an inner moral substance.

Confucius distinguished between two levels of transmitting and interpreting his philosophy, as synthesized in his famous phrase: "My studies lie on the physical level, and my penetration rises to a metaphysical one" (*xia xue er shang da*).[63] The former approach was exemplified in the moral teachings for the uneducated and mostly agrarian population, where in order to express his concept of immanent transcendence Confucius relied on traditional notions that were already familiar to his listeners in order to denote specific aspects of the inner substance. In applying this dual approach, he used real human experience in order to elaborate a philosophical discourse on the concept of a morality which transcends the one-dimensional nature of human existence.

Confucius expressed concepts such as Heaven/Nature, the Heavenly Mandate or the Way of Nature with the most direct and simple language; but he was actually talking about a morality which supersedes experience (Xu Fuguan 2005, 81).

In order to spread his teachings, these moral-philosophical concepts assumed the function of appropriate symbols that people could apply in their lives through moral conduct and rituality. The Heavenly Mandate could thus become a part of everyday life, while thanks to their familiarity with this traditional idea the common people could become aware of their unity with its moral dimension, and its relevance for them in terms of moral responsibility.[64]

The fulfillment of these internalized moral-humanistic values thus gained the dimension of perfecting one's personality.[65] By linking the innate personal attributes of individuals (*xin*) with the Heavenly Mandate (*tian ming*), Confucius created a new moral content with a deeper significance that superseded the traditional idea of "righteousness" (*yi*). This concept, with which all Confucian discourses were permeated and which constitutes their conceptual core, was expressed by the idea of humanity or mutuality (*ren*), as representing a state of complete individual and social consciousness.[66]

Thus, in Xu Fuguan's reading, Confucianism is not a religion, but a discourse that represents both a practical moral teaching and an abstract philosophy of immanent transcendence. While Confucius' works have generally been understood and interpreted in the former sense, it was primarily the Neo-Confucian philosophers of the Song and Ming Dynasties who would develop its philosophical aspects. We might well ask therefore, and notwithstanding his detailed and painstaking philological research into original Confucianism, whether Xu Fuguan has not projected the discoveries and results of later Confucian philosophies and interpretations onto the original teachings.[67]

However, if we take Modern Confucianism as a whole, the reinterpretation of this teaching as embodying something sacred is clearly evident. Although it has been described as a religion without God, i.e. as an atheistic religion (similar to Buddhism) the correctness of this interpretation remains open to debate.

While using a very different approach from Xu, Heiner Roetz (2008, 370) has also contextualised original Confucianism within the transition from a religiously determined to a purely pragmatic ethics. He points out that in original Confucianism, "Heaven" (*tian*) never appears in the function of external provisions or regulations, since it "never speaks".[68] Another reason for his scepticism as to the religious dimension of original Confucianism is that a non-religious reading of these ancient texts can, if based on a proper interpretation and adaptation, allow for a unitary conceptualization of modernization which is not limited to instrumental rationality, but which also does not negate social progress, understood as a necessary consequence of enlightenment.

However, Roetz's arguments appear a bit tenuous here, precisely because based on a very specific way of reading the original Confucian texts which does not take into account the broader socio-political context which the second generation theorists elaborated so exhaustively in their own socio-philological researches. And while his basic argument is both comprehensible and reasonable, Roetz tends to become entangled in the toils of his own rhetoric, which sometimes appears as logically unsound. Because his own views run counter to the highly suspect and theoretically unfounded euphoria observable in the works of certain third generation Confucian thinkers who are intent on creating a synthesis between Confucianism and the Christian foundations of modernization, the impression is that his arguments ultimately seek to confute Modern Confucian interpretations in view of their possible consequences for the future development of Chinese philosophy.

7. The Modern Confucian Legacy and the New Confucian Ideologies in the People's Republic of China: The Case of Harmony

As we have indicated throughout this study, the last two decades have witnessed a lively revival of Confucian thought in the P. R. China. However, this revival and its most influential approaches differ in many ways from the Modern Confucian theories examined thus far. While in Taiwan and Hong Kong, this revival represented a continuous discourse that developed and refined the basic approaches delineated by the pioneers of this intellectual movement, i.e. the representatives of the so-called first generation, in the P. R. China this stream of thought was ignored or silenced for more than 30 years.[1] In my opinion, one of the basic differences between mainland and island Modern Confucianism is that, in the P. R. China, the widespread revival of traditional thought was—at least to a certain extent—instigated from above. In mainland China, it was one of the new ideologies that were designed to fill the axiological rift or gap that gradually appeared in Chinese society as a result of the explosive economic liberalization. As we explained above, these new ideologies were necessary in order to compensate the loss of the normative authority of the Chinese Communist party, and from the mid-1980s onwards, these ideologies were utilized in order to fill the so-called "vacuum of values", a function which had previously been entrusted to the orthodox socialist and communist values systems.

Clearly, we do not mean to imply that the mainland Confucian revival was motivated only by ideology. Following the period of gradual liberalization, numerous brilliant new Confucian scholars appeared in the P. R. China, who focused on many previously neglected or overlooked aspects of original Confucian thought, while also developing new approaches for its modernized integration into contemporary Chinese society. These scholars include important figures, such as Guo Qiyong, Chen Lai, Zheng Jiadong, Li Zehou, Tang Yijie, Zhang Liwen, Meng Peiyuan, and Mou Zhongjian.

However, these innovative approaches were often overshadowed by ideological initiatives that were intended to reestablish a modern Chinese cultural identity. The figure of Confucius provided a symbol or icon which fit into this scheme quite well, representing as it did "3,000 years" of a cultural heritage that had been shared by all strata and classes of society. As we shall see, this figure—together with others—became the vehicle for another idea that was functional to creating this new, ideal Chinese society: that of harmonious unity and the avoidance of conflict.

7.1 Confucianism in the People's Republic of China—A Brief Historical Overview

The idea of "harmonious society" represents one of the core elements of the social ideology in contemporary China. Although the concept of harmony which underpins this idea has often been explicitly denoted as originating in Confucian thought, Confucian discourses did not form part of the public intellectual debate in the P. R. China before the last two decades of the twentieth century. Prior to that time, the historical figure of Confucius, and the entire Confucian tradition, were the targets of severe criticism by official governmental ideologists. Confucian teachings were seen as a reactionary "feudalistic" ideology which had mainly served the interests of the exploitative ruling classes of the previous social orders, while Confucius himself was seen—in the light of the tradition of the May Fourth cultural renewal movement[2] and Marxist modernization theories—as a symbol of the ultra-conservative tradition that had blocked Chinese modernization and as thus "responsible" for the country's backwardness.

Such criticism reached its peak in the campaign "Criticize Lin, Criticize Confucius" (Pi Lin pi Kong) which followed Lin Biao's death in an airplane accident in 1971. In this campaign, Confucius and his thought were seen as a prototype of reactionary ideology and traditionalism, although it was mainly directed against Lin Biao and the moderate politician, Zhou Enlai. (Motoh 2009, 91)

Less than two decades later, however, and to the complete surprise of many experts in Chinese studies, such criticism was completely reversed. As Helena Motoh (2009, 91) points out, one of the first indications of this turnabout was Gu Mu's official address on the occasion of the 2540th anniversary of Confucius' birth. In his speech (1989), Gu Mu, who was one of the chief ideologues of Chinese modernization, indicated the importance of a "correct" (or rectified) relation to traditional national culture and urged a revival of the positive elements of Confucian thought within the framework of a synthesis with Western ideas. At the same time, he stressed that in this synthesis the Chinese tradition should predominate over the Western one.

This "official" turning towards Confucianism manifested itself in changes in official Party language, the founding of numerous departments and chairs of "national studies"[3] and the establishment of a network of "Confucius institutes" throughout the world (Motoh 2009, 91). However, Confucianism was also rediscovered by many intellectuals who hoped to find in it a useful tool for re-evaluating (traditional) social practices, thereby contributing to the solution of the many socio-political problems facing contemporary China.

In recent years, Confucian teachings have been valued primarily in terms of their possible contribution to the idea of a "harmonious society".

> The need for a policy rethink spurred Hu's "harmonious society/world" idea. China now needs to adjust its attitude: a more proactive role is now necessary if the country is to shape its own destiny, both internally and externally. "Scientific development" (*kexue fazhanguan*) and "harmonious society" serve to provide Hu's

domestic audience with new developmental objectives "harmonious world" sends the signal that China is now moving into a new stage of development. This new mentality and approach—China finally "going out"—is applicable to both China's domestic and foreign policies, three decades into its 'open door' policy. (Zhen and Tok 2007, 2)

Although in the reports of the Seventeenth Communist Party Congress, the concept of the harmonious society would be overshadowed somewhat by the slogan of "scientific development", the "construction of a harmonious society" (*hexie shehui jianshe*) still represents one of the main principles of the continental government, and was even applied in the new reform of Chinese legislation.

7.2 A Harmony of Peace and Order

This link between harmony and law was often the focus of Chinese academic articles dealing with the legal implications of the (planned) harmonious society:

> In establishing its legal and judicial system, the ancient Chinese society in which Confucian culture predominated laid stress upon the concepts of "applying rituality, respect for harmony and consideration of the methods of ancient rulers". In its method of following "the middle way", Confucianism strove for the consolidation for these concepts. The "respect for harmony" represents the core of ancient Chinese culture and, at the same time, the basic value tendency on which rests the classical Chinese idea of a legal system. Nowadays, we have re-established this idea of "constructing harmonious society" and emphasized the content of the notion "harmony"… Thus, the foundation of modern societies is law, which is based upon regulations, the wisdom of the people, equality and justice. A harmonious society lays stress upon peace and order, sincerity, friendship, love and also upon a coherent development. It strives for the unification of man and nature and for a healthy sustainable development. Thus, if we want to establish a harmonious society, we must first establish the rule of law. (Zhou Jiayi 2010, 285)

As Leila Choukrone and Antoine Garapon point out, in this context the concept of harmony is seen primarily as an instrument of social discipline, a view which comes to the forefront in discussions on the linkage between harmony and law:

> This theoretical framework turns law into a disciplinary principle dedicated to society's moral construction. If law is seen as an instrument for legitimizing power, it remains implicitly but primarily subordinate to the regime's durability... Thus, at the current juncture, "harmony" is also essential for a Party concerned over retaining its grip on the country. (Choukrone and Garapon 2007, 3)

This position was already made explicit in an article by Xiao Zhuoji, a professor of the School of Economics of Peking University and vice-chairman of the Social and Legal Affairs Committee of the Chinese People's Political Consultative Conference, whose comments on the new political direction appeared in the English edition of the official *China Daily* soon after Hu Jintao's announcement of the new "harmonious path": "In addition, we will crack down on various social ills, which are a poisonous tumour in a harmonious society and must be eliminated" (Xiao Zhuoji 2007, 2).

Similar passages can also be found in various academic articles that, within the context of the harmonious society, stress the importance of discipline, self-restraint and a "correct" attitude towards superiors and the community (see Li Ning 2010, 9). If, as Choukrone and Garapon argue (2007, 3), the idea of harmony serves as an ideological support for a legal model which is used as a disciplinary and moral tool for preserving the present regime, then harmony (as an ostensibly essential aspect of Confucian teachings) also serves as a symbol for Confucius, seen as a thinker who propounded a "proper" morality that manifested itself in the subordination of individuals to "higher" social goals and in the unconditional obedience to superiors.

Such notions of harmony are often shared by many Western scholars, and are based not only on contemporary Chinese ideologies, but on the much older, Weberian interpretation of this concept:

> The cosmic orders of the world were considered fixed and inviolate and the orders of society were but a special case of this. The

great spirits of the cosmic orders obviously desired only the happiness of the world and especially the happiness of man. The same applied to the orders of society. The "happy" tranquility of the empire and the equilibrium of the soul should and could be attained only if man fitted himself into the internally harmonious cosmos. (Weber 1951, 152–3)

Li Chenyang (2014, 8) points out that in such (mis)understandings, Confucian harmony is just to fit into fixed and inviolate orders. In such a view, harmony is nothing more than mere conformity. In his brilliant analysis, however, Li shows that the Confucian notion of harmony is neither pure accord, nor conformity. In fact, it is rather founded on diversity and formulated with creative tension (Li Chenyang 2014, 9).

Here, we have to lay stress upon the fact that Confucian notion of harmony is multilateral and multifaceted. Although official publications dedicated to promoting the idea of a harmonious society often indicate Confucius and/or Confucianism as the source of this concept, at first glance the connotations indicated above do not seem to derive from the original Confucian canon, but from the discourses of the post-Confucian Legalist school of thought. However, we should recall that for Dong Zhongshu, the Han scholar and reformer who elaborated the later traditional Confucian state doctrine, the normative function of "propriety" (*zheng*), which manifests itself through the implementation of rituals (*li*), provided a basic means (together with the hierarchical social structure) for integrating legalist elements into the ideal framework of original Confucianism. In order to understand the implications of this position, let us briefly examine the semantic connotations of the concept of harmony (or harmonization) in the context of the most relevant classical texts.[4]

7.3 Classical Harmony

In the *Analects* (*Lun yu*), Confucius makes a radical distinction between sameness (in the sense of uniformity, *tong*), and harmony or harmonization (*he*), and criticizes the former in the following terms: "The nobleman creates harmony, not sameness. Ordinary men, on the contrary, are all the same and cannot create harmony" (Confucius 2012, Zi lu 23).

The idea that diversity is a condition of harmony (Motoh 2009, 99) can also be found in the Confucian classics *The Annales of Spring and Autumn* (*Chun qiu lu* 春秋錄):

> If the ruler approves something, everyone approves it. And if he is against something, everyone is against it. This is like adding water to water. Who would like to eat (such a watery soup)? This is like all instruments (in an orchestra) playing the same musical tune. Who would like to listen to such music? (Confucius 2012b, Shao gong ershi nian 1)

Underlying this view is the assumption that social harmony is merely a projection or metaphor for the mutual coherence of tones that forms the basis of any good music. Rituals, of which it is part, also have a regulatory function. Thus, any kind of harmony that was not in accordance with rituals was deemed inappropriate by the Confucians and could not represent a positive value: "To know the harmonious coherence and still create harmony without regulating it by the rules of propriety, this likewise should not be done" (Confucius 2012a, Xue er 12).

Here, we find the regulatory or normative function of the central Confucian concept *li*. Although music is an important part of Confucian ritual, not every kind of music is appropriate for cultivated people. The function of the ritual fusion of nature and culture, men and nature, individuals and society can only be fulfilled by "proper", or "sublime" music (*ya yue*). Given the similarity with the Confucian understanding of harmony,[5] it cannot be claimed that the disciplinary function of harmony—in a broader sense—derives exclusively from legalist discourses.

As it is well known, the interpretations of the original teachings of Confucius by his most important followers, Mencius and Xunzi, differed in their specific approach towards innate human qualities. This naturally influenced their divergent views on the relation between individuals and society, as well as their interpretation of social harmony. We should bear in mind that Xunzi also provided the interpretative foundation of Dong Zhongshu's reformist thought, which implied various legalistic elements. On the other hand, Neo-Confucian philosophy mainly followed the Mencian interpretations of the original Confucian teachings, and provided a basis for the later Modern Confucian theorists. In the framework of the present study, it is worth noting that while the concept of harmony often appears in the works of the more rigid philosopher Xunzi, it is scarcely mentioned by the "humanistic"[6] Mencius, who always understood the concept *he* in the sense of mutual human harmony and coherence:

> Opportunities of time provided by Heaven are not equal to advantages of situation provided by the Earth, and advantages of situation arising from the Earth are not equal to the union arising from the harmony between people. (Mencius 2012, Gongsun Chou III/10)

Mencius explains this view with the following example, in which he analyses the reasons for a city's decline:

> The city walls were distinguished for their height, and its moats were deep enough. Its arms were distinguished for their strength and sharpness, and the stores of rice and grain were large enough. Yet it was given up and abandoned. This is because advantages of situation provided by the Earth are not equal to the union arising from the harmony between people. (Mencius 2012, Gongsun Chou III/10)

Such a harmonious coherence is conditioned by adaptation, for he also applied the term *he* with this connotation: "Hui of Liu Xia could adapt harmoniously to the sages" (Mencius 2012, Wang zhang II/10).

In his understanding of the concept *he*, Xunzi adhered to its original meaning, which is linked to musical harmony: "Rituality is grounded in the respect of culture, and music in harmony" (Xunzi 2011, Quan xue 12).

Further, he often explicitly connects the harmonious compliance among people with the concept of regularity (*jie*).[7]

> If we want our government to function well, our efforts, will and thoughts have to follow rituality. If not, then chaos will prevail and people will suffer. Our food, clothes, homes and actions must all follow rituality, because only in this way can harmony be achieved. Otherwise, we will experience unhappiness and illness. (Xunzi 2011, Xiu shen 2)

According to Xunzi, this regularity which was meant to order human relations in a harmonious society, was based upon the regular order of Nature. In fact, it manifested itself in the orderly sequence of the four seasons:

> To act in accordance with Heaven/Nature means that there is no drought on the heights and no floods in the lowlands. Winter and summer follow each other with an orderly, harmonious constancy and the crops mature in their proper time. (Xunzi 2011, Xiu shen 3)

This orderly harmony must be strengthened by culture (Xunzi 2011, Ru xiao 1). Xunzi thus distinguishes between "good" and "bad" harmony: "When harmony among people is established by the means of goodness, everything will flow smoothly. If somebody wants to establish harmony by means of evil, he is nothing but an opportunist" (Xunzi 2011, Rongru 11).

Hence, "good" harmony is based on a regulative order of nature, which also manifests itself in a proper hierarchic structure of society. Such connotations, which are already rather legalistic, are expressed explicitly in the following passage, in which this Confucian philosopher links an orderly social hierarchy to the concept of unification. This concept is, of course, fundamental to the functioning of a centralist state, while also clearly contradicting Confucius who, as we noted above, advocated diversity:

> It is therefore reasonable to create harmony by the means of divisions. (Such) harmony allows unification and unification allows superiority. In this way, the farthest borders (of the state) can be reached and our enemies can be defeated. (Xunzi 2011, Wang zhi 19)

But Xunzi goes even further, and links the creation of harmony to the idea of punishment: "With the establishment of forms of punishment, the governing [of society] will become balanced and people will live in harmony" (Xunzi 2011, Wang zhi 26).

The disciplinary connotation that prevailed in the understanding and propagation of a "harmonious society" in China under Hu Jintao, thus derives directly from Xunzi's interpretations of this notion. They can thus be regarded as Confucian, but in terms of their fundamental aims they derive from elaborations of the original Confucian teachings which were functional to the integration of despotic elements into the new state doctrine formulated in the Han period.

7.4 Modern Confucian Harmony as Balance and Equilibrium

In the context of the present study, it is of particular interest to determine whether (and to what degree) the modern concept of a "harmonious society", which represents an important element of current ideologies and is often denoted as a Confucian heritage, may also be linked to the theoretical conclusions of Modern Confucianism.

As noted, Modern Confucians have generally followed a Neo-Confucian philosophy based upon Mencius', rather than Xunzi's development of the original teachings. Xunzi was thus often viewed as something of a heretic who did not profess or elaborate a "proper" Confucianism in his own discourses. Xiong Shili, who taught many of the representatives of the second generation of Modern Confucianism, identifies what he considers the fundamental failing in Xunzi:

> Confucianism upholds original human goodness, that is, the shining aspect of human nature. Orthodox Confucianism, from Mencius to Wang Yangming, insists that there is original benevolence in human nature (with the exception of Xunzi). Xiong concludes that Xunzi fails to reach the essence of Confucianism. (Yu Jiuyuan 2002, 131)

In order to better understand this basic division, we will briefly examine the meaning and interpretations of the concept of harmony

The Modern Confucian Legacy and the New Confucian Ideologies 203

in the context of the second generation of Modern Confucianism. The main representatives of this generation are Mou Zongsan, Xu Fuguan, Tang Junyi and Fang Dongmei. Although the present study is devoted to the specific theoretical concepts relating to modernization (and it is in this context that these philosophers will be discussed below), given their relevance to our chosen topic, we will provide a brief survey of their views on the legitimization of Confucianism and harmony.

One of Xiong Shili's most gifted students was Mou Zongsan, who is generally regarded, especially in philosophical terms, as the leading representative of the second generation of Modern Confucians. With respect to the legitimacy of Confucian teachings and the definition of a "proper" Confucianism, Mou agrees with his teacher Xiong Shili, in terms of the criteria of autonomous ethics and the unity of reason and emotions. Consequently, only Confucius, Mencius and the authors or commentators of the classical works, *The Doctrine of the Mean* (*Zhong yong*) and *The Book of Changes* (*Yi jing*) can be considered as "legitimate" heirs to pre-Qin Confucianism. Xunzi instead belongs to a lateral (i.e. not completely legitimate) current, due to his advocacy of the so-called "ethics of heteronomy" (Lee Ming-huei 2001a, 73).

While Mou does not give much attention to the question of harmony, at least explicitly, some clues to harmonious living in society can be found in his work, *On Summum Bonum* (*Yuan shan lun*), in which he attempts to explain the method of the harmonization (or unification) of happiness and goodness. In this study, he also briefly considers the interpretation of the original Confucian phrase "the harmony of balance" (*Zhong he*); a phrase which, however, has nothing to do with the social connotations of harmony that are at the heart of present day continental ideologies. On the contrary, this phrase refers to the ideal foundations of harmony, which are grounded in the completeness of the individual (and integral) moral Self.

> The existence of my individual life is a completed fact, but it still implies possibilities of improvement. Therefore, it is not a kind of fixed or determined existence. This existence is, according to the Buddhists, a non-defined existence of everything that exists.

Everything that exists is in this completed fact of existence, but, at the same time, this existence is undefined (i.e. it is not of a fixed, determined nature). All existence is permeated by reason and grows out from it. The *Doctrine of the Mean*[8] refers to this, for it says: "When the harmony of balance is achieved, Heaven and Earth are in their proper places and everything that exists develops". (Mou Zongsan 1985, 306)

In his discussion of the *Doctrine of the Mean* (*Zhong yong*), Xu Fuguan likewise deals with this concept (i.e. the harmony of balance, *zhong he*), which he views as a notion that:

refers to the "nature" that unifies the internal and the beyond and to the harmonizing function of the nature that consummates both the self and the things around (it). The internal aspect is what consummates the self, and the beyond is what consummates the things around. (Ni 2002, 287)

Xu explains this notion as follows:

Here, the notion "balance (*zhong*)"[9] does not only refer to a foundation of some external balance, but rather to a common basis for both "balance" (*zhong*) and "one's own way". In the third commentary of Guang Ya we can read: "One's own way is harmony". This means that harmony can be equated to one's own way. The expression "harmony" which forms a part of the compound "harmony of balance" (*zhong he*), is not only an effect of the "own way", but a joint effect of balance and the own way. The balance that appears in the expression "harmony of balance", acts outwards as the way of the mean (or the middle way), but on a higher level it connects the innate qualities of each individual with their life. Therefore, it can be denoted as the "great foundation". The notion "harmony", which appears in the phrase "harmony of balance", is an effect of the middle way (or the own way of balance). The middle way (or the own way of balance) therefore implies the actual effect (or substantial impact) of "harmony" and thus is capable of reaching everything under heaven... Hence, we can say, that the concept of harmony refers to something which describes "the effect of that which is called dao". At the same time, this concept expresses the very entity which makes the inherent connection with the middle way (or the own way of balance) possible. (Xu Fuguan 2005, 127)

The harmony of balance is thus the most basic foundation of each individual, which enables them to achieve/maintain a harmonious co-existence with other individuals and society as a whole. As we shall see, in Modern Confucian philosophy the moral Self represents both the foundation of each individual and the core of the universal reason. This is naturally preconditioned by the complementarity of the relation between the individual and their natural/social environment. This means that social harmony is necessarily linked to the harmonious inwardness of the individual.

Given that, in the Modern Confucian view, the universe (or all that exists) is permeated with the virtue of goodness, both the phenomenal forms of reality, as well as its substantial nucleus that manifests itself in the idea of the "things in themselves" (noumenon) are axiological notions. The harmony of human existence is thus strictly bound with moral premises. For Xu Fuguan, these values are closely linked to the aesthetics of perceiving beauty, which is one of the fundamental functions or effects of harmony. Xu argues that this is why music was considered of paramount importance in the ideal framework of original Confucianism. A profound musical sensation enables us to simultaneously project its harmony into the sphere of social reality: "In Confucianism, balance (*zhong*) and harmony were the central aesthetic criteria of music. Behind balance and harmony there is the meaning of goodness; thus, they can move human hearts and awaken goodness in them" (Xu Fuguan 2001a, 14).

In the field of concrete social politics, Xu Fuguan envisioned a system that would enable society to achieve "rational harmony" on the basis of a reasonable competition. A co-existence that was not merely a question of the individual should be premised on the independence of each individual, with the collective rights of the community grounded in individual rights (Ni 2002, 296–7).

> However, when the maturity of the people and the other conditions are sufficiently present so that people who enjoy political

> rights can live together harmoniously, the system of rights may become less important or even unnecessary. As Chenyang Li suggests, between well-related family members, "it is meaningless or even destructive to talk about their rights against one another". Yet between the stage that relies on sage rulers and the stage at which harmony prevails, Confucianism must provide room for something less ideal. As Shu-hsien Liu says, in the current historical situation "we have to negate the tradition in order to reconfirm the ideal of the tradition". (Ni 2002, 298)

Xu Fuguan was thus advocating a harmony of human communities based upon the individuality of each person.

> In the chapter "The twentieth year of Duke Zhao", in *Zuo's Commentary on the Spring and Autumn Annals*, Yanzi says: "Harmony is like a stew". A stew contains various kinds of tastes that blend together into a delicious unity. Therefore, "harmony" is composed of many different combinations of particular individual qualities. In harmony, none of these individual qualities will be lost: instead, they blend harmoniously with one another. (Xu Fuguan 2005, 127)

The morality offered to the individual by Tang Junyi, is not based on either the uniqueness of their individual existence (as in Xu Fuguan's political philosophy), nor on the autonomous freedom of the moral Self and its infinite mind (as in Mou Zongsan). Tang's idea of morality is much more directly rooted in the individual sense of the innate responsibility which—similarly to the neo-Confucian concept of "innate knowledge"/*liang zhi*/—can guide human beings through the opaque thickets of all the ethical dilemmas and doubts they will encounter during their actual lives. But the individual can contribute to the higher goal of social harmony only if they obey this inner gnomen of responsibility:

> You need not ask what you should do, because you alone know what is to be done. However, sometimes you might sense the possibility of acting in more than one way. You might even feel that these different possibilities are in contradiction with one

another. You might not know immediately which one to choose, or how to unify them in order to achieve a higher level of harmony... And yet all these questions must be resolved exclusively by you, for you alone can recognize the reason for acting in one specific way. (Tang Junyi 1985, 53–54)

However, this form of responsibility does not condition individual interests based on those of society (or groups). A morally conscious person will always act in accordance with their responsibility, regardless of their own interests, or the interests of the broader social community.

> A human being is not a thing; a human being is a goal in and of itself. This means that individuals are not tools of society, nor tools of the state. And the people of today are not tools for the people of tomorrow... But if we say that people are not tools of society, this does not mean that we are outside of it, and individuals should not look upon society and the state as the means for achieving their own interests... I believe that the conflict between individuals and society can only be solved by educating people to develop to the utmost their innate moral nature. (Tang Junyi 2000, 61–62)

This is clearly not about obedience to external authorities. As his choice of language indicates, Tang remains loyal to the fundamental principles of Chinese ethics, which consciously strives to transcend the boundaries between the Self and Others through harmonious action in the sphere of interpersonal relations (Chan 2002, 320).

However, since the ethical Self or the morally conscious mind of an individual also strongly influences the specific features of the culture in which they were born and live, Tang believes that the prevailing orientation in a given culture is rooted in the attitudes that predominate in the minds of the persons within that culture. Hence, one of the main differences between Chinese and Western culture is to be found in the Chinese focus on ethics and art, while the West was instead founded on religion and science. A difference which, Tang adds, derives from the Chinese stress upon harmony, as opposed to the Western emphasis on distinctions.

A similar (albeit more biased) view on "cultural" difference[10] can also be found in the works of Fang Dongmei (Thomé Fang), whose thought is essentially based upon the "typically Chinese" concept of "creative harmony". He considers Western philosophy to be trapped in a mesh of continuous contradictions, from which it seeks to escape through nihilism (Li 2002, 265). If the Chinese tradition is far more sophisticated, then this is due precisely to its concept of harmony and harmonization: "In contrast, Chinese philosophy maintains a balance between *qing* and *li*.[11] Through cultivation, Chinese philosophy aims at a grand harmony in life; it is like a symphony, with all notes contributing to its harmonious unity" (Fang Dongmei 1980, 93).

This "harmonious unity" is rooted in Fang's core concept of "comprehensive harmony", which is grounded in turn in a view of the universe as a balanced and harmonious system. And because he considers this paradigm as the very bedrock of Chinese philosophy, the Chinese ideal of life must be harmonious, as well. In this ideal, there is no room for either conflicts or selfishness. This kind of harmony is not limited to the universe, but also represents a criterion for the formation of behavioural patterns and political ideals (Fang Dongmei 1980, 93).

But given the idealistic nature of his philosophy, Fang did not devote much attention to questions regarding the social reality. Harmony, which is at the centre of his idealistic theory, is mostly confined to the harmony of the unification of men and nature, in contrast with other representatives of the second generation of Modern Confucians who, as we have seen, addressed questions of social harmony in a more comprehensive and detailed way.

Even though the modern ideologies in the P. R. China that proclaim the ideal of a harmonious society, and the treatises on harmony by theorists from Taiwan and Hong Kong both refer to Confucianism as their main template for achieving such social coherence, it is manifestly evident that certain fundamental distinctions divide these two discourses. The most obvious difference is to be found in an ideal of harmony which, for the continental theorists, is rooted in the tradition of the Xunzi, who was often denoted as a kind of an ideological link between Confucian and legalist approaches,[12] while Modern Confucianism instead tends to follow the more humanistic line of Mencian discourses. The ideology of this emergent, neo-liberal superpower is thus grounded upon an authoritarian discourse which has the obedience of its citizens as its prime concern, whereas for Modern Confucians influenced by Mencian philosophy, the autonomy of the individual is at the forefront of their theorizing. The Mencian approach certainly offers a much better basis for the development of a "democratic"[13] society composed of free individuals. But given that the Modern Confucian concept of a harmonious society is still unachieved and remains mostly at the theoretical level, while the more disciplinary discourse is supported by a well-equipped, highly efficient and at times very aggressive propaganda apparatus, this latter may very well prevail. Ultimately, the question of what kind of "harmony" awaits the Chinese people in the near future remains an open one.

8. Conclusion—Modern Confucianism Between Past and Future

As we have seen, while Modern Confucians can imagine a human existence without God, they have great difficulty in imagining human existence without meaning (or purpose). Some of the representatives (especially Mou and Xu) of the second generation agreed with Kant's supposition that a meaningful conception of existence necessarily demands the concept of a free subject. The freedom of this subject is rooted in its autonomy, which is primarily understood in terms of self-cultivation.[1]

Modern Confucians thus tried to formulate an articulated and advanced concept of the traditional moral Self which in the new global philosophies was meant to assume the function of a "truly" autonomous subject. In this sense, "true" autonomy means that this subject is both particular and universal. It acts as an individual, necessarily forming part of the social community, but is ennobled by an infinite heart-mind which enables it to be aware of its unity with the cosmos. Through free will, it derives its freedom from its own inborn moral imperative, which is likewise infinite. Nevertheless, this infinite nature is not defined by the existence of God, but by the organic, structurally defined wholeness of the subject (in the sense of the moral Self) with all physical and metaphysical elements of being.

Despite their skepticism regarding the existence of God, the Modern Confucians never denied absolutely the possibility of his/her existence. However, they were never particularly interested in this "higher instance", which they considered an issue that was marginal, if not utterly redundant. In their view, the issues with which every human being should be engaged were instead primarily linked to the Self and to the quality of human existence. In their philosophical world, free will, autonomy and the immortality of the soul (like intellectual intuition and infinite heart-mind) were not abstract theorems or empty clichés, but authentic elements of real human life. They all form part of human existence, which is *a priori* moral and endows every individual life with meaning.

The human subject contemplated and pursued by the representatives of the second generation of Modern Confucianism, is an active subject that seeks to fulfill or complete its Self in moral terms, even though this Self is already, in and of itself, complete.

In this sense, the Modern Confucians dressed the Western concept of the subject in completely new semantic clothes. To avoid a too easy confusion with Andersen's fable of the emperor's new clothes, it should be stressed that this allusion must be understood at a more profound level. The "clothes" of which we speak remain invisible in this context if viewed from a habitual perspective, which permits only the perception of forms, and not of substance. A viewpoint, which cannot transcend the boundary between subject and object, and statics and dynamics, or between ethical concepts and real human beings, will merely see in this newly clothed subject a hybrid concept, stripped of its previous dignity. However, if we immerse ourselves in the world of immanent transcendence, these new clothes become visible. And while they may not be cut to the latest fashion, they are still new, pleasing to look at, and challenging. Therefore, we could even presume that they were somehow provocative. But nevertheless, this provocativeness is purely assumed, for provocation as such was quite alien to the thinkers of the second generation of Modern Confucianism, who elaborated their syntheses of Western and Chinese philosophy in a calm, modest and, at times, almost humble manner. Their often quite substantive criticisms of Western philosophers are always low-key and courteous, sincere and made with implicit respect. Their dialogues with Western thought aimed primarily at the possibility of mutual growth.

This general attitude of the Modern Confucians is consistent with the traditional Chinese worldview, which sees the individual as an organic element of a dynamic and unified, but also structurally ordered universe. The Mencian interpretation of the Confucian teachings, which can be found more or less directly in all the representatives of the second generation, did not stress the individual's normative limitations, but their moral-ethical foundations. This approach was especially evident in the central virtue of humanity or mutuality (*ren*) which not only represents the possible realization of the inborn reason of each individual, but also their natural striving towards the good (*shan*). Here, the good is not understood as an imperative by a higher, incomprehensible force, but as a real, actual necessity (and pragmatic reason) within each individual. The good is thus perceived and understood as life itself in a dual dimension: in moments of silence, contemplation and introspection, and in the constant awareness of co-existence with one's fellow human beings. At the same time, the good is perceived as the core of every existence, human being and spirit.

The spirit of goodness which manifests itself in the moral Self seeks to refine itself, though, is already perfect in its being. Its intrinsic perfection notwithstanding, the search for refinement is at the heart of its *a priori* perfection, for the existence of the spirit (as the core of the moral Self) is defined by the dynamics of the continuous processes of existence. The process of cultivating personality and the insight into its necessity are preconditions for this refinement. I therefore disagree with Sin yee Chan's (2002, 317) critique, in which she accuses these discourses of failing to substantiate the concept of Self, as compared with Hegel's concept of absolute spirit. In her criticism of Tang Junyi, Chan states that although Tang's idea of heart-mind as transcendent at first glance resembles Hegel's spirit, this resemblance is only apparent, for while Hegel's spirit must undergo a long process of development in order to achieve absolute freedom, the Modern Confucian Self was already intrinsically perfect (Chan 2002, 317).

However, this paradox is only virtual, because grounded in a static perception of the metaphysical. If the concept of moral Self is understood in terms of complementary binaries (which include the binary opposition of static and dynamic or, "in Chinese", of movement and stillness), then the process of its perfection and refinement occurs within a complementary, and not a contradictory relation. The perfection of the moral Self is, of course, eternal and limitless (or infinite), just as in the perfection of Hegel's absolute spirit. Nevertheless, here it is important to recall that in the European tradition, the concept of eternity has always been equated with a static immutability. The eternal must remain forever as it is, as we find, for example, in the concept of the "Word of God". Instead, eternity (or the absolute) within dynamic complementary systems is a concept which can only exist in (and through) continuous change.

This new, moral and simultaneously infinite, limitless subject, which represents an elaboration of the "traditional" Confucian concept of the moral Self, can potentially become an active personality capable of sustaining the idea of modernization. Because its reason, as a tool of intuitive, concrete bodily comprehension is unlimited, it is not contingent or dependent upon any kind of spiritual connection between the world and itself. This moral subject or its Self is truly autonomous, for its autonomy has not been determined by anything external to itself.

In the framework of the original and, partly also Modern Confucianism, this Self is autonomous precisely due to its structural (*li*) connection with the whole of its natural and social environment. And since this connection is also dynamic and organic, it permits infinitely varied forms of communication and cooperation. For a human modernity, i.e. for a modernity permeated with humanism or mutuality (*ren*), these forms of communication and cooperation are much more important than formal economic and political laws. Such a Confucian conception of the Self is often criticized as being unable to provide the basis for the individual within a democratic society, because it is inevitably premised by a fundamentally hierarchical conceptualization of society. Hierarchy is, in fact, one of the fundamental concepts of original Confucian thought. However, irrespective of the general critique of the universal concept of hierarchy (see the chapter on Asian values)[2] our understanding of this concept is perhaps too one-dimensional, in the sense that we tend to view it in terms of its exclusively negative connotations of suppression and dependence. We therefore tend to overlook its positive connotations, such as the proper or appropriate forms of responsibility towards the subordinates, of love towards those we feel close to, or the intimate sense of belonging to them.

The representatives of the second generation of Modern Confucianism have always been seen as advocating neo-conservative ideologies because they failed to create a model of Confucian revival wholly rooted in their own tradition, thereby making it possible to produce a genuine discourse of "Chinese modernization". Such possibilities certainly exist, and we are thus still awaiting an interpretation of original "Confucian democracy" which is not necessarily linked to liberal or neo-liberal theories and practices.

If we turn back to the start of the third century A.D. and the very beginnings of Confucianism and then attempt to evaluate the function and significance of the modernized forms of this body of thought, as manifested in Modern Confucian intellectual contributions to the development of Chinese culture in the era of modernization and globalization, we are confronted with a very complex image.

In 1905, when the Chinese Empire abolished the system of official state examinations, Confucianism, which had served as the official state doctrine since the Han Dynasty, lost its institutional foundations. This has led Yu Yingshi (1988, 1) to describe all subsequent Confucian discourses as those of a "wandering ghost" (*you hun*³). Han Qiang and Zhao Guanghui (1994, 274), instead called Confucian philosophers of the modern era the "lonely new Confucians" (*jimode xin rujia*), due to their reformulations of the Chinese tradition and its syntheses with Western ideas, and within a context which differs totally from the many centuries in which traditional Confucianism dominated the whole of Chinese culture, due to its being firmly rooted in state institutions. Modern Confucianism can thus no longer be seen as a state-building, national ideology comparable to the traditional discourses, which for almost two thousand years had, to a great extent, determined the social and moral codes, as well as the political and economic paradigms of the mighty Chinese Empire. However, it was precisely this domination of traditional Confucian state doctrine that, together with other factors, contributed to the stagnation and lack of innovative flexibility, which led to its inglorious demise in the first years of the twentieth century. The new position in which Confucian thought found itself after the collapse of the official Confucian state doctrine, can thus be seen as an opportunity for its revitalization and further development, in the sense of establishing new philosophical foundations for the modern and post-modern era.

> With the decline of the empire, Confucianism lost its institutional support (the systems of despotic rule, family clans and traditional examinations). But this historical event also marked a shift in the history of Confucianism, for once deprived of its position as state ideology, it re-emerged as an independent intellectual current which can definitely take its place within the pluralistic culture of future humanity. (Lee Ming-huei 2001a, 89)

Despite the "uneasy nature" of this new position, it certainly gave the members of this current much more freedom to re-elaborate old concepts and ideas, and create new ones. In general, Modern Confucians have fulfilled these hopes and expectations, creating a variety of new visions and syntheses, and it is no accident that the Modern Confucian current is one of the most influential philosophical discourses in present-day China.[4] At the same time, it must be stressed that in their theoretical efforts, the second generation of Modern Confucianism focused primarily on the areas of metaphysics, philology and classical Chinese texts, as well as the sociology of culture. Its contributions to the theories of the cultural conditionality of modernization were thus limited to abstract debates on the main concepts of the transformation of modern society. As noted in our discussion of the harmonious society, no member of this group formulated (or even projected) a critical social theory in which these new concepts could provide constitutional elements within modern Asian social systems.[5] This is also the central reason why Han Qiang and Zhao Guanghui labelled this group as the lonely new Confucians.

> In this regard, Modern Confucians still have not left the "bosom of lonely solitude" and have failed to create any kind of "major Modern Confucian movement". While some believe that "their general recognition and praise is long overdue", for the most part their teachings are still seen as a "recycling of remote discourses without any connection to the current reality". They remain, in fact, "lonely new Confucians". (Han and Zhao 1994, 274)

While the characterization as a "wandering lonely ghost" might seem exaggerated in describing this current, it is certainly true that Modern Confucians are still not included (at least directly) within the most popular intellectual streams of contemporary China. Debating the projects and strategies for the future development of this undeniably significant current and considering ways to put its key ideas into practice, not only theoretically but also in concrete ways within society, thus seems to be a worthwhile ambition. For as Yu Yingshi (2001, 1), has noted,[6] reasoning is the beginning of problem solving.

Appendix 1. A Chronology of China's History of Dynasties and Republics

夏 Xia   2100–1600 B.C.

商 Shang   1600–1066 B.C.

周 Zhou   1066–256 B.C.

西周 Western Zhou   1066–771 B.C.

    東周 Eastern Zhou   770–256 B.C.

    春秋 Chun Qiu (Spring–Autumn)   770–476 B.C.

    戰國 Zhan Guo (the Warring States)   475–221 B.C.

秦 Qin   221–206 B.C.

漢 Han   206 B.C.–220 A.D.

    西漢 Western Han   206 B.C.–23 A.D.

    東漢 Eastern Han   25–220 A.D.

三國 San Guo (Three Kingdoms)

    魏 Wei   220–265

    蜀 Shu   221–263

    吳 Wu   222–280

西晉 Western Jin   265–316

東晉 Eastern Jin　　　　　　　　　　　　317–420

十六國 Sixteen States　　　　　　　　　304–439

南北朝 Northern and Southern Dynasties

　　　南朝 Southern Dynasties

　　　　　宋 Song　　　　　　　　　　420–479

　　　　　齊 Qi　　　　　　　　　　　479–502

　　　　　梁 Liang　　　　　　　　　 502–557

　　　　　陳 Chen　　　　　　　　　　557–589

　　　北朝 Northern Dynasties

　　　　　北魏 Northern Wei　　　　　 386–534

　　　　　東魏 Eastern Wei　　　　　　534–550

　　　　　北齊 Northern Qi　　　　　　550–577

　　　　　西魏 Western Wei　　　　　　535–557

　　　　　北周 Northern Zhou　　　　　557–581

隋 Sui　　　　　　　　　　　　　　　　581–618

唐 Tang　　　　　　　　　　　　　　　 618–907

五代十國 Five Dynasties and Ten States

　　　後梁 Late Liang　　　　　　　　 907–923

　　　後唐 Late Tang　　　　　　　　　923–936

　　　後晉 Late Jin　　　　　　　　　 936–946

　　　後漢 Late Han　　　　　　　　　 947–950

　　　後周 Late Zhou　　　　　　　　　951–960

　　　十國 Ten states　　　　　　　　 902–979

宋 Song	960–1279
北宋 Northern Song	960–1127
南宋 Southern Song	1127–1279
遼 Liao	916–1125
西夏 Western Xia	1032–1227
金 Jin	1115–1234
元 Yuan	1271–1368
明 Ming	1368–1644
清 Qing	1644–1911
中華民國 Republic of China (remains in Taiwan)	1911–1949
中華人民共和國 People's Republic of China	from 1949

Appendix 2. A Chronology of the Developmental Phases of Confucianism

I. **Original Confucianism:**

from ca. 525 to 221 B.C. (from the end of the Spring and Autumn period and during the Warring States period until the establishment of the Qin Dynasty).

II. **The first reform of Original Confucianism, the integration of Legalist elements through Xunzi's interpretations, the imposition of Confucianism as the official state doctrine and the period of formalized stagnation:**

from ca. 155 to 1050 (from the middle of the Western Han until the middle of the Northern Song Dynasty).

III. **The second reform of Original Confucianism, the appearance and development of the Neo-Confucian philosophy (through Mencian interpretations):**

from ca. 1050 to 1911 (from the middle of the Northern Song Dynasty until the end of the Chinese empire).

IV. **The third reform of Confucian teachings: Modern Confucianism as the elaboration and upgrading of Neo-Confucianism and as the search for syntheses with Western thought:**

from 1911 to the present time. First generation: from 1859 until 1992; second generation: from 1899 until 1995; and third generation: from 1930 onwards.

Notes

1 Introduction

1. 新儒學，現代新儒學， 現代儒學，當代新儒學．
2. Since the dominant discourses in Western philosophical theory are based on the concept of truth, the awareness that there are very few objective, universally valid values is of utmost importance for those Western scholars who are concerned with Chinese philosophy. While the value-systems that shape modern Western societies are based upon concepts like individualism and free will, in East Asian societies a strong sense of familism and belonging to a community was (and, to a certain extent, still is) prevalent. These concepts and identification patterns represent the foundations of a different values system(s), which should thus be seen as being relative.

2 China's Confrontation with the West and Processes of Modernization: From the Liberalization of the Subject to a Free Market

1. For Arif Dirlik, for instance, the reasons for this phenomenon are linked to the very nature of global capitalism: "I think it is arguable (as I will argue here) that the apparent end of Eurocentrism is an illusion. Capitalist culture, as it has taken shape, holds Eurocentrism in the very structure of its narrative, which may explain why, even as Europe and the United states lose their domination of the capitalist world economy, culturally European and American values are still dominant globally. It

226 Notes

is also noteworthy that what makes something like the East Asian Confucian revival plausible is not its offer to alternative values to those of Euro American origin, but its articulation of native culture into a capitalist narrative. Having said this, it is important to reiterate nevertheless that the question of world culture has become much more complex than in earlier phases of capitalism." (Dirlik 1994, 51–52)

2. For a more detailed description of this line of thought and its connection to current ideologies, see chapter 7.

3. Especially Fang Dongmei and to a certain extent also Tang Junyi.

4. Gloria Davies exposes that, with the further acceleration of the state led market expansion during the nineties, "there was plenty of social commentary about the large numbers of people who were using party membership to advance their careers and make money" (Davies 2012, 131).

5. Here, the term Confucianism does not refer to the original Confucian teachings, nor to Confucian philosophy as such, but rather to the official Confucian state doctrine.

6. Because the term modernity, which generally denotes a period of social transformation, was developed within Euro-American discourses, defining the "general" theoretical evolution of this concept means (once again) addressing the development of Western theory. We should also stress that we are not referring to classic modernity, i.e. the Western "New era", but to modernity understood as a process of general social transformation or social revival, and linked to certain specific conditions that dictate modernization (e.g. the Enlightenment, the dominant role of the intellectual in philosophy, industrialization, etc.). This process followed diverse pathways depending on the specific cultural environment or tradition, but always involved the transformation of the specific conditions of transitional societies.

7. Although some scholars, including Liang Shuming in his *Dogxi wenhua jiqi zhexue* (1921) were claiming exactly the opposite.

8. It should be stressed that the Eurocentric discourses of the dominant Western social sciences still focus on the Western paradigms of social development. These discourses conclude that China would never have produced an industrial revolution on its own, due to its inadequate technological development. However, as the research for the

well-known theory of the "germs of capitalism in China" (*Zhongguo zibenzhuyi mengya*) has clearly shown, China already possessed the means for an industrial revolution in the twelfth century. The fact that this revolution did not occur can be explained by the inability of the traditional Chinese political and economic system to bring about such a transformation, also due to the fact that China—unlike Europe—did not face an economic crisis in that period.

9. In this regard, we need to distinguish between Modern Confucians and the more conservative stream, which is comparable to the radical conservative current that exists in contemporary China, and can be seen as a follower of the "School of the revival of the past" (*Fu gu pai*). While not advocating a complete return to the pre-modern period, many of the scholars belonging to this current, e.g. Jiang Qing, Kang Xiaoguang, and Zhang Xianglong, reject some essential elements of modernity and therefore can be considered as anti-modern.

10. These were mainly intellectuals (of both genders), who studied in Europe or Japan, or at least at one of the modern universities that adopted the Western curriculum.

11. From the Han dynasty onwards (206 B.C.–A.D. 220), the state thoroughly actively intervened in agricultural production, which constituted the base of the economic system in traditional Chinese society. These interventions were not limited to the creation of numerous state monopolies in various areas of production, but also included active implementation of an inheritance system that implied and supported both, moral and family/clan motives as well as the interests of the state. The state thereby guaranteed its fiscal and budgetary power by preserving the highest possible number of independent agricultural holdings, while also preventing the division of assets through inheritance. Landowners were further tied to the state by the offer of official positions, once they had manifested their acceptance and mastering of the Confucian ideology. In this way, the state patronage made it possible to reduce the division of arable lands through inheritance (see Moritz 1933, 64).

12. The reform oriented into the gradual introduction of the market-capitalist economy, began in 1978 under the leadership of Deng Xiaoping. Like the first two social modernization programs, Deng's reforms also began in the areas of technology and economics, and avoided cultural

reforms as such. However, Hua Shiping (2001, 4) has shown how the increasingly successful reforms were often reflected in cultural terms, as confirmed by phenomena such as the "Cultural fever" (*Wenhua re*) and the "Great debate on culture" (*Wenhua da taolun*). Of course, following Tiananmen, these theoretical reflections on modernization processes were violently suppressed.

13. In most cases, the epistemological sources that formed the basis for New Enlightenment theory derived from (predominantly liberal) Euro-American economic, political and legal theories. In the historic perspective it is evident that the New Enlightenment thought processes served as the fundamental ideology for economic reforms (Wang Hui 2000, 16).

14. During the last two decades, we have begun to see livelier debates and more intense research emerging from the assumptions of the new Confucianism, also in the PRC. Here, we should mention the role of the academic organization for "Research in the intellectual current of Contemporary New Confucianism (*Xiandai xin rujia sichao yanjiu* 现代新儒家思潮研究)", founded in November 1986 by two philosophy professors, Fang Keli 方克立 and Li Jinquan 李锦全. Nicolas Bunnin has described this integration of mainland China into the discourses of Modern Confucianism in optimistic terms: "With a renewal of officially sanctioned Confucian philosophy in China and greater contact among philosophers in China, Hong Kong and Taiwan, New Confucianism can contribute to the reintegration of Chinese philosophical life after the politically enforced divisions of half a century. Other Chinese and Western influences can also contribute to this reintegration. In addition, the schools of Chinese philosophy, from their origin to their modern interpretation, provide grounds for fusion with Western philosophy and a standpoint from which Western philosophy can be constructively criticized. In these circumstances, Chinese philosophers, holding diverse views but sharing a complex intellectual culture, can display subtlety, dynamism and openness to dialogue as Chinese philosophy takes its place in world philosophy." (Bunnin 2002, 13)

15. Taiwan was a Japanese colony from 1895 to 1945.

16. At this point we should mention the general issue of the concept of national identity in Taiwan. As mentioned by Lai Ming-Yan (1995, 104): "What constituted the nation in Taiwan was (and continues to be) a

highly contentious issue." While the Nationalist government claimed representation of the Chinese "nation" against the Communist regime in mainland China, some local people came to see Nationalists as "colonializers" of their Taiwan (Formosa) "nation", especially after the bloody events of the "February 28 incident" in 1947, which saw considerable deaths and persecutions of local people, particularly social elites, at the hands of the Nationalist Army, and the subsequent imposition of a highly repressive regime as the Nationalists "retreated" to Taiwan in 1949.

17. The last dynasty Qing (1644–1911).

18. The functions and the theoretical contributions of them will be treated in greater detail in the following chapter.

19. David Elstein (2011, 391) also draws attention to the debate concerning the hierarchical structure implied in the so-called "Five relations" (*wu lun*) and exposes that it is an overstatement to say that they provide templates for all social relations even in Confucian thought, and much less in Chinese culture in general. The argument of understanding all relations in terms of such paradigms come not from Confucian texts, but instead from those texts conventionally known as Legalist.

20. The idea of "negative freedom" denotes freedom from something in the sense of lack of heteronomy, while the term "positive freedom" denotes freedom to something in the sense of ensured rights. Berlin's definition of negative liberty is absence of external control and interference. Positive liberty, on the other hand, is rooted in self-mastery. Negative liberty is quite compatible with heteronomy; positive liberty is not. For a more detailed explanation, see Angle (2012b, 68, 97–98).

21. Stephen Angle (2012a, 399) points out, that in traditional China, the political problem was actually that by conceiving politics as ethics-writ-large, meaning that Confucians were in a particularly difficult situation when rulers turned out not to be sages. This is the route from the sage-ideal to despotism, which has been "a well-trodden route in Chinese history, both ancient and modern" (Angle 2012a, 399).

22. On the one hand, Lee Ming-huei exposes (2005, 14) that a new, communitarian interpretation of Confucianism could doubtless offer new sense and meaning to contemporary societies, which are suffering under the listlessness of the post-modern cultural nihilism. On the

other, he warns of an absolutisation of communitarian ideas, pointing out that some (particularly Sandel's) communitarian critiques of the liberal values were much too exaggerated (Lee Ming-huei 2005, 29).

3   Modern Confucianism

1. Tu Weiming, a prominent member of the third generation of Modern Confucianism, has described this in the following way: "The scholarly tradition envisioned by Confucius can be traced to the sage-kings of antiquity. Although the earliest dynasty confirmed by archaeology is the Shang dynasty (18th–12th century B.C.), the historical period that Confucius claimed as relevant was much earlier. Confucius may have initiated a cultural process known in the West as Confucianism, but he and those who followed him considered themselves part of a tradition, later identified by Chinese historians as the rujia, 'scholarly tradition', that had its origins two millennia previously, when the legendary sages Yao and Shun created a civilized world through moral persuasion" (Tu 2014, 1). In addition to Tu, many other scholars have noted the wider connotational scope of the term "ruxue." Roger Ames, for example, has shown how this notion refers to a general classical "scholarly tradition" (see Ames 2014, 5). This, of course, does not mean that Daoist and Buddhist texts were included in the Confucian canon, but only confirms how inextricably intertwined these three major idea systems were. In most forms of Confucian state orthodoxy, e.g. the Shiji and Hanshu, the term Ru basically signifies an expert in the Five Classics. In her book on Confucianism and women, Li-Hsiang Lisa Rosenlee also writes: "The concept of Ru 儒… denotes the inexact Chinese counterpart of the term Confucianism used by Jesuits in the eighteenth century… The ambiguity of its semantic origins in ancient, pre-Confucian times obscures the connection between Ru as an intellectual discipline and Confucius, as its most prominent spokesperson. Unlike the term Confucianism—its secularized and simplified representation in the West—the complex term Ru can only be approximated as the teaching of the sages and the worthies wherein the ethical teaching of Confucius—the Supreme sage and the First teacher—forms a part, but an important part nevertheless." (Rosenlee 2006, 4)

2. For example, the concepts of the subject and object of recognition

(*neng-suo*), originating in Buddhist epistemology, which were often applied even by the most rationalistic philosophies within the School of Structure (*li xue*). Even Zhu Xi, the leading figure this school, incorporated several Daoist ideas and procedures into his own philosophy (e.g. the idea of the ultimate pole or *taiji*, the concept of non-action or *wu wei*, etc), whereas the theories of the more idealistic current ("The School of Mind", *Xin xue*) were practically based upon Buddhist and Daoist onto-epistemologies.

3. It is difficult to say to what extent this process was a conscious one, but the contemporaneous integration and "discharging" of Buddhist and Daoist philosophy certainly constituted a challenge for Neo-Confucian philosophers. By the tenth century, the formalized classical Confucian doctrine was an empty husk, and was studied and mastered only in order to pass the official state examinations, which for the successful candidates (and their clans) gave access to political power. But because this doctrine was incapable of satisfying the intellectual needs of the educated classes, these classes turned to the study of Daoist and Buddhist philosophies, a tendency which threatened both Confucianism as such, and the entire ideological system on which the traditional state institutions were based. In this sense, the Neo-Confucian reform was absolutely necessary for the preservation of Confucianism, in terms of its function as the main social, ethical and philosophical system of thought in China.

4. Modern Confucians rarely relied on Daoism, and understandably so, for this current emerged not only in order to preserve cultural identity, but also with the goal of modernizing and "saving" the institutional framework of Chinese society. The anarchic classics of Daoism are eminently unsuited for such goals. That said, several Modern Confucian philosophers have devoted considerable effort to the study and integration of Buddhist thought into their own theories (e.g. Xiong Shili, Liang Shuming and Mou Zongsan).

5. See note 1.

6. In considering specific features of traditional Chinese philosophy that are common to all schools of ancient and classical Chinese thought, of primary importance are the concept of transcendent immanence (or immanent transcendence), binary structured holism which functions by means of binary categories (for example *yin-yang*, *you-wu*, *ti-yong*,

ming-shi etc), as well as the principle of complementarity which represents the method of interactions between both implied antipodes.

7. Carsun Chang (Zhang Junmai), whom most categorizations include in the First generation of Modern Confucianism, is the exception here. He is also the only representative of the First generation who did not stay in mainland China, but fled to the USA after 1949, where he would remain until his death in 1969.

8. The thesis of the defeat of Confucianism has yet to be fully verified. Ideological elements of this ancient tradition are still evident not only in the Chinese educational system and in the axiological framework of rights and duties within the family, but also in the hierarchies of professional politics and modern economic structures.

9. However, as noted above, the state ideologies of present day P. R. China are still rooted in the same Confucian tradition which prevailed in traditional China in the form of the dominant state doctrine and which followed Xunzi's interpretation of the original teachings. Taiwanese Modern Confucians instead mainly follow the neo-Confucian (i.e. Mencian) model of Confucianism.

10. The disputes on the religious aspects of Confucianism will be examined below (see "The Unemployed God").

11. 內聖外王之道 (Zhuangzi 2012, Tianxia 1). In this chapter, Zhuangzi warns that the Way can become hidden or blurred if one is unable to conform to the cosmic order of dao. Here, *neisheng waiwang* serves as a metaphor for the refined person, seen as someone who cultivates their intimate spiritual self while also being actively engaged in social matters.

12. Chung-ying Cheng, (Cheng Zhongying), Liu Shu-hsien (Liu Shuxian), Tu Weiming (Du Weiming), Yu Ying-shih (Yu Yingshi).

13. Roger T. Ames rather cynically summarizes his critique as follows: "Arif Dirlik rues what he takes to be an unholy tryst between Confucianism as an indictable 'post-colonialist discourse' and the devil himself, capitalism. For him, the revival of Confucianism in modern Asia is oriental 'Orientalism'. It is, at best, a conspiracy between the State and freeloading intellectuals, or, as he says, 'a foremost instance ... of intellectual discourse creating its object'". He dismisses Dirlik's interpretations, in general, as being essentialist, generalizing and destructive. (Ames 2001, 71)

14. For a more detailed explanation of Reotz's arguments, see the section "The unemployed God".
15. He claims that this was also the opinion of Fang Dongmei (Chen Guying 1998, 95).
16. This is Mou Zongsan, the leading exponent of the second generation of Modern Confucianism.
17. As we shall see in later chapters, Feng Yaoming overreaches somewhat in his critique of the essential semantic structure of Modern Confucian philosophy. As a strictly analytical thinker, he does not consider the possibilities of change in the semantic nuances of particular terms with respect to their context or the categorical sector in which they have been applied. This semantic flexibility and situationally conditioned structural modification of semantic units is one of the key characteristics of classical Chinese philosophy as such, and was thus applied not only in its "mystical" discourses, but also in the works of the classical Chinese rationalists.
18. We should note here that his central claim that "not every 'infinite' necessarily implies 'values'", likewise cannot be scientifically proven.
19. Although wide strata of Malaysian population are Islamic, the concept of Asian values is compatible with this religion, as it mainly refers to principles of behavioral ethics and political ideals.
20. The despotic line in Confucianism was established during the Han Dynasty, which had inherited the enormous, centralized, legalist and despotic Qin state. Because ruling such a state required a centralized doctrine, and because the new rulers could not simply appropriate Legalism, which had represented the central ideology of the defeated Qin empire, the new state doctrine was based upon Dong Zhongshu's reinterpretation of the original Confucian teachings. This reinterpretation was rooted primarily in Xunzi's elaboration of original Confucianism, such that Xunzi appears as the bridge between Confucian and Legalist teachings.
21. A suitable ruler will consider the decrees of the Heavenly Mandate and obey the Mandate; a ruler, who ignores it, is unsuitable for his position.
22. We should also recall that the Confucian tradition—in various forms—has only had an influence on the East Asian countries. For example, in

India and other South Asian countries it had no influence at all, even before colonialization. It would therefore be more correct to speak of "East Asian values".

23. Here, we should mention two additional aspects of Huntington's theory: "...That the civilizations he referred to, while they represented long-standing cultural traditions, were not relics of the past but were products of modernity that were empowered by their claims on modernity. Second, that to impose the values of the modern West on these societies would not only not work, but also represented a kind of imperialism". (Dirlik 2001, 22)

4 The "Second Generation"

1. Bresciani (2001, 20) called the period in which most works by the second generation appeared, "the developing years".
2. The title of Feng's Dissertation is *A Comparative Study of Life Ideals*.
3. Here, we should mention the influence of W.P. Montague in particular.
4. This title is also used to denote his philosophical system.
5. This designation derives from Guy Alitto's (1979) celebrated study, *The Last Confucian—Liang Shuming and the Chinese Dilemma of Modernity*.
6. This should not surprise us, given that the Neo-Confucian theory of knowledge (especially the solipsistic current of the School of Mind / Xin xue 心學) incorporated many epistemological and methodological paradigms from the chan-Buddhist philosophic system.
7. Chinese intellectuals found it easier to understand American pragmatism than analytical and formal logical discourses in the European tradition, given that the most influential discourses in the Chinese philosophical tradition are also pragmatic. The new philosophical currents were greatly influenced by social Darwinism, as its concept of the connection between nature and society was much closer to the traditional Chinese, holistic understanding of the world, than theories based on a strict separation between the two. The idea of evolution (*jinhua*) was especially interesting to Chinese thinkers, for it included the concept of progress, which had never been part of the Chinese tradition.

8. *Kritik der reinen Vernunft* (1781), *Kritik der praktischen Vernunft* (1788), *Kritik der Urteilskaft* (1790).

9. In this realm, Mou's teacher Xiong Shili has salso distinguished between the two categories of internal (*nei xiu* 內修) and external cultivation (*waixiu* 外修); in his system, each of the categories were subdivided into three subcategories, the first one into a) exploration of things (*gewu* 格物), b) obtaining the perfect knowledge (*zhi zhi* 致知), and c) sincere attitude (*cheng yi* 誠意); and the second into a) regulating the family (*qi jia* 齊家), b) ruling the state (*zhi guo* 治國), and c) pacification of the world (*ping tian xia* 平天下), see Heubel (2014, 44).

10. Wei Jin Southern and Northern Dynasties 魏晉南北朝 (220–589).

11. As is well-known, Mou greatly admired Kant's moral philosophy and argued that only with Kant did Western philosophy begin to have a real understanding of the nature of morality. Kant was the first in the West to say that "being moral is determined by moral rule, and is not determined by external objects". However, he sharply criticized Kant's claim that the existence of God was a necessary precondition for the existence of an integral realm of morality and happiness (*Summum bonum*, Mou 1985, 239–40).

12. In the Chinese holistic tradition ontology is inseparable from epistemology, as in its view of the world every object of cognition is also cognition itself; the manner of its existence is thus linked to our understanding of it. Because this connection goes both ways, i.e. their relation is not a relation of single sided dependency and determination, but an interaction that includes mutual co-dependency, we cannot state that this is a solipsistic conceptualisation of the world. The same as for the perception of the existing world holds true also for its perception and interpretation. This can also not be separated from the wholesome, but changeable and totally individualised existence of objects of cognition; this is clearly manifested in the theoretical system of the so-called onto-hermeneutics (*benti quanshi xue*), which was developed by Chung-ying Cheng, a representative of the third generation of modern Confucianism (see Ng On-cho, 2011).

13. Lee Ming-huei (2001, 68) ascertained that Mou cannot be considered an expert in Kant's philosophy, for he did not know how to read German, thus his translations into Chinese were based on the English translations of this philosopher. However, even if his translations were

secondary and thus surely less reliable, we have to admit that Mou's comments, with which he equipped them, represent valuable additions to Kant's philosophy, with which he opened quite a few new, philosophically innovative problems and issues.

14. The Neo-Confucian idealistic philosopher Wang Yangming called this type of cognitive perception a "clear understanding of the substance of knowledge" (*zhiti mingjue* 知體明覺).

15. Mou finds similar notions to original heart-mind (*ben xin*) also in Daoist (heart-mind of the Way, *dao xin*) and Buddhist (empty heart-mind / *kong xin*) discourses. He understands the three terms as various forms or manners of naming infinite (or unlimited) heart-mind (*wuxian zhixin*, Mou Zongsan 2010, 198–205). This pure, primary and unlimited heart-mind is a heritage with which every person is born. Unfortunately—at least in Mou's opinion—most of us do not know how to preserve it. He who manages to preserve it, becomes a Confucian saint (*sheng ren*), a Daoistic truly perfected man (*zhen ren*) or a Buddha.

16. To the question as to which philosophical school he belongs to, Fang responded that his family tradition makes him a Confucian, his character is Daoist, his religious inspiration is Buddhist and his education makes him a Westerner (Li Chengyang 2002, 264).

17. *Li* and *qi* are commonly being translated as "structural principle" (or "structural pattern") and "vital creativity".

18. Numerous theoreticians share the opinion that Neo-Confucian philosophers headed by Zhu Xi represented a turnaround in Chinese tradition. This was often expressed through the optics of its alleged "germs of dualism" (see for instance Forke 1934, 173). Feng Yaoming also discusses the new paradigm, which was supposedly established by Neo-Confucians in comparison to the classical theoreticians of this school; in his article "Zhongguo ru xuede dianfan zhuanyi" (Paradigmatic turn in Chinese Confucianism) Feng argues that the referential frame within which Neo-Confucian philosophers established their theory differed from the referential frames of classical Confucians to an extent where we can no longer talk merely about a theoretical, but also about a paradigmatic turnaround, which means that Neo-Confucian philosophers addressed totally new and different Confucian theories, which were thus in their essence no longer comparable to the older ones.

19. For a brilliant account of the historical coherence of East Asian Confucianism, see Huang Chun-chieh (2010, 9–13) and Huang Chun-chieh (2011, Foreword).
20. Cheng Chung-ying and Liu Shu-hsien.
21. The pragmatic philosophy of John Dewey (1859–1952) had a great influence on young Chinese intellectuals during this period. For example, Hu Shi (1891–1962) and Feng Youlan (1895–1990) both earned their PhDs at Columbia University, with Dewey as their advisor.
22. In his study, *Three Types of Philosophical Wisdom* (*Zhexue san hui*), he begins by comparing ancient Greek, modern European and traditional Chinese philosophy.
23. Void, or lack of substance, is a concept that derives primarily from the Buddhist and Daoist classics. However, even though classic Confucianism focused mainly on the here and now, and thus on political philosophy and pragmatic ethics, under the influence of early Buddhism the concept of void began to enter Confucian discourses shortly after the end of the Han dynasty. Later on, it became one of the core concepts of the idealist Neo-Confucian school.
24. He elaborated the tradition of Confucius and Mencius (Kong-Meng), i.e. the tradition, which was based upon the belief that Mencius was the true successor of original Confucianism (in contrast to the first reform, which took place during the Han dynasty within the frame of Dong Zhongshu's thought and was grounded on the belief that Xunzi was the true successor of original Confucianism).
25. Xunzi, in his English language works Fang used the Wade-Giles transcription.
26. We have to keep in mind that the term "method" might be a better translation of the notion "Dao", which of course does not merely represent the heart of Confucianism, but also stands in the centre of Daoist, Legalistic and numerous other classic Chinese philosophies. Not only are the etymological cores of the two words almost identical, they also both emphasise a certain (possibly the most sensible and "right") manner of a certain activity. Taking into account the central meaning of the term Dao in traditional Chinese culture it is not surprising that Ancient Greek or traditional European discourses differ from traditional Chinese ones also in the specifics of the central research methods

or the semantic framing of the basic questions of reality. For instance, according to Roger T. Ames (2001, 19–72), the basic question of the analytical methods, which dominated the history of European philosophy, has sought the answer as to "what" something is, while classical and traditional philosophers preferred to ask "how" to achieve something. The concept of the proper Confucian path (*daotong*) originates from this notion.

27. In the political aspect Xu's enthusiasm for the Marxist theory was substituted by the studies of Sun Yat-sen's *Three Principles of the People* (*San min zhuyi*). He stuck to Sun's political ideals until his death.

28. In Western countries, commonly known as Chiang Kai-Shek.

29. According to Bresciani (2001, 333) Xu moved from Hong Kong to Taiwan as late as 1961. This information is most likely wrong, for there is precise data which shows that he lectured at the Donghai University in Taizhong from 1955 onwards. According to Li Weiwu (1995, 587) he even started to teach at the Agricultural institute as early as 1952.

30. As we shall see a bit later, however, he changed his views about mainland China after the beginning of its economic liberalization.

31. This academy, established in 1950 by two leading representatives of modern Confucianism (the philosopher Tang Junyi, who we will discuss in the next chapter and the renowned Taiwanese new Confucian historian and sinologist Qian Mu) and some other Confucian intellectuals. Alongside Xu Fuguan, Mou Zongsan, the most important philosopher of the second generation of modern Confucianism also occasionally lectured at this academy. Bresciani describes it as a central institution (2001, 20) of contemporary modern Confucianism: "For over two decades the college was the main bastion of research and promotion of Chinese culture in the whole world. Beside these scholars' activity of training disciples, writing, and lecturing, one activity much worth remembering is that of the Seminars on Chinese Culture organized by Tang Junyi and held every Saturday at the new Asia Research Institute. Specialized scholars from all over the world were invited to offer these seminars, and the seminars enjoyed a high esteem for their scholarly value. The intellectuals affiliated with this activity were united into a Humanistic research Association". (Bresciani 2001, 20–21)

32. 實事求是—We should note that even Mao Zedong used this phrase occasionally, especially after the failure of the Cultural Revolution.

33. During the first unification of the Chinese state, i.e. during the Qin dynasty (221–206 B.C) original Confucianism was forbidden. At the time the despotic legalist school, which defended the interests of the absolute ruler, represented the only permitted political theory and served as the exclusive state ideology. Following the domination of the Han dynasty (206 B.C.–A.D.220), which controlled most of the vast territories that previously belonged to the preceding dynasty, the court ideologists searched for a new state doctrine that would manage to preserve central control over the state. As they could not adopt the central ideology of the defeated, which would in fact be more than appropriate for the task, the political philosopher Dong Zhongshu—most likely due to the hierarchical system and the emphasised principle of obeying the superiors—chose Confucianism, into which he skilfully included all of the most important legalist elements, as the new state doctrine. Numerous despotic measures, which appeared under the name of Confucianism (such as for instance the principle of collective responsibility or the principle of denunciation) throughout Chinese history, are thus in their essence a heritage of legalism.

34. The pragmatic orientation of the pre-Qin philosophy can be explained with the conditions that governed the area of China at the time. This area was divided into a series of small feudal states that fought for domination. For a detailed description of the socio-political background of this philosophy see Rošker (2010, 321).

35. This orientation is expressed by the following quotes from the Discussions by Confucius: 未能事人，焉能事鬼？ (We do not know how to serve people, how can we possibly serve their spirits?) and "未知生，焉知死？ (We do not even know life, how could we possibly know death?) see Confucius (2012a, Xianjin: 12).

36. See Xu's standpoints as regards the reasons and consequences of this declination in the chapter "Unemployed God."

37. The term *xin* 心 is traditionally a Chinese epistemological term, which in its basic meaning equals the Western understanding of consciousness. Because it is linked to the connotation of ethical or moral valuation, emotions and intuition, which are supposedly—similar to intellect and other cognitive mechanisms—based in the heart, and because it differs from the Western understanding of consciousness (it "surpasses" it), I usually use the term "heart mind". In most academic discourses in the English language the term "heart-mind" has become standard.

38. For a more detailed description of the conception behind implementing reworked Confucianism into a new state doctrine see Rošker (2010, 50).

39. Xu called this process "the humanization of heaven" (天的人文化 1982, 589).

40. Following the outbreak of the Chinese-Japanese war he returned to Chengdu in 1937. There he lectured at the Huaxi University and a series of secondary schools. Due to his unfavourable financial situation he moved to Chongqing (the provisional capital) one year later, where he found employment as a proof-reader at the Ministry of Education. In 1940, he started his work as a lecturer at the Central University, which had moved to Chongqing. Following the war, he returned to Nanjing together with the entire University (Lee Ming-huei 2001b, 58).

41. Lee Ming-huei (2001a, 59) divided his works into four categories. The first includes the early works, in which he explained his view of the world. The second category deals with his reflections on cultural philosophy and his intercultural research. The third category consists of two philosophical works, out of which the first is of a more general nature and deals with most central philosophical issues, while the second deals with the development of the basic ideas and the concepts of Chinese philosophy. The fourth category represents a synthesis of all Tang's academic works.

42. The nine forms are:

萬物散殊境 (the horizon of differentiating between the characteristics of various different forms of the existing)

依類成化境 (the horizon of the evolution of species)

功能序運境 (the horizon of causes and effects)

感覺互攝境 (the horizon of mutual reflection of the perception objects)

關照凌虛境 (the horizon of mirroring in a total void)

道德實踐境 (the horizon of realisation in moral operation)

歸向一神境 (the horizon of returning to the Divine unity)

我法二空境 (the horizon of void self and dharma)

天德流行境 (the horizon of the circle of the Divine/of natural virtues)

5 Science and Democracy

1. To confirm this point, we can cite two additional sayings (among many others) from the same source: "Heaven feels compassion for the people and thus fulfils their desires." (*Shu jing* 2012, Zhou shu, Qinshi shang). (天矜于民，民之所欲，天必從之). "Heaven loves the people, and the ruler should have reverence for this fact." (*Shu jing* 2012, Zhou shu Qinshi zhong 2). (惟天惠民，惟辟奉天).

2. In Mengzi, we find several hints in this direction, though he never explicitly states the right of the people to overthrow an unjust ruler. For example: "Mencius said: People cannot be treated heedlessly… People are relieved when they have enough work and food to survive. If they don't, they become upset and capable of anything" (Mencius 2012, Teng wen gong shang, 3). (孟子曰：民事不可緩也⋯民之為道也，有恆產者有恆心，無恆產者無恆心。苟無恆心，放辟邪侈，無不為已)." He who afflicts his people greatly, will be killed and his country will collapse. He who afflicts it less, will always live in danger and his country will be in constant crisis" (Mencius 2012, Li lou shang, 2) (暴其民甚，則身弒國亡；不甚，則身危國削). "Even if a ruler who does not follow the proper way, or act in accordance with humanity and refuses to change, obtains power over the whole world, he will not be able to maintain this power for a single night" (Mencius 2012, Gaozi xia, 29). (君不鄉道，不志於仁 ⋯ 由今之道，無變今之俗，雖與之天下，不能一朝居也). Much more explicit affirmations of the right of the people to overthrow their ruler can be found in the work of Mencius' rival, Xunzi, e.g.: "The ruler is a boat, and the people water. A boat can be carried by water, but it can also be overturned by it" (Xunzi 2012, Wang zhi, 5). (君者、舟也，庶人者、水也；水則載舟，水則覆舟) These classical citations should probably not be understood as the expression of a natural right of the people, but rather as advice to rulers on to how to rule if they did not wish to lose their power.

3. In these views, collectivism is closely related to individualism because it represents a society of individuals who were deprived of their individual interests and rights and re-moulded into groups in a mechanistic fashion (see Abbeg 1970, 210).

4. There are several such passages in Mencius. We can cite two of the best known: the first counsels the ruler on how to choose his ministers, while the second speaks of a ruler who was chosen by the people and

Heaven, instead of inheriting his throne: 1) "It is not enough that all your courtiers are in agreement. But if all the citizens believe that a certain man is capable, then you should look into this matter. And if you find out that this is true, you should choose this person" (Mencius 2012, Liang Hui wang xia, 14). (左右皆曰賢，未可也；諸大夫皆曰賢，未可也；國人皆曰賢，然後察之；見賢焉，然後用之). 2) "In the past, Yao introduced Shun to the people and they accepted him" (Mencius 2012, Wan zhang shang, 5) (昔者堯薦舜於天而天受之，暴之於民而民受之). Of course, passive acceptance is and consultations are not the same as exercising sovereignty. However, even if we consider that such passages were only about advices given to the ruler who makes the final choice of a counselor, they still clearly tend towards democratic thinking, especially regarding the early times in which they were written. And last, but not least: even in modern, existing democracies, people can neither directly appoint their leaders or representatives. All they can do, is participating in the votes.

5. 人心所同然 Here, Xu Fuguan refers to Mencius' famous saying "What is common to the heart-mind of every human being? I say it is the structural principles of reason and justice" (心之所同然者何也？謂理也，義也。Mencius 2012, Gaozi: 7). Mencius viewed this innate goodness as a kind of natural law, for innate goodness, like water, always flowed downwards, i.e. there was no human being who could not possess this innate goodness, just as there was no water that did not flow downwards (人性之善也，猶水之就下也。人無有不善，水無有不下。Mencius 2012, Gaozi: 2)

6. In this regard, Tang limited his elucidations to cultural or ideal factors which had determined these problems, ignoring the material and political conditions which underlie the academic debate on the "germs of capitalism" (*zibenzhuyi mengya*) in the Chinese tradition.

7. We should mention the thinkers of the so-called new methodologies and the members of the Donglin Academy. See Rošker (2008, 206).

8. This question was problematized by many of Tang's commentators, as for instance by Sin yee Chan (2002, 322) and He Xinquan (2000, 109).

9. In this context, Tang Refeng (2002, 340) translates the term *jiao* as religion. But given that the correct translation of this notion (religion) into modern Chinese is the compound *zongjiao*, the term *jiao* used here

must be applied in both a broader and yet more specific sense. In the absence of a more appropriate term, I translate it as teachings.

10. This is also a question of a proper evaluation and distinction between qualitative and quantitative scientific methodologies.

11. Elstein (2012, 198) prefers the term "self-restriction" and explains the reasons for it as follows: "Mou believes that although functional reason is superior to constructive reason, it nevertheless needs to limit itself to allow for constructive reason. Although China did not develop democracy and science, 'this is because it surpassed them, not because it could not attain them. Functional reason thus has to restrict itself to a lower level' (Mou Zongsan 1991, 51–52)—one reason I favour 'self-restriction.'" But since Mou's own gloss is "self-negation" (*ziwo fouding*), and since it has most often been translated with this latter term, we will also stick to it.

12. Mou's concept of reason is described in the chapter on reason and intuition below.

13. Here, Mou Zongsan is referring to the saying by Mencius: "Therefore, structure and justice are pleasing to my heart-mind, just as the flesh of grass and grain-fed animals are agreeable to my mouth". (Mencius 2012, Gaozi shang, 7) (故理義之悅我心，猶芻豢之悅我口).

14. The concept of "two functions" was borrowed by Mou Zongsan from the Neo-Confucian philosopher Liu Jishan, for whom this phrase denotes the love of goodness and hatred of evil. As Mou noted, in Kantian terminology this concept is defined as passive freedom. The idea of "two functions" instead implies both good and evil.

15. In a more detailed elucidation of this phrase, Mou Zongsan cites Mencius again: "What belongs by his nature to the nobleman cannot be increased by his sphere of action, nor diminished by his dwelling in poverty and seclusion—for it is his (self-)apportioning" (Mencius 2012, Jinxin shang, 21). (君子所性，雖大行不加焉，雖窮居不損焉，分定故也). Hence, all these characteristics pertain to individual predispositions, which are limited.

16. See the chapter on reason and intuition.

17. The word *yiyi* 意義 can also mean sense, significance or importance.

6 The Midwives of Modern Cultures: Reason, Subjectivity and their Philosophical Connotations

1. Because of the semantic ambiguity of this term (which can also be understood as being in dichotomous opposition to the notion of objectivity), Li Zehou (1996) has replaced the term subjectivity (*zhuguanxing*) with the term subjectivity (*zhutixing*). (For a detailed discussion see Rošker 2008, 231).

2. For this reason, the exponents of this intellectual movement often linked criticism of Mao Zedong's socialist model with a general criticism of the Chinese "feudalist" tradition which hindered any progress (see Wang Hui 2000, 18).

3. A comparative survey of Taiwanese and Central European students shows that the Taiwanese understand the concept of autonomy in the Kantian sense (i.e. as a morally determined self-control), whereas the Central Europeans perceive this notion in terms of freedom, liberation, independence and an absence of heteronomy.

4. For example, see Mencius's (孟子) (2012, Tan Wengong I, 4) dictum: 或勞心，或勞力；勞心者治人，勞力者治於人；治於人者食人，治人者食於人：天下之通義也. (Some labor with mind, and some with strength. Those who labor with mind govern others; those who labor with strength are governed by others. Those who are governed by others feed them; those who govern others are fed by them. This is a universally recognized principle).

5. Nietzsche can also be mentioned here as the forerunner of postmodern philosophies, which include the works of Lyotard, Deleuze, Derrida, Guattari, but also Umberto Eco.

6. Here, we can mention Ai Siqi, Jin Yuelin, He Lin and Feng Qi.

7. The semantic connotations of the term *ming* suggest that the notions "decree", "command" and "destiny" are essentially identical. In ancient Chinese philosophy, the Heavenly Mandate or the Decree of Heaven (*tian ming*) appears as similar—especially within the postulate of continuity and determination—to the idea of natural law, though with certain significant differences. These differences derive from the fact that the former is conceived within a holistic worldview, while the latter is dualistic. Thus, *ming* represents a principle or law situated within the

framework of the "unity of men and nature" (*tian ren heyi*), which is intrinsic to all human beings, while a natural law is a phenomenon which influences the individual externally.

8. 外在超越性，內在超越性.(Lee Ming-huei 2001a: 118).

9. Here, Lee Ming-huei is referring to Modern Confucians.

10. For the full controversy between Lee, Hall and Ames, see Lee Ming-huei, (2001a and 2002, especially Chapter 1), as well as Hall and Ames (1987 and 1998, especially Chapter 9).

11. Lee Ming-huei also mentions another aspect which is related to Hall and Ames' remarks. Clearly, he finds this misunderstanding to be rooted in the claim that Mou has applied the term transcendence in the strict sense, which is obviously not true. However, it is helpful to know that traditional Chinese notions of immanent transcendence like *tian*, *dao*, *tianming* or *tiandao*, can be understood as representing both the source of values and the basis of existence (Lee Ming-huei 2002, 229). Its axiological and creative connotations are thus of utmost importance in Chinese philosophy. In the history of Western philosophy, however, transcendence is generally understood either in the epistemological or the ontological sense. In the first instance, this term signifies going beyond certain cognitive abilities (or possibilities of recognition—especially those linked to experience) in order to reach the realm of an integrated or comprehensive recognition (*quanbu renzhi nengli* 全部認知能力, Lee Ming-huei 2002, 229). Hall and Ames, however, only consider the ontological connotations of the Western notion—which primarily denotes a separation and isolation from the world (or existence), while also implying the notion of creatio ex nihilo (*wu zhong chuangzao* 無中創造, Lee Ming-huei 2002, 229)—and do not take into account the equally significant epistemological connotations of the term. It is important to stress that the concept of transcendence as applied in the notion of "immanent transcendence" is primarily linked to its epistemological connotations, and is by no means limited to the strict sense of the Western ontological scope.

12. The Chinese holistic worldview is traditionally expressed by the phrase "unity of men and nature" (*tian ren heyi*).

13. For example, distinctions between subject and object, substance and phenomena, creator and creation, etc.

14. The analogical model used in the context of traditional Chinese logic differs from the classical European model in terms of both its methods and functions (Cui and Zhang 2005, 25–41).

15. Some well-known binary categories are: *yinyang* (sunny/shady), *tiyong* (substance/function), *mingshi* (concept/actuality), *liqi* (structure/phenomena), *benmo* (roots/crown).

16. Several interpreters (e.g. Ng 1996, I), especially those seeking a connection between Christian and Confucian ethics, see transcendence (in the sense of a possibility of transcending) as proof that Confucian ethics is not secular, but contains religious elements.

17. Collectivism is the polar opposite of individualism, which represents a mechanistic ideology that is based upon the dichotomy between the individual and society. In the relationship between individual and society that predominated in China, the individual was not seen as being alien to the society as a whole, but rather as a specific inmixing or differentiation of functions and abilities which are, as such, universal (Rošker 1996, 21).

18. These arguments are being applied not only by Western thinkers, but also by the Chinese. Fang Dongmei, for example, one of the leading figures of the second generation of Modern Confucianism, states that "in the whole history of Chinese philosophy, Yang Chu (521?–442? B.C.) was the only who spoke out boldly for the actual individual. But all other thinkers looked at him askance. For the Confucians, the individual had to be ceaselessly edified; for the Taoists, he had to be constantly liberated; and for the Buddhists, he had to be endlessly purified before he could be firmly established in the transfigured world of moral, aesthetic and religious perfection. In their view, any other way of affirming the status of the individual would be a premature mode of thought and betray an essential lack of wisdom" (Fang Dongmei 1980, 33).

19. As we shall see in the next chapter, the second generation of Modern Confucians (especially Mou Zongsan) clearly showed that this understanding of a highly individualized Self is hardly the only basis for the elaboration of such notions.

20. This claim, of course, has to be relativized. At least for Mou Zongsan, the moral self is basically stripped of everything that might mark him as

a unique person: there is just pure legislating free will giving the law to itself, and this law is universal. It also harks back to Mencius's claim that sages would all act the same way under the exact same circumstances. There isn't much uniqueness (in the Western sense) there.

21. As opposed to Hall and Ames, who propose an "autonomous" vs. a "unique" self, I would instead distinguish between an "isolated" and a "relational" or "contextualized" self (Lai 2006, 169–70).

22. As Lee Ming-huei (2001a, 17) points out, as opposed to Mou's complementary model, the problem of Weber's concept of modern rationalization is that it remains trapped in the phase of targeted rationalization (*Zweckrationalität*), which instead should always remain rooted in the axiological choice of the main aims or goals which have produced it. Thus, Weber's model of rationality remains trapped in the static framework of an isolated and static moral subject: "'Instrumental rationality' as found in the developmental processes of Western social technology, first arose from the 'rationality of values' that underlies the choice of its aims (or goals). The exaggerated emphasis on 'targeted rationality', however, has gradually led to completely forgetting the reasons for which technology was originally developed".

23. However, we must not forget that Mou often also uses the term "dialectic" to describe the non-analytic method employed in "perfect teachings". In such contexts, he refers not to the dialectical synthesis of two discrete opposites as employed by Georg Hegel (1770–1831), but to the nullification of opposition as employed in the Buddhist exposition of *prajñāpāramitā* (i.e. "perfect wisdom", Chan 2003, 143).

24. The term *ren xing*, which is generally translated as "human nature", actually implies all innate human qualities and impulses, as opposed to those that are acquired through education and socialization. These a posteriori properties are called "artificial" (*wei*).

25. The first partial horizon at the level of subjectivity is composed of the mutual projection of feelings deriving from individual subjects; the second implies abstract meanings which manifest themselves in the use of language and signs, arithmetic, geometry, logic and philosophy; while the third is defined by the consolidation of an integral, moral personality.

26. Judaism and Christianity belong to this sphere.

27. Tang's main reference here is to Buddhism.

28. The notion of culture is applied in the broadest possible sense here, as denoting anything produced by human beings, as opposed to untransformed nature.

29. Tang, like Churchill, considered democracy as the best possible, albeit imperfect, system. He stresses that abuses are also possible in democracy, in which the general interest is violated for the benefit of the few.

30. This is a principle of moral valuation which determines the admissibility or obligatory nature of the performance or omission of a certain act.

31. This principle offers incentives for the performance of acts, determined by the *principium dijudicationis*.

32. Heart and mind, a consciousness connecting reason, feelings and values.

33. According to Wang, "There is no knowledge without action. To know and not to act, means not to know". (未有知而不行者，知而不行，只是未知)" (Wang Shouren 1929, I/6a). A similar idea can be found in Hegel (1986a, 32). Wang, however, argues that actions cannot be performed after gaining knowledge, for they are indivisible parts of the same entity: "If we search structural principles outside of heart-mind, knowledge and action will be split into two pieces. Only the search for structural principles within heart-mind can refer to the teachings of the unity of knowledge and action". (外心以求理，此知行之所以為二也，求理於吾心，此圣門知行合一之教 ." (Wang Shouren 1933, II. Chuanxi lu zhong, Da Gu Dongqiao shu, 40)

34. Of course, this holds true only for the dominant discourses. In Chinese intellectual history we find a number of philosophical schools or individuals who tried to elaborate realistic methods of recognition that were based upon rational and analytical approaches, and who were critical of the introspective method and its exponents. In ancient China, the best known advocates of realism were the Nominalist and Mohist schools, while in Confucianism we find many members of the School of Structure (*li xue*) and later, many opponents of the dominant current within Confucianism and the "new methodologies", who were known collectively as the Academy of the Eastern Forest (Donglin shuyuan). An exemplary critique of intuitive methods can be found in the works of Wang Fuzhi (1619–2), a realist philosopher who in his commentaries

on the Daoist classic Laozi does not conceal his contempt for this approach: "How can things simply grant knowledge to me without any effort on my part? It is like a blind man trying to catch a galloping horse. This is a stupid waste of energy. Where under the sun is it possible to not do anything but still gain knowledge, to name things without perceiving them with the senses, and to reach perfection without acting?" (Wang Fuzhi, Laozi Yan in Xia Zhentao 1996b, 372)

35. Making a dualistic separation between idealism and materialism when exploring traditional Chinese philosophy is inappropriate, given that the distinction between matter and idea was often completely absent in the metaphysical discourses of most early Chinese philosophers. It thus never became a criterion of philosophical thought.

36. This was a pseudonym; his actual name was Wang Shouren.

37. This item is relative, because in Zhu Xi's realism, the structural principle *li* has also often functioned in a very rational way; however, since it is embedded in a different onto-epistemological paradigm, it still cannot be compared to the modern rationality. Besides, Wang has also often mentioned this Neo-Confucian concept of structural rationality, which manifested itself in the omnipresent (thus also mental) structure (*li*). However, he always stressed his belief that reason was merely that part of heart-mind which perceived and recognized the external world or reality in a more comprehensive way, i.e. through introspection and intuition. According to Wang, reason or the mental structure within heart-mind were the same as objects in the external reality: "There are no structures (structural principles) outside heart-mind, and there are no objects outside heart-mind. (Wang Yangming 1929, I/8b)

38. Bergson's most important works were translated into Chinese at the turn of the twentieth century (An 1997, 337).

39. Another closely related modern term is *lizhi*, which has also been translated as reason.

40. Weishi jia yu Bogesen 唯識家與柏格森 (*The Theoreticians of Pure Consciousness and Bergson*).

41. Li originally means structure (Rošker 2012a). In the ancient Chinese worldview, it represented an all-embracing order which, among other forms, also manifests itself in human heart-mind and is compatible with the structure of the external world. Although this understanding of the

concept of *li* differs in many ways from the connotations it has acquired in the history of European philosophy (Rošker 2011, 113–23), in the nineteenth century it was applied as the first (and most important) part of the compound by which the "Western" type of reason was translated into Chinese.

42. This essay was followed by another text in 1960, in which Chang, proceeding from the same premises, examined the application of intuitive methods within traditional Chinese philosophy (Chang 1960, 35–49).

43. This supposition is generally viewed as forming part of the Mencian ideal heritage. Xu, however, tried to prove that it could already be found in the works of Confucius.

44. Xu adopted *tiren* from Wang Yangming by way of Xiong Shili. See Gao Ruiquan (2001, 110).

45. For instance, the researches of the third generation theorists, Tu Wei-ming and Cheng Chung-ying.

46. In academic literature, this school is often denoted as the "Lu and Wang School", after Lu Jiuyuan (or Lu Xiangshan) and Wang Yangming (or Wang Shouren). While generally labeled as idealistic, it is problematic to transfer the unqualified categories of idealism and materialism into Chinese philosophy. The label of idealism derives from the School's focus on understanding the cultivation and functions of heart-mind recognition (see Chan 2002, 305).

47. Lee Ming-huei (2001, 67) notes that in Mou's *The Philosophy of History* (*Lishi zhexue*), which appeared in 1962, he denotes this pair of notions as "the spirit of synthetic rationality" and "the spirit of analytical rationality" (Part 3, Chapter 2). Despite the different denotations, Lee believes that both pairs of notions are identical in content.

48. In his principal work, *Intellectual Intuition and Chinese Philosophy* (*Zhide zhijue yu Zhongguo zhexue*), through a detailed study of Kant's Critique of pure reason Mou Zongsan comes to the conclusion that Kant's system also offers possibilities for the functioning of intellectual intuition, though Kant himself (in contrast to traditional Chinese philosophy) did not allow human beings access to it (Lee Ming-huei 2001, 69). Mou therefore concludes that the "transcendental" metaphysics precluded by Kant, was instead possible. Although Mou identified

various forms of this metaphysic in Confucianism, Daoism and Buddhism, he believed that Heidegger's attempt to constitute a "fundamental ontology" was a dead end (Lee Ming-huei 2001, 69).

49. According to Mou, this holds true not only for Kant, but also for the entire Western philosophical tradition, in which the cognitive abilities of intellectual intuition have always been exclusively reserved for God. In Western thought, intellectual intuition (like the immortal soul or free will) was thus always perceived as a postulate and never as reality. (For Mou's proof that the autonomous and free will forms part of the phenomenal actuality /*chengxian*/ and is not merely a postulate, see Mou Zongsan 1983, 77ff). In Mou's view, the prevailing separation of reality into the spheres of appearances and substance is also a consequence of this inconsistency (Han Zhao 1994, 170).

50. This concurs with Zhang Zhidong's famous slogan "Preserve the substance of Chinese teachings, while applying Western teachings" (Zhongxue wei ti, xixue wei yong 中學為體，西學為用).

51. Literary: original heart-mind, *xin*.

52. In this context, Mou's argument regarding the existence of the concept of autonomy within traditional Chinese or Confucian thought is of special importance. With this hypothesis, Mou could rather successfully counter the central critiques of the May Fourth movement, for which personal autonomy was necessarily linked to individualism. Mou Zongsan has namely demonstrated that Menciu's concept of innate morals (*renyi neizai*) corresponds to Kant's understanding of autonomy (Mou Zongsan 1985, 1–58). This conclusion is significant, because it shows that Weber's criticism of Confucianism is mistaken, for it is rooted in a misapprehension of the core of Chinese philosophy. In his (and also already in Hegel's) view, Confucianism was a kind of folk morality that did not offer any potential for speculative philosophy, an uncreative ideology that merely served the goal of adapting people to the conditions of the external world. Mou's analysis shows how biased and prejudiced these views were.

53. See the chapter on Tang Junyi.

54. The "Chinese" (*Han ren*) were first mentioned as a people with a distinct culture during the early centuries of the Zhou Dynasty (1066–221 B.C.). While we cannot speak of state borders in the modern sense,

this term indicates that already at that early date there existed a clear boundary between the agrarian culture of the Chinese Dynasties and various nomadic tribes. The emerging Chinese civilization was also linked to a unified cultural domain by the language and script, which the rulers of the Zhou Dynasty took over from the cultures of the Shang (Yin) Dynasty, and introduced throughout their territories. The bronze inscriptions of the Zhou period with their long texts simplified the ideographs, reduced strokes and standardized the characters. From the mid-Zhou period on, bamboo slips became a widespread writing material. However, the characters still differed from region to region, for the script became standardized only with the unification of the empire in 221 B.C.

55. While the nomadic origin of the Zhou continues to be debated in both the Chinese academic world and in Western Sinology, strong support for this thesis can be found in the chapter Zhou benji, of *Shi Ji* (*Historical Notes*, see next footnote). In their philosophical and religious approaches, the representatives of the second generation generally subscribed to Xu Fuguan's historical researches, especially those found in the chapter, The pre-Qin Period (Xian Qin bian), in his study, *The History of Human Nature Theories in China* (*Zhongguo renxing lun shi*). For my own part, in the present study I will focus primarily on the interpretations of the Modern Confucian scholars.

56. Of course, this point is still open to further discussion. We can interpret his famous saying "If we cannot comprehend the living, how can we comprehend the spirits? (Confucius 2012a, Xian jin 12)" as a clear statement that the afterlife was *a priori* inaccessible to human perception or comprehension. On the other hand, this sentence could also be translated as "If you cannot comprehend the living, how can you comprehend the spirits?"

57. E.g. as in the following two poems: "The Great Heaven is not righteous, and the ruler cannot find peace. And yet, he does not calm his heart, but instead tries furiously to alter Heaven". (*Shi jing* 2012, Xia ya, Jie nan shan 9). "Heaven does not feed us and we are doubtful, because we do not know where to go". (天不我將。靡所止疑) (*Shi jing* 2012, Da ya, Sang rou 3).

58. 795–771 B.C.

59. Chen Lai (1996, 4), for instance, explains this counter-tendency by the

fact that in China, the great religious crisis occurred before the emergence of the "axial period". Because this morally defined religion dating from the early Zhou Dynasty had gradually lost all its moral lustre and Heaven itself, in the role of the highest God and the ultimate moral instance, had lost all credibility, overcoming the prevailing scepticism in the population and reestablishing some form of theological thought that would permit the development of a monotheistic faith was extremely difficult. This "religious" faith was instead replaced by a faith in the rational structure of the universe, and "Heaven" became "Nature".

60. Or a hope in paradise and a fear of suffering in hell.

61. According to Xu Fuguan, the idea of reverence predominated precisely because of the "consciousness of concern" (*youhuan yishi*), which he sees as a fundamental psychological feature of ancient Chinese society (Xu Fuguan 2005, 24).

62. Hence, this discourse cannot be considered merely in terms of the explicit formulation of moral discourses, but must be understood as the internalization and awareness of one's moral Self. The following saying by Confucius makes this explicit: The Master said, "I would rather not speak." Zi Gong replied, "If you do not speak, what can we, your disciples, narrate?" The Master replied: "Does Heaven speak? The four seasons pursue their courses, and all things are constantly being produced, but does Heaven say anything?" (Konzi 2012a, Yang huo 19)

63. See Confucius (2012a, Xian wen 35).

64. Confucius expressed this concept as: "My inner virtue was produced by Heaven" (Confucius 2012a, Shu er 23). Also: "I do not blame Heaven. I do not complain against men. My studies lie on the physical level, and my penetration rises to the metaphysical one. But only Heaven knows me!" (Confucius 2012a, Xian wen 35)

65. According to Confucius, unity with Heaven could only be reached by a nobleman (*junzi*): "Yao as a sovereign was a true nobleman! He was extraordinarily majestic! Only Heaven is truly grand, and only Yao corresponded to it". (Confucius 2012a, Tai bo 19)

66. Confucius stressed that humanity was established in each person through the realization of a moral life: "True humanity means being able to practice five virtues everywhere under heaven" (Confucius 2012a, Yang huo 6). Proper moral conduct also manifests itself in

overcoming oneself (i.e. one's selfish interests) and in rituality as a symbolic identification with Heaven/Nature and the universe: "To subdue one's self and turn to rituality, is perfect virtue. If you can do this for one day, all under heaven will ascribe perfect virtue to you" (Confucius 2012a, Yan yuan 1). This clearly indicates the possibility of obtaining unity with one's natural and social environment through experiencing humanity.

67. That Confucius' philosophy was more than a set of simple regulations within a body of moral teaching is evident in the following saying: "At fifteen, I was eager to learn. At thirty, I stood firm on my own legs. At forty, I had no doubts. At fifty, I understood the Heavenly Mandate. At sixty, my ears were open for following the truth. At seventy, I could follow what my heart desired, without violating what was right." (Confucius 2012a, Wei zheng 4)

68. See Confucius (2012a, Yang huo 19); and Mencius (2012, Wang zhang 5).

7 The Modern Confucian Legacy and the New Confucian Ideologies in the People's Republic of China: The Case of Harmony

1. For a more detailed explanation of this issue and of the differences between the two regional currents see Chapter 7. However, many scholars have different opinions about this. Makeham, for instance, rather points out the independent, critical and cohesive attitude of the Confucian revival: "Successfully transcending the geographical and political boundaries of China, Taiwan and Hong Kong, since the mid-1980s, New Confucianism has increasingly played a leading role in bridging the cultural and ideological divide separating mainland and overseas Chinese scholars by providing a shared intellectual discourse". (Makeham 2003, 2)

2. In his article, "How to understand the slogan 'Let's close the Confucian store'", Zhang Yixing wrote: "This slogan of the May Fourth cultural revolution gives the impression that the representatives of the May Fourth movement were totally opposed to Confucian thought and traditional culture." (Zhang Yixing 2004, 1)

3. *Guo xue* 國學. In contemporary China, we can also cite the so-called "National studies fever" (*Guo xue re* 國學熱).

4. Li Chenyang (2006, 583) points out that the character *he* 和 has been applied mostly in the verbal form ("to harmonize") or as an expression that denotes the process of harmonization (often in the sense of tuning). However, this kind of mixed usage is true for the majority of classical Chinese notions (especially if abstract), which can assume different grammatical functions depending on the context. In addition, there are many passages in ancient Chinese texts, in which the notion *he* can be best translated by the noun harmony (e.g Confucius 2012a, Xue er 12, 2. Sentence; *Li ji* 2012, Tan gong I, 59, or Zhuangzi 2012, Shan xing 1 etc). Even the modern term harmony (*hexie* 和諧) can appear in both the adverbial and nominal form.

5. As one can easily imagine, the harmonious coherence between unmarried lovers does not find an unconditional approval in Confucian ideology.

6. In Mengzi, it is mentioned only three times, while in Xunzi not less than seventy-six times.

7. The contemporary meaning of the term *jie* 節 refers to festivals or celebrations. Originally, it meant respect for proper social rituals. Even the modern compound that denotes a feast, implies the word for ritual (*lijie* 禮節). The regulative function of the word *jie* is also evident in its classical connotation of "saving".

8. The Confucian classic, the *Doctrine of the Mean* (*Zhong Yong* 2012) is a text rich with symbolic meanings that provide implicit guidelines for the improvement and cultivation of human personality. Ezra Pound defined it as an "unswerving" or "unwobbling pivot", in the sense that the mean (*zhong*) is a balance, without oscillations or inclinations to either side. The second part of this compound (*yong*) generally refers to something common, familiar or domestic. It is changeless, but not static; rather, it can be regarded as continual. I have decided to translate it with the term "own way". One of the first translators of this text, James Legge, understood the purpose or goal of this mean as the preservation of a harmonious balance that keeps the mind in a state of continuous concentration. Someone who follows these principles can never stray or deviate from their "own way", meaning that they can always act in accordance with their unique or individual position within the natural and social world. These principles apply to everyone, and help each person to live in accordance with the natural order (see *Li ji* 2012; *Zhong yong* 2012, 233).

9. *Zhong* is "the mean, the middle". Due to its very specific and concrete use in the text, we have translated it with the more appropriate term "balance".

10. Gross generalizations applied to different cultures (and without entering into the definition of this complex and semantically vague notion) are a characteristic of the Modern Confucians and, to a certain extent, of modern Chinese theoreticians in general.

11. Emotions and reason.

12. Although Xunzi mainly taught about transforming people through ritual, he is often considered to be a bridge between Confucianism and Legalism. His most notable disciples were Li Si and Han Feizi. The first one was a prime minister to Qin shi huangdi, the first Qin emperor, who has established legalist ideology as a state doctrine, and the latter a scholar who developed the quasi-authoritarian aspects of Xunzi's thought into the theoretical framework of the legalist system. Because both of them were known for their anti-Confucian stances, Xunzi's reputation as a Confucian philosopher has often come into question.

13. Here, the notion of "democracy" is not understood in its prevailing sense of a multiparty system with diverse forms of parliamentary and political decision-making, but in much broader terms. In keeping with its original denotation, democracy is seen as a social system founded upon a complementary and equal relation between society and free individuals.

8 Conclusion—Modern Confucianism Between Past and Future

1. For a more detailed explanation of the Kantian (and Chinese) understanding of autonomy and for an analysis of the different ways in which this notion has been understood in Europe and China, see Rošker (2012b, 30).

2. This primarily concerns specific concepts of mutual responsibility and a more objective evaluation of the concept of authority.

3. John Makeham (2008) has translated this notion as "Lost Soul".

4. The other two main discourses can be broadly defined as the sinization of (neo) Marxist thought and the elaboration of liberal pragmatism (see Han and Zhao 1994, 273).

5. In this context, we should mention Lin Anwu, who proposes a development of a "Post New Confucianism" (*Hou xin ru jia*, 後新儒家 , see Lin Anwu 2006) which should pay more attention to the social issues and to a subject as a concrete existing moral being; the real experiences of human beings should thus represent a new basis for the further development of Confucian philosophical discourses. A similar critique can be found in the works of the mainland scholar Zheng Jiadong (2001, 192–4, 406–7), who reproaches Modern Confucians for an exaggerated intellectualisation of Confucianism to the detriment of social and political praxis. For a good analysis and a detailed introduction of these critiques see Elstein (2014, 60).

6. Literary: "Reasoning is the beginning of liberation from a difficult situation". In this regard, Modern Confucians still have not left the "bosom of lonely solitude" and have failed to create any kind of "major Modern Confucian movement". While some believe that "their general recognition and praise is long overdue", for the most part their teachings are still seen as a "recycling of remote discourses without any connection to the current reality". They remain, in fact, "lonely new Confucians" (Han Qiang in Zhao Guanghui, 1994, 274).

Bibliography

Abbeg, Lily. 1970. *Ostasien denkt anders—eine Analyse der West-Östlichen Gegensätze (East Asia Thinks Differently—an Analysis of the East-West Contrast)*. München: Verlag Kurt Desch.

Adorno, Theodor, and Horkheimer, Max. 1969. *Dialektik der Aufklärung*. Frankfurt: S. Fischer.

Alitto, Guy S. 1979. *The Last Confucian—Liang Shuming and the Chinese Dilemma of Modernity*. Berkeley and London: University of California Press.

Ames, Roger T. 2001. "New Confucianism: A Native Response to Western Philosophy." In *Chinese Political Culture 1989–2000*, edited by Shiping Hua, 70–99. New York: M.E. Sharpe.

Ames, Roger T. 2014. "Classical Daoism in an Age of Globalization." In *Classics and College Education in an Age of Globalization*, edited by Chun Chieh Huang, 5–17. Taibei: Institute for Advanced Studies in Humanities and Social Sciences, National Taiwan University.

An, Yanming. 1997. "Liang Shuming and Henri Bergson on Intuition: Cultural Context and the Evolution of Terms." *Philosophy East and West* 47(3): 337–62.

Angle, Stephen C. 2009. *Sagehood: The Contemporary Significance of Neo-Confucian Philosophy*. Oxford: Oxford University Press.

———. 2012a. "A Response to Thorian Harris." *Philosophy East and West* 62(3): 397–400.

———. 2012b. *Contemporary Confucian Political Philosophy*. Cambridge: Polity Press.

de Bary, William Theodore. 1998. *Asian Values and Human Rights: A Confucian Communitarian Perspective*. Cambridge, MA: Harvard University Press.

de Bary, William Theodore, and Haboush, JaHyun Kim. 1985. *The Rise of Neo-Confucianism in Korea*. New York: Columbia University Press.

de Bary, William Theodore, Carol Gluck, and Arthur E. Tiedemann, eds. 2002. *Sources of Japanese Tradition, 1600–2000*. New York: Columbia University Press.

Bell, Daniel A. 2008. *China's New Confucianism: Politics and Life in a Changing Society*. New Jersey: Princeton University Press.

Bellah, Robert. 1985. *Tokugawa Religion: The Cultural Roots of Modern Japan*. New York: The Free Press.

Berger, Peter. 1988. "An East Asian Development Model?" In *In Search of an Asian Development Model*, edited by Peter Berger and Michael Hsiao Hsin-huang, 5–6. New Brunswick, N.J.: Transaction Books.

Berthrong, John H. 1994. *All Under Heaven: Transforming Paradigms in Confucian-Christian Dialogue*. Albany, NY: State University of New York Press.

———. 1998. *Transformations of the Confucian Way*. Boulder, CO: Westview Press.

Billioud, Sebastien. 2012. *Thinking through Confucian Modernity: A Study of Mou Zongsan's Moral Metaphysics*. Leiden and Boston: Brill.

Bloom, David E., and Williamson, Jeffrey G. 1998. "Demographic Transitions and Economic Miracles in Emerging Asia." *The World Bank Economic Review* 12(3): 419–55.

Bresciani, Umberto. 2001. *Reinventing Confucianism—The New Confucian Movement*. Taipei: Taipei Ricci Institute for Chinese Studies.

Bunnin, Nicholas. 1996a. "Fang Dongmei (Thomé H. Fang)." In *Biographical Dictionary of Twentieth-Century Philosophers*, edited by Stuart Brown, Diane Collinson and Robert Wikinson, 223–4. London and New York: Routledge.

———. 1996b. "Mou Zongsan (Mou Tsung-san)." In *Biographical Dictionary of Twentieth-Century Philosophers*, edited by Stuart Brown, Diane Collinson and Robert Wilkinson, 549–50. London and New York: Routledge.

———. 1996c. "Tang Junyi (T'ang Chun-i)." In *Biographical Dictionary of Twentieth-Century Philosophers*, edited by Stuart Brown, Diane Collinson and Robert Wikinson, 768. London and New York: Routledge.

———. 2002. "Introduction." In *Contemporary Chinese Philosophy*, edited by Cheng Chung-Ying and Nicholas Bunnin, 1–15. Oxford: Blackwell Publishers.

Calder, Kent E. 2006. "China and Japan's Simmering Rivalry." *Foreign Affairs* 85(2): 129–39.

Chaibong, Hahm. 2000. "How the East Was Won: Orientalism and the New Confucian Discourse in East Asia." *Development and Society* 29 (1): 97-109.

Chan, Serina N. 2003. "What is Confucian and New about the Thought of Mou Zongsan?" In *New Confucianism*, edited by John Makeham, 131–65. New York: Palgrave.

———. 2011. *The Thought of Mou Zongsan*. Leiden: Brill.

Chan, Sin yee. 2002. "Tang Junyi: Moral Idealism and Chinese Culture." In *Contemporary Chinese Philosophy*, edited by Cheng Chung-Ying and Nicholas Bunnin, 235–346. Oxford: Blackwell Publishers.

Chang Carsun (Zhang Junmai 張君勱). 1932. "Guojia minzhu zhengzhi yu guojia shehuizhuyi 國家民主政治與國家社會主義 (State Democratic Politics and State Socialism)." *Zaisheng* 再生 1(3): 1–40.

———. 1954. "Reason and Intuition in Chinese Philosophy." *Philosophy East and West* 4(2): 99–112.

———. 1957. *The Development of Neo-Confucian Thought*. Vol.1. New York: Bookman Associates.

———. 1960. "Chinese Intuitionism: A Reply to Feigl on Intuition." *Philosophy East and West* 1(2): 35–49.

———. 1963. *The Development of Neo-Confucian Thought*. Vol. 2. New York: Bookman Associates.

Chen, Grant. 2002. "The Concept of Ultimate Reality in Tu Wei-ming and Cheng Chung-ying: A Comparative Study of new Confucian and Christian Understandings." PhD Dissertation. Deerfield, Illinois: Trinity International University.

Chen Guying 陳鼓應. 1998. "Chen Guying ping dangdai xin rujia 陳鼓應評當代新儒家 (Chen Guying on Contemporary Modern Confucianism)." In *Taiwanzhi zhi zhexue geming—zhongjie sanzhong wenhua weiji yu ershi shiji zhi gaobie* 台灣之哲學革命 —— 仲介三種文化危機與二十世紀之告別 (*The Philosophical Revolution in Taiwan—an Introduction of the Three Kinds of Cultural Crisis and the Farewell from the 20th Century*), edited by Wang Yingming, 95–98. Taibei: Shuxiang wenhua shiye.

Chen Lai 陳來. 1996. *Gudai zongjiao yu lunli—ru jia sixiangde genyuan* 古代宗教與倫理 —— 儒家思想的根源 (*Ancient Religions and Ethics—the Foundation of Confucian Thought*). Beijing: Sanlian shudian.

———. 2006. "On the Universal and Local Aspects of Confucianism." *Frontiers of Philosophy in China* 1(1): 79–91.

Cheng Chung-ying 成中英. 1985. *Zhongguo zhexuede xiandaihua yu shijiehua* 中國哲學的現代化與世界化 (*Modernization and Globalization of Chinese Philosophy*). Taibei: Lianjing.

———. 1988. *Zhongguo wenhuade xiandaihua yu shijiehua* 中國文化的現代化與世界化 (*Modernization and Globalization of Chinese Philosophy*). Beijing: Zhongguo heping chuban she.

———. 1991. *New Dimensions of Confucian and Neo-Confucian Philosophy*. New York: State University of New York Press, Albany.

———. 1991a. "Genyuan yu pianxiang 根源與偏向 (Foundations and Trends)." In *Zhongguo siwei pianxiang* 中國思維偏向 (*The Trends of Chinese Thought*), edited by Zhao Ping, 190–200. Beijing: Zhongguo shehui kexueyuan.

———. 1991b. *Lun Zhongxi zhexue jingshen* 論中西哲學精神 (*On the Spirit of Chinese Philosophy*). Shanghai: Dongfang.

———. 1991c. *Wenhua lunli yu guanli—Zhongguo xiandaihuade zhexue xingsi* 文化倫理與管理 —— 中國現代化的哲學省思 (*Cultural Ethics and Management—a Philosophical Reflection of Chinese Modernization*). Guian: Guizhou renmin chuban she.

———. 1998. "Dui Taiwan zhexue jiede fanxing 對臺灣哲學界的反省 (A Reflection on the Taiwanese Philosophical Circles)." In *Taiwanzhi zhexue geming—zhongjie sanzhong wenhua weiji yu ershi shiji yhi gaobie* (*The Philosophical Revolution in Taiwan—an Introduction of the Three Kinds of Cultural Crisis and the Farewell from the 20th Century*), edited by Wang Yingming, 14–32. Taibei: Shuxiang wenhua shiye.

———. 2003. "Confucianism: Twentieth Century." In *Philosophy, Chinese—Encyclopedias*, edited by Antonio S. Cua, 160–72. New York: Routledge.

———. 2008. *Yixue benti lun* 易學本體論 (*The Ontology of the Book of Changes*). Taibei: Kant Publishing House.

Cheng, Chung-ying, and Bunnin, Nicholas, eds. 2002. *Contemporary Chinese Philosophy*. Oxford: Blackwell Publishers.

Cheng Chung-ying 成中英, and Ma Sang 麻桑. 2008. *Xinxin ruxue qisi lu—Cheng Zhongying xianshengde benti shijie* 新新儒學啟思錄——成中英先生的本體世界 (*Records of the Modern Confucian Revival—the Ontological World of Sir Cheng Chung-ying*). Beijing: Shangwu yinshiguan

Choe, Yong. 2000. *Sources of Korean Tradition, Vol. 2: From the Sixteenth to the Twentieth Centuries*. New York: Columbia University Press.

Choukrone, Leila, and Garapon, Antoine. 2007. "The Norms of Chinese Harmony: Disciplinary Rules as Social Stabiliser." *China Perspectives* 3: 36–49. Accessed July 18, 2012. http://chinaperspectives.revues.org/1933.

Ci, Jiwei. 2002. "He Lin's Sinification of Idealism." In *Contemporary Chinese Philosophy*, edited by Cheng Chung-Ying and Nicholas Bunnin, 258–80. Oxford: Blackwell Publishers.

Ciaudo, Joseph. "Zhang Junmai (Carsun Chang, 1877–1969)." In *Internet Encyclopedia of Philosophy*. Accessed August 10, 2014. http://www.iep.utm.edu/zhang-ju/.

Clower, Jason. 2010. *The Unlikely Buddhologist—Tiantai Buddhism in Mou Zongsan's New Confucianism*. Leiden and Boston: Brill.

———. 2014. "Mou Zongsan (Mou Tsung-san) (1909–1995)." In *Internet Encyclopedia of Philosophy*. Accessed August 11, 2014. http://www.iep.utm.edu/zongsan/.

Collcutt, Martin. 1991. "The Confucian Legacy in Japan." In *The East Asian Region: Confucian Heritage and Its Modern Adaptation*, edited by Gilbert Rozman, 111–54. Princeton: Princeton University Press.

Confucius. 2012a. *Lunyu* 論語 (*The Analects*). Available at Chinese Text Project. Pre-Qin and Han. Accessed July 7, 2012. http://chinese.dsturgeon.net/text.pl?node=3925&if=en.

———. 2012b. *Chunqiu lu* 春秋錄 (*The Annals of Spring and Autumn*). Available at Chinese Text Project. Pre-Qin and Han. Accessed July 7, 2012 http://chinese.dsturgeon.net/text.pl?node=3925&if=en.

Cotton, James. 1991. "The Limits to Liberalization in Industrializing Asia: Three Views of the State." *Pacific Affairs* 64(3): 311–27.

Cui, Qingtian, and Xiaoguang, Zhang. 2005. "Chinese Logical Analogism." *Asian and African Studies* 9(2): 27–54.

Dai Liyong 戴立勇. 2008. *Xiandaixing yu Zhongguo zongjiao* 現代性與中國宗教 (*Modernization and Chinese Religions*). Beijing: Zhongguo shehui kexue chuban she.

Dallmayr, Fred. 1993. "Tradition, Modernity, and Confucianism." *Human Studies* (Postmodernity and the Question of the Other) 16(1/2): 203–11.

Davies, Gloria. 2010. "Affirming the Human in China." *Boundary 2* 37(1): 57–90.

———. 2012. "Discontent in Digital China." In *Red Rising, Red Eclipse*, edited by Geremie R. Barme, Jeremy Goldkorn, and Carolyn Cartier, 119–23. Canberra: The Australian National University, Australian Center on China in the World.

Day, Wan-Wen. 1999. "The Pathology of Modernity? Cultural Dialogue & Taiwan Small-Scale Media." PhD Dissertation. Boulder: University of Colorado Boulder.

Derrida, Jacques. 1994. *Izbrani spisi* (*Selected Writings*), translated by Tine Hribar and Uroš Grilc. Ljubljana: Študentska organizacija univerze (Krt).

Dirlik, Arif. 1994. *After the Revolution: Working to Global Capitalism*. Hanover, London: Wesleyan University Press.

———. 1995. "Confucius in the Borderlands: Global Capitalism and the Reinvention of Confucianism." *Boundary 2* 22(3): 229–75.

———. 1996. "Chinese History and the Question of Orientalism." *History and Theory* 35(4): 96–118.

———. 2001. "Postmodernism and Chinese History." *Boundary* 4(28): 19–60.

———. 2002. "Modernity as History: Post-Revolutionary China, Globalization and the Question of Modernity." *Social History* 27(1): 16–39.

Eisenstadt, Shmuel Noah. 2000. "Multiple Modernities." *Daedalus* 129(1): 1–29.

Eisenstadt, Shmuel Noah, and Schluchter, Wolfgang. 1998. "Introduction— Paths to Early Modernities —A Comparative View." *Daedalus* 127(3): 2.

Elstein, David. 2010. "Why Early Confucianism Cannot Generate Democracy." *Dao* 9: 427–43.

———. 2011. "Beyond the Five Relationships: Teachers and Worthies in Early Chinese Thought." *Philosophy East and West* 63(3): 375–91.

———. 2012. "Mou Zongsan's New Confucian Democracy." *Contemporary Political Theory* 11(2): 192–210.

———. 2014. *Democracy in Contemporary Confucian Philosophy*. New York: Routledge.

Fan, Ruiping, and Yu, Erika, eds. 2011. *The Renaissance of Confucianism in Contemporary China*. Dodrecht: Springer.

Fang Dongmei 方東美. 1931. "Shengming qinggan yu meixue 生命情感與美學 (Life Emotion and Aesthetics)." *Wenyi Zhongbao* 1(1): 17–36.

———. 1936. *Kexue, zhexue yu rensheng* 科學, 哲學與人生 (*Science, Philosophy and Human Life*). Beijing: Shangwu yinshu guan.

———. 1937. *Zhongguo xian zhe rensheng zhexuegaiyao* 中國先哲人生哲學概要 (*An Philosophical Outline of Ancient Chinese Philosophers*). Taibei: Shangwu yin shu guan.

———. 1959. "Jianyao zishu 簡要自述 (A Brief Self Introduction)." *Zhexue yu wenhua yuekan* 4(8): 15–17.

———. 1978. *Fang Dongmei xiansheng yanjiang ji* 方東美先生演講集 (*A Collection of Sir Fang Dongmei's Lectures*). Taibei: Liming wenhua shiye gongsi.

———. 1979. *Shengshengzhi de* 生生之德 (*The Virtue of Continuous Organic Creativity*). Taibei: Liming wenhua shiye gongsi.

———. 1980. *Zhongguo rende rensheng guan* 中國人的人生觀 (*The View of Life of Chinese People*). Taibei: Youshi wenhua shiye gongsi.

———. 1982. *Zhongguo rensheng zhexue (Fang Dongmei quanji zhi yi)* 中國人生哲學（方東美全集之一）(*Chinese Philosophy of Human Life /The Complete Collection of Fang Dongmei, Part 1*). Taibei: Liming wenhua shiye gongsi.

———. 1983. *Yuanshi rujia daojia zhexue* 原始儒家道家哲學 (*The Original Confucian and Daoist Philosophy*). Taibei: Liming wenhua shiye gongsi.

———. 1984. *Zhongguo zhexuede jingsheng jiqi fazhan* 中國哲學的精神及其發展 (*The Spirit and Development of Chinese Philosophy*). Taibei: Chengjun chuban she.

———. 1989. "Zhongguo zhexuezhi gejia tedian yu huitong 中國哲學之各家特點與會通 (The Particular Characteristics and the Representatives of Chinese Philosophical Schools)." In *Xiandai xin ruxue xue'an* 現代新儒家學案 (*The Records of Modern Confucianism*), Vol. 3, edited by Fang Keli 方克立 and Li Jinquan 李錦全, 1055–9. Beijing: Zhongguo shehui kexue chuban she.

———. 1992. *Shengming lixiang yu wenhua leixing: Fang Dongmei xin ruxue lunzhu jiyao* 生命理想與文化類型：方東美新儒學論著輯要 (*The Ideal of Life and the Types of Culture: an Edited Collection of Sir Fang Dongmei's Confucian Studies*). Taibei: Zhongguo guangbo dianshi chuban she.

———. 2004a. *Xin rujia zhexue shiba jiang* 新儒家哲學十八講 (*Eighteen Lectures on Modern Confucianism*). Taibei: Liming wenhua chuban she.

———. 2004b. *Zhongguo zhexue jingshen jiqi fazhan—shang* 中國哲學精神及其發展——上 (*The Spirit and the Development of Chinese Philosophy—Part 1*). Taibei: Liming wenhua chuban she.

———. 2004c. *Zhongguo zhexue jingshen jiqi fazhan—xia* 中國哲學精神及其發展——下 (*The Spirit and the Development of Chinese Philosophy—Part 2*). Taibei: Liming wenhua chuban she.

———. 2007. *Zhexue sanhui* 哲學三慧 (*Three Philosophical Wisdoms*). Taibei: Sanmin shuju.

Fang Keli 方克立. 1997. *Xiandai xin ruxue yu Zhongguo xiandaihua* 現代新儒學與中國現代化 (*Modern Confucianism and Chinese Modernization*). Tianjin: Tianjin renmin chuban she.

Fang Keli 方克立, and Li Jinquan 李錦全, eds. 1989. *Xiandai xin ruxue yanjiu lunji* 現代新儒學研究論集 (*A Collection of Research Studies in Modern Confucianism*). Beijing: Zhongguo shehui kexue chuban she.

———. 1995. *Xiandai xin rujia xue'an* 現代新儒家學案 (*The Records of Modern Confucianism*), Vol. 3. Beijing: Zhongguo shehui kexue chuban she.

Fang, Thomé H. (Fang Dongmei 方東美). 1957. *The Chinese View of Life*. Hong Kong: The Union Press.

———. 1980a. *Creativity in Man and Nature: A Collection of Philosophical Essays*. Taipei: Linking Publishing.

———. 1980b. *The Chinese View of Life: The Philosophy of Comprehensive Harmony*. Taipei: Linking Publishing.

———. 1981. *Chinese Philosophy: Its Spirit and its Development*. Taibei: Linking Publishing.

Feng Yaoming 馮耀明. 1992. "Cong 'zhitong' dao 'qucheng'—dangdai xin ruxue yu xiandaihua wenti 從「直通」到「曲成」——當代新儒學與現代化問題 (From the 'Straight' to the 'Crooked'—Contemporary Modern Confucianism and the Question of Modernity)." *Hanxue yanjiu* 10(2): 227–51.

———. 2000. "Dangdai xin rujiade zhuti gainian 當代新儒家的主體概念 (The Concept of Subject in Contemporary Modern Confucianism)." *Dalu zazhi—The Continent Magazine* 101(4): 145–65.

———. 2007. "Zhongguo ruxuede dianfanzhuanyi 中國儒學的典範轉移 (The Paradigmatic Shift in Chinese New Confucianism)." *Rujiao wenhua yanjiu—Journal of Confucian Philosophy of Culture* 2007(8): 2–33.

Feng Youlan 馮友蘭. 1999 (1939). *Xin lixue* 新理學 (*The New School of Principle*). Shanghai: Fudan daxue chuban she.

Fetzer, Joel S., and Soper, Christopher J. 2007. "The Effect of Confucian Values on Support for Democracy and Human Rights in Taiwan." *Taiwan Journal of Democracy* 3(1): 143–54.

Forke, Alfred. 1934. *Geschichte der mittelalterlichen chinesischen Philosophie (II)* (*A History of Medieval Chinese Philosophy*). Hamburg: R. Oldenbourg Verlag.

Fricker, Amanda. 1995. "Intuition and Reason." *The Philosophical Quarterly* 45(179): 181–9.

Geist, Beate. 1996. *Die Modernisierung der Chinesischen Kultur. Kulturdebatte und kultureller Wandel im China der 80er Jahre* (*The Modernization of Chinese Culture. Cultural Debate and Cultural Change in China in the 80s*). Hamburg: Institut für Asienkunde.

Goto-Jones, Christopher S., ed. 2008. *Re-Politicising the Kyoto School as Philosophy*. New York: Routledge.

Graham, A. C. 1989. *Disputers of the Tao—Philosophical Argument in Ancient China*. Chicago: Open Court Publishing.

Gao, Ruiquan. 2001. "On Xiong Shili's Intuitional Theory." *Journal of East China University* (Philosophy and Social Sciences) 1: 106–14.

Guo Qiyong 郭齊勇. 2014. "Chuantong wenhua jiaoyu xianzhuangde fansi 傳統文化教育現狀的反思 (A Reflection on the Contemporary Situation of Traditional Education)." *E hu* 3: 50–52.

Gussfield, Joseph R. 1967. "Tradition and Modernity: Misplaced Polarities in the Study of Social Change." *American Journal of Sociology* 72(4): 351–62.

Habermas, Jürgen. 1973. *Legitimationsprobleme im Spätkapitalismus* (*Problems of Legitimation in Late Capitalism*). Frankfurt/Main: Suhrkamp.

———. 1986. *Der philosophische Diskurs der Moderne—zwölf Vorlesungen* (*The Philosophical Discours of Modernity—Twelve Lectures*). Frankfurt/Main: Suhrkamp.

———. 1998. *Die postnationale Konstellation—Politische Essays* (*The Postcolonial Constellation—Political Essays*). Frankfurt/Main: Suhrkamp.

Hall, David L., and Ames, Roger T. 1987. *Thinking through Confucius*. Albany, New York: State University of New York Press.

———. 1998. *Thinking from the Han: Self, Truth and Transcendence in Chinese and Western Culture*. Albany, New York: State University of New York Press.

Han Qiang 韓強, and Zhao Guanghui 趙光輝. 1994. *Wenhua yishi yu daode lixing—Gang Tai xin rujia Tang Junyi yu Mou Zongsande wenhua zhexue* 文化意識與道德理性——港台新儒家唐君毅與牟宗三的文化哲學 (*Cultural Awareness and Moral Self—The Philosophy of Tang Junyi and Mou Zongsan from Hong Kong and Taiwan*). Shenyang: Liaoning renmin chuban she.

Hanafin, John J. 2003. "The 'Last Buddhist': the Philosophy of Liang Shuming." In *New Confucianism*, edited by John Makeham, 187–219. New York: Palgrave.

He Lin 賀麟. 1938. *Zhixing heyi—xin lun* 知行合一新論 (*A New Study on the Unification of Knowledge and Action*). Beijing: Beijing daxue chuban she.

He Xinquan 何信全. 1996. *Ruxue yu xiandai minzhu—Dangdai xin rujia zhengzhizhexue yanjiu* 儒學與現代民主——當代新儒家政治哲學研究 (*Confucianism and the Modern Democracy—Research in the Political Philosophy of the Contemorary New Confucians*). Taibei: Zhongyang yanjiu yuan.

Hegel, Georg Wilhelm Friedrich. 1969. *Vorlesungen über die Geschichte der Philosophie (Lectures on the History of Philosophy)*. Frankfurt/Main: Suhrkamp.

———. 1970. *Phänomenologie des Geistes (The Phenomenology of the Spirit)*. Frankfurt/Main: Suhrkamp.

———. 1986a. *Jenaer Schriften (The Jena Writings)*. Frankfurt/Main: Suhrkamp.

———. 1986b. *The Jena System, 1804–5: Logic and Metaphysics.* Kingston and Montreal: McGill-Queen's University Press.

Heubel, Fabian. 2011. "Immanente Transzendenz im Spannungsfeld von europäischer Sinologie, kritischer Theorie und zeitgenössischem Konfuzianismus (Immanent Transcendence in the Field of Tension between European Sinology, Critical Theory and Contemporary Confucianism)." *Polylog* 26: 91–114.

———. 2014. "Gebrochene Kontinuität: Selbstkultivierung und Demokratie im zeitgenössischen Neokonfuzianismus (Broken Continuity: Self-Cultivation and Democracy in Contemporary New Confucianism)." In *Kontinuität und Umbruch in Chinas Geschichte und Gegenwart (Continuity and Change in Chinese History and Presence*), edited by Philipp Mahltig and Eva Sternfeld, 41–60. Wiesbaden: Harrassowitz.

Hill, Michael. 2000. "'Asian Values' as Reverse Orientalism: Singapore." *Asia Pacific Viewpoint* 41(2): 177–90.

Hobsbawm, Eric, and Ranger, Terence, eds. 1995 (1983). *The Invention of Tradition*. Cambridge: Cambridge University Press.

Hu Shi 胡適. 1990. *Hu Shi wencun* 胡適文存 *(Hu Shi's Essays)*, Vol 2. Taibei: Yuandong chuban she.

Hua, Shiping, ed. 2001. "Introduction: Some Paradigmatic Issues in the Study of Chinese Political Culture." In *Chinese Political Culture 1989–2000*, 3–17. New York: M.E. Sharpe.

Huang Chun-chieh 黃俊傑, ed. 2006. *Dongya ruxue yanjiude huigu yu zhanwang* 東亞儒學研究的回顧與展望 *(Retrospects and Prospects of the East Asian Confucianism)*. Taibei: Taida chuban she.

———. 2009. *Humanism in East Asian Confucian Context*. Bielefeld: Transcript Verlag.

———. 2010. *Mencian Hermeneutics. A History of Interpretation in China*. New Jersey: Transaction publishers.

———. 2011. *Dongya ruxue shiyue zhongde Xu Fuguan ji qi sixiang* 東亞儒學視域中的徐復觀及其思想 *(Xu Fuguan and His Thought from the Viewpoint of East Asian Confucianism)*. Taibei: Taida chuban zhongxin.

Huntington, Samuel P. 1993. "The Clash of Civilizations." *Foreign Affairs* 2: 22–49.

Jaspers, Karl. 2003. *The Way to Wisdom: An Introduction to Philosophy*. New Haven, CT: Yale University Press.

Jiang Guobao 蔣國保, and Yu Bingyi 余秉頤. 1995. "Fang Dongmei xue'an 方東美學案 (Fang Dongmei's Academic Record)." In *Xiandai xin rujia xue'an* 現代新儒家學案 *(The Records of Modern Confucians)*, Vol. 3, edited by Fang Keli 方克立 and Li Jinquan 李錦全, 867–1128. Peking: Zhongguo shehui kexue chuban she.

Jiang Qing 蔣慶. 2003. *Zhengzhi ruxue: Dangdai ruxuede zhuanxiang, tezhi yu fazhan* 政治儒學：當代儒學的轉向，特質與發展 *(Political Confucianism: the Directions, Characteristics and the Development of Contemporary Confucianism)*. Beijing: Sanlian chuban she.

———. 2011. "From Mind Confucianism to Political Confucianism." In *The Renaissance of Confucianism in Contemporary China*, edited by Ruiping Fan, 17–32. Dordrecht: Springer.

Kahn, Hermann. 1979. *World Economic Development: 1979 and Beyond*. Boulder: Westview Press.

Kant, Immanuel. 1924. *Kritik der reinen Vernunft (The Critique of Pure Reason)*. Leipzig: Reclam.

Kim, Joo Yup, and Nam, Sang Hoon. 1998. "The Concept and Dynamics of Face: Implications for Organizational Behavior in Asia." *Organization Science* 9(4): 522–34.

Kuhn, Thomas. 1970 (1962). *The Structure of Scientific Revolutions*. Chicago: University of Chicago Press.

Kupke, Christian. 2007. "Subjekt und Individuum: zur Bedeutsamkeit ihres philosophischen Unterschieds in der psychiatrischen Praxis (The Subject and the Individual: on the Significance of their Philosophical Difference in the Psychiatric Practice)." *e-Journal Philosophie der Psychologie* June: 1–11. Accessed July 6, 2012. http://www.jp.philo.at/texte/KupkeC2.pdf.

Kwon, Keedon. 2007. "Development in East Asia and a Critique of the Post-Confucian Thesis." *Theory and Society* 36(1): 55–83.

Lai, Karyn. 2006. *Learning from Chinese Philosophies—Ethics of Interdependent and Contextualised Self*. Burlington: Ashgate.

Lai, Ming-Yan. 1995. "Family Troubles—Contestation and Non-Western Modernity in the Cases of China, Taiwan and Japan." PhD Dissertation. Madison: University of Wisconsin.

Lai Xianzong 賴賢宗. 2010. *Xin rujia quanshixue* 儒家詮釋學 (*Confucian Hermeneutic*). Beijing: Beijing daxue chuban she.

Lee, Hong-jung. 2003. "Development, Crisis and Asian Values." *East Asian Review* 15(2): 27–42.

Lee Ming-huei 李明輝. 1990. *Ru jia yu Kangde* 儒家與康德 (*The Confucians and Kant*). Taibei: Lianjing.

———. 1991. *Ruxue yu xiandai yishi* 儒學與現代意識 (*Confucianism and Contemporary Awareness*). Taibei: Wenjin chuban she.

———. 1994. *Kangde lunlixue yu mengzi daode sikaozhi chongjian* 康德倫理學與孟子道德思考之重建 (*A Reconstruction of the Kantian Ethics and Mencian Thought*). Taibei: Zhongyang yanjiuyuan.

———. 2001a. *Der Konfuzianismus im modernen China* (*Confucianism in Modern China*). Leipzig: Leipziger Universitätsverlag.

———. 2001b. *Dangdai ruxuede ziwo zhuanhua* 當代儒學的自我轉化 (*The Self-Transformation of Contemporary Confucianism*). Beijing: Zhongguo shehui kexue chuban she.

———. 2002. "Zai lun Rujia sixiang zhongde 'neizai chaoyuexing' wenti 再論儒家思想中的「內在超越性」問題 (A Revisited View of the Problem of 'Immanent Transcendence' in Confucian Thought)." In *Zhongguo sichao yu wailai wenhua* (*Chinese Thought Currents and Foreign Cultures*), edited by Liu Shu-hsien, 223–40. Taibei: Zhongyang yanjiu yuan, Zhongguo wenzhe yanjiusuo.

———. 2005. *Rujia shiye xiade zhengzhi sixiang* 儒家視野下的政治思想 (*Political Thought from the Confucian Viewpoint*). Taibei: Taiwan daxue chuban zhongxin.

Lee Ming-Huei 李明輝. 2006a. "Guanyu 'Haiyang ruxue' yu 'fazheng zhuti' de xingsi 關於「海洋儒學」與「法政主體的」省思 (A Reflection on the 'American Confucianism' and on the 'Subject of Legal Politics')." *Dangdai* 當代 28(8): 60–73.

———. 2006b. "Kangde zhexue zai xiandai Zhongguo 康德哲學在現代中國 (Kant's Philosophy in Modern China)." In *Zhonghua wenhua yu yuwai wenhuade hudong yu ronghe* 中華文化與域外文化的互動與融合 (*The Mutual Impact and the Fusions of Chinese and Foreign Cultures*), edited by Huang Chun-chieh, 89–134.Taibei: Ximalaya yanjiu fazhan jijinhui.

———. 2006c. "Liu Shuxian xiansheng yu Zhong Xi bijiao zhexue 劉述先先生與中西比較哲學 (Sir Liu Shuxian and the Chinese Comparative Philosophy)." In *Ruxue, wenhua yu zongjiao—Liu Shuxian xiansheng qishi shouqing lunwen ji* 儒學、文化與宗教：劉述先先生七十壽慶論文集 (*Confucianism, Culture and Religion—a Collection of Essays Dedicated to the 70th Birthday of Sir Liu Shuxian*), edited by Li Minghui, Ye Haiyan, Guo Zongyi, 215–24. Taibei: Taiwan xuesheng shuju.

———. 2007a. "Xu Fuguan lun rujia yu zongjiao 徐復觀論儒家與宗教 (Xu Fuguan's Religious Studies)." In *Renwen Luncong* 人文論叢 (*Studies in*

Humanities), edited by Feng Tianyu, 402–12. Wuchang: Wuhan daxue chuban she.

———. 2008. "Wang Yangming's Philosophy and Modern Theories of Democracy: A Reconstructive Interpretation." *Dao: A Journal of Comparative Philosophy* 7(3): 283–94.

———. 2009. "Mou Zongsan xiansheng yu Zhong Xi bijiao zhexue 牟宗三先生與中西比較哲學 (Sir Mou Zongsan and Chinese—Western Comparative Philosophy)." *Zhongguo quanshi xue* 中國詮釋學 (*Chinese Hermeneutics*) 6(1): 86–97.

———. 2010. "Ruxue zhishihua yu xiandai xueshu 儒學知識化與現代學術 (Confucian Knowledge and Modern Academia)." *Zhongguo Renmin daxue xuebao* 中國人民大學學報 (*The Journal of Renmin University*) 6(1): 2–7.

———. 2013. *Konfuzianischer Humanismus—Transkulturelle Kontexte* (*The Confucian Humanism—Transcultural Contexts*). Bielefeld: Transcript Verlag.

Lee Ming-Huei 李明輝, and Lin Weijie 林維杰, eds. 2007. *Dangdai ruxue yu xifang wenhua: huitong yu zhuanhua* 當代儒學與西方文化：會通與轉化 (*Contemporary Confucianism and Western Culture: Coherence and Transformation*). Taibei: Zhongyang yanjiuyuan.

Lee, Su-san. 1989. *Xu Fuguan and New Confucianism in Taiwan (1949–1969): A Cultural History of The Exile Generation*. PhD Dissertation. Rhode Island: Brown University.

Leung, Thomas In-Sing. 1986. "The Fang-fa (Method) and Fang-fa-lun (Methodology) in Confucian Philosophy." PhD Dissertation. Honolulu: University of Hawaii.

Li, Chenyang. 2002. "Philosophy of Life, Creativity and Inclusiveness." In *Contemporary Chinese Philosophy*, edited by Cheng Chung-Ying and Nicholas Bunnin, 258–80. Oxford: Blackwell Publishers.

———. 2006. "The Confucian Ideal of Harmony." *Philosophy East and West* 56(4): 583–603.

———. 2014. *The Confucian Philosophy of Harmony*. New York: Routledge.

Li ji 禮記 (*The Book of Rituals*). 2012. Available at Chinese Text Project. Pre-Qin and Han. Accessed July 7, 2012. http://chinese.dsturgeon.net/text.pl?node=3925&if=en.

Li Ning 李寧. 2010. "Goujian hexie shehui zhongde hexie xintai wenti 構建和諧社會中的和諧心態問題 (The Problem of Harmonic Mind in the Construction of Harmonious Society)." *Jiaoyu jiaoxue luntan* 教育教學論壇 22: 8–14.

Li Weiwu 李維武. 1995. "Xu Fuguan Xue'an 徐復觀學案 (Xu Fuguan's Record)." In *Xiandai xin rujia xue'an* 現代新儒家學案, Vol. 3, edited by Fang Keli 方克立 and Li Jinquan 李錦全, 579–866. Beijing: Zhongguo shehui kexue chuban she.

Li Zehou 李澤厚. 1996. *Zou wo zijide lu* 走我自己的路 (Going my Own Way). Taibei: Sanmin shudiuan.

Liao Xiaoping 廖小平. 1994. "Lun Zhongguo chuantong zhexue daode renshilunde tezheng 論中國傳統哲學道德認識論的特質 (On the Specific Features of Traditional Chinese Philosophical and Ethical Epistemology)." *Hebei Xuekan* 河北學刊 94(4): 43–47.

Liang Shuming 梁漱溟. 1921. *Dong Xifang wenhua jiqi zhexue* 東西文化及其哲學 (*Eastern Cultures and Philosophies*). Shanghai: Shangwu yinshuguan.

———. 1924. *Liang Shuming sanshi qian wenlu* 梁漱溟三十前文錄 (*Liang Shuming's Works, Written Before He Was Thirty Years Old*). Shanghai: Dongfang Wenku.

———. 1993. *Liang Shuming jiang Kong Meng* 梁漱溟講孔孟 (*Liang Shuming's Lectures on Kongzi and Mengzi*), edited by Li Yuanting 李淵庭. Beijing: Heping chuban she.

Lin Anwu 林安梧. 2003. *Daode cuozhi—Zhongguo zhengzhi sixiangde genben kunjie* 道的錯置——中國政治思想的根本困結 (*Misplaced Dao—the Basic Problem of Chinese Political Thought*). Taibei: Taiwan xuesheng shuju.

———. 2006. *Ruxue zhuanxiang—cong "Xin ruxue" dao "Hou xin ruxue" de guodu* 儒學轉向——從「新儒學」到「後新儒學」的過渡 (*The Shift in Confucianism—from 'New Confucianism' to 'Post-New Confucianism'*). Taibei: Taiwan xuesheng shuju.

Lin Guoxiong 林國雄. 2007. "Xin ruxue zhishi lun 新儒學知識論 (Modern Confucian Theory of Knowledge)." In *Xin ruxue zhishi lun* 新儒學知識論 (*Modern Confucian Theory of Knowledge*), edited by Lin Guoxiong and Yi Xiangquan, 1–82. Taibei: Zhongguo cihui hongdao gongde hui.

Liu Huiru. 1993. "Die 4. Mai Bewegung aus heutiger Sicht (The May 4th

Movement from the Present Point of View)." In *Chinesische Intellektuelle im 20. Jahrhundert: Zwischen Tradition und Moderne* (*Chinese Intellectuals in the 20th Century: between Tradition and Modernity*), edited by Karl-Heinz Pohl, Wacker, Gudrun, and Liu Huiru, 37–55. Hamburg: Institut für Asienkunde.

Liu, Shu-hsien, Berthrong, John, and Swidler, Leonard, eds. 2004. *Confucianism in Dialogue Today—West, Christianity and Judaism*. Philadelphia, PA: Ecumenical Press.

Liu, Shu-hsien. 1996. "Confucian Ideals and the Real World." In *Confucian Traditions in East Asian Modernity*, edited by Tu Wei-ming, 45–67. London: Harvard University Press.

———. 2001. "Introduction." In *Reinventing Confucianism—The New Confucian Movement*, edited by Umberto Bresciani, i–ii. Taipei: Taipei Ricci Institute for Chinese Studies.

———. 2003. "Mou Zongsan (Mou Tsung-san)." In *Encyclopedia of Chinese Philosophy*, edited by Antonio S. Cua, 480–5. New York: Routledge.

Liu Shu-hsien 劉述先. 2005. "Chaoyue yu neizai wentide zai xingsi 超越與內在問題的再省思 (Rethinking the Problem of Transcendence and Immanence)." In *Dangdai ruxue yu xifang wenhua—zongjiao pian* 當代儒學與西方文化——宗教篇 (*Contemporary Confucianism and Western Cultures—the Volume on Religions*), edited by Liu Shu-hsien and Lin Yuehui, 11–43. Taibei: Zhongyang yanjiuyuan—Zhongguo wenzhe yanjiusuo.

Lubmann, Stanley. 1999. *Bird in a Cage: Legal Reform in China after Mao*. Stanford: Stanford University Press.

Luo Rongqu 羅榮渠, ed. 2008. *Cong "Xihua" dao xiandaihua* 從「西化」到現代化 (*From Westernization to Modernization*). Hefei: Huangshan shu she.

Ma Dongyu 馬東玉. 1993. "Jianlun dangdai xin rujiade 'xiandaihua' licheng 簡論當代新儒家的「現代化」歷程 (A Short Debate on the Modern Confucian 'Modernization' Process)." *Liaoning shifan daxue xuebao* 遼寧師範大學學報 5: 74–80.

Makeham, John. 2003, ed. *New Confucianism. A Critical Examination*. New York: Palgrave Maximilians.

———. 2008. *Lost Soul: "Confucianism" in Contemporary Chinese Academic Discourse*. Vol. 64. Council on East Asian Studies, Harvard University.

McCormick, Peter. 1979. "The Concept of the Self in Political Thought." *Canadian Journal of Political Science/Revue Canadienne de science politique* 12(44): 689–725.

Mencius. 2012. *Mengzi* 孟子. Available at Chinese Text Project. Pre-Qin and Han. Accessed July 7, 2012. http://chinese.dsturgeon.net/text.pl?node=3925&if=en.

Meng Peiyuan 蒙培元. 1989. *Lixue fanchou xitong* 理學範疇系統 (*The System of Structural Categories*). Beijing: Xinhua shudian.

Metzger, Thomas A. 1991. "Confucian Thought and the Modern Chinese Quest for Moral Autonomy." In *Confucianism and the Modernization of China*, edited by Silke Krieger and Rolf Trauzettel, 266–307. Mainz: Hase & Koehler.

———. 2005. *A Cloud across the Pacific—Essays on the Clash between Chinese and Western Political Theories Today*. Hong Kong: The Chinese University Press.

Moody, Peter R. Jr. 1996. "Asian Values." *Journal of International Affairs* 50(1): 166–92.

Moritz, Ralf. 1993. "Denkstrukturen, Sachzwänge, Handlungsspielräume—Die chinesische Intelligenz im Konflikt der Ordnungsmuster (Structures of Thought, Constraints, Maneuvers—Chinese Intellectuals in the Conflict of the Patterns of Order)." In *Chinesische Intellektuelle im 20. Jahrhundert: Zwischen Tradition und Moderne* (*Chinese Intellectuals between Tradition and Modernity*), edited by Karl-Heinz Pohl, Gudrun Wacker and Liu Huiru, 59–108. Hamburg: Institut für Asienkunde.

Motoh, Helena. 2009. "Harmonija konfliktov—klasična kitajska kozmologija v sodobnem političnem kontekstu." *Dialogi* 9(9): 88–104.

Mou Zhongjian, ed. 2013. *General History of Religions in China*. Vol. 1. London: Paths international Ltd.

Mou Zhongjian 牟鍾鑒, and Zhang Jian 張踐. 1994. *Zhongguo minguo zongjiao shi* 中國民國宗教史 (*The History of Religions in Republican China*). Beijing: Renmin chuban she.

Mou Zongsan 牟宗三. 1941. *Luoji dianfan* 邏輯典範 (*Logical Paradigms*). Hong Kong: Shangwu yinshu guan.

———. 1962. *Lishi zhexue* 歷史哲學 (*Philosophy of History*). Taibei: Xuesheng shuju.

———. 1963. *Caixing yu xuanli* 才性與玄理 (*Material Nature and Profound Principle*). Taibei: Xuesheng shuju.

———. 1969. *Xinti yu xingti* 心体與性體 (*Substance of Heart-Mind and the Innate Moral Substance*). Taibei: Zhengzhong shuju.

———. 1971. *Zhide zhijue yu Zhongguo zhexue* 智的直覺與中國哲學 (*Intellectual Intuition and Chinese Philosophy*). Taipei: Taiwan shangwu yinshu guan.

———. 1975. *Xianxiang yu wu zishen* 現象與物自身 (*Phenomena and the Things as Such*). Taibei: Xuesheng shuju.

———. 1979. *Cong Lu Xiangshan dao Liu Jishan* 從陸象山到劉蕺山 (*From Lu Xiangshan to Liu Jishan*). Taibei: Xuesheng shuju.

———. 1983a. *Zhongguo zhexue shijiu jiang* 中國哲學十九講 (*Nineteen Lectures on Chinese Philosophy*). Taibei: Xuesheng shuju.

———. 1983b. *Kangde de chuncui lixing pipan* 康德純粹理性批判 (*On Kant's Critique of Pure Reason*), 2 vols. Taibei: Xuesheng shuju.

———. 1984. *Shengmingde zhexue* 生命的哲學 (*Philosophy of Life*). Taibei: Sanmin shuju.

———. 1988. *Zhou yide ziran zhexue yu daode hanyi* 周易的自然哲學與道德涵義 (*The Meaning of Natural Philosophy and Morality in the Zhou Yi*). Taibei: Wenjin chuban she.

———. 1989a. *Wushi zishu* 五十自述 (*The Autobiography at Fifty*). Tabei: Penghu chuban she.

———. 1989b. "Gainiande xinling yu zhizhi zhijue xingtai ji zhixingxingtai 概念的心靈與智之直覺形態及知性形態 (The Conceptual Spirit, the Form of Intellectual Intuition and the Form of Knowledge)." In *Xiandai xin ruxue yanjiu lunji* 現代新儒學研究論集 (*A Collection of Research Essays on Modern Confucianism*), edited by Fang Keli and Li Jinquan, 527–33. Beijing: Zhongguo shehui kexue chuban she.

———. 1990. *Zhongguo zhexuede tezhi* 中國哲學的特質 (*Specific Features of Chinese Philosophy*). Taibei: Taiwan xuesheng shuju.

———. 1995. "Zhengdao yu zhidao, di san zhang 政道與治道, 第三章 (The Ways of Politics and Governance, Chapter Three)." In *Xiandai xin ruxue xue'an* 現代新儒家學案 (*Records of Modern Confucians*), Vol. 3, edited by Fang Keli 方克立 and Li Jinquan 李錦全, 450–545. Peking: Zhongguo shehui kexue chuban she.

———. 2010 (1985). *Yuanshan lun* 圓善論 (*On Summum Bonum*). Changchun: Jilin chuban jituan zouxian zeren gongsi.

Ng, On-cho, ed. 2011. "The Imperative of Understanding: Chinese Philosophy, Comparative Philosophy, and Onto-Hermeneutics—A Tribute Volume Dedicated to Professor Chung-ying Cheng." *Journal of Chinese Philosophy* 38(1): 151–6.

Ng, Yau-Nang William. 1996. "T'ang Chun-I's idea of Transcendence." PhD Dissertation. Toronto: University of Toronto.

Ni, Peimin. 2002. "Practical Humanism of Xu Fuguan." In *Contemporary Chinese Philosophy*, edited by Cheng Chung-Ying and Nicholas Bunnin, 281–304. Oxford: Blackwell Publishers.

Ouchi, William G. 1978. "The Transmission of Control through Organizational Hierarchy." *The Academy of Management Journal* 21(2): 173–92.

Peerenboom, Randall. 2002. "Social Networks, Rule of Law and Economic Growth in China: The Elusive Pursuit of the Right Combination of Private and Public Ordering." *Global Economic Review* 31(2): 1–19.

Pfister, Lauren. 1986. "The Different Faces of Contemporary Religious Confucianism: an Account of the Diverse Approaches of Some Major Twentieth Century Chinese Confucian Scholars." *Journal of Chinese Philosophy* 22(3): 5–80.

Qi Liang 豈良. 1995. *Xin ruxue pipan* 新儒學批判 (*A Critique of Modern Confucianism*). Shanghai: Sanlian shudian.

Qiu Feng 秋風. 2011. "Zunzhong Kongzi, xiandaihua cai you yiyi 尊重孔子，現代化才有意義 (Only through Respecting Confucius the Modernization Gains a Significance)." In *Gongshi wang*. Accessed July 2012. http://www.21ccom.net/articles/sxpl/sx/article_2011020729358.html.

Roetz, Heiner. 2008. "Confucianism between Tradition and Modernity, Religion, and Secularization: Questions to Tu Weiming." *Dao—Journal for Comparative Philosophy* 2008(7): 367–80.

Rosenlee, Li-Hsiang Lisa. 2006. *Confucianism and Women: A Philosophical Interpretation*. Albany, New York: State University of New York Press.

Rosemon, Henry Jr. 1986. "Kierkegaard and Confucius: On Finding the Way." *Philosophy East and West* 36(3): 201–12.

Rošker, Jana S. 2006. *Na ozki brvi razumevanja—metodologija medkulturnih raziskav v sinoloških študijah* (*On the Tiny Bridge of Understanding—Methodology of Intercultural Research in Sinological Studies*). Ljubljana: Oddelek za azijske in afriške študije, Filozofska fakulteta Univerze v Ljubljani.

———. 2008. *Searching for the Way: Theory of Knowledge in Pre-Modern and Modern China*. Hong Kong: The Chinese University Press.

———. 2010. *Odnos kot jedro spoznanja: kitajska filozofija od antičnih klasikov do modernega konfucijanstva* (*Relation as a Core of Comprehension—Chinese Philosophy from the Ancient Classics till Modern Confucianism*). Zbirka Čas misli. Ljubljana: Cankarjeva založba.

———. 2012a. *Traditional Chinese Philosophy and the Paradigm of Structure (Li)*. Newcastle upon Tyne: Cambridge Scholars Publishing.

———. 2012b. "Cultural Conditionality of Comprehension: The Perception of Autonomy in China." In *Reinventing Identities: The poetic of language use in contemporary China* (Nankai huayu yanjiu xilie congshu), edited by Qing Cao, Hailong Tian and Paul Chilton, 26–42. Tianjin: Nankai daxue chuban she.

Rozman, Gilbert, ed. 1991. *The East Asian Region: Confucian Heritage and Its Modern Adaptation*. Princeton: Princeton University Press.

———. 2002. "Can Confucianism Survive in an Age of Universalism and Globalization?" *Pacific Affairs* 75(1): 11–37.

Said, Edward W. 1995 (1978). *Orientalism—Western Conceptions of the Orient*. Harmondsworth, Middlesex: Penguin Books.

Sandel, Michael. 1984. "The Procedural Republic and the Unencumbered Self." *Political Theory* 12(1): 81–96.

Scalapino, Robert A. 2002. "Democracy in Taiwan and Asia—Advances and Challenges." In *Taiwan's Modernization in Global Perspective*, edited by Peter C.Y. Chow, 29–44. Westport, Connecticut-London: Praeger.

Schmidt-Glintzer, Helwig. 1983. "Max Weber's Interest in Confucius." In *Confucianism and the Modernization of China*, edited by Silke Krieger and Rolf Trauzettel, 243–8. Mainz: Hase & Koehler.

Shu jing 書經 (*Shang shu* 尚書). 2012. Available at Chinese Text Project. Pre-Qin and Han. Accessed July 7, 2012. http://chinese.dsturgeon.net/text.pl?node=3925&if=en.

Tang Junyi 唐君毅. 1953. *Zhongguo wenhua zhi jingshen jiazhi* 中國文化之精神價值 (*The Spiritual Value of Chinese Philosophy*). Taibei: Zhengzhong shuju.

———. 1975a. *Xin wu yu rensheng* 心物與人生 (*Heart-Mind, Objects and Human Life*).Taibei: Xuesheng shuju.

———. 1975b. *Zhonghua renwen yu dangjin shijie* 中華人文與當今世界 (*Chinese Humanities and the Contemporary World*). Taibei: Xuesheng shuju.

———. 1977. *Shengming cunzai yu xinling jingjie* 生命存在與心靈境界 (*The Existence of Life and the Spiritual World*). 2 Vol. Taipei: Xuesheng shuju.

———. 1985. *Daode ziwozhi jianli* 道德自我之建立 (*Establishing the Moral Self*). Taipei: Xuesheng shuju.

———. 1986. *Wenhua yishi yu daode lixing* 文化意識與道德理性 (*Cultural Awareness and Moral Reason*). Taibei: Xuesheng shuju.

Tang Junyi 唐君毅, 1989: *Renshengzhi tiyan* 人生之體驗 (*The Experience of Human Life*). Taibei: Taiwan xuesheng shuju.

———. 1991. *Zhongxi zhexue sixiangzhi bijiao lunji* 中西哲學思想之比較論集 (*A Collection of Essays on Chinese and Western Comparative Philosophy*). Taipei: Xuesheng shuju.

———. 2000. *Renwen jingshenzhi chongjian* 人文精神之重建 (*The Reconstruction of the Spirit of the Humanities*). Taipei: Xuesheng shuju.

———. 2008. *Tang Junyi xin ruxue lunji* 唐君毅新儒學論集 (*A Collection of Tang Junyi's Essays on Modern Confucianism*). Nanjing: Nanjing daxue chuban she.

Tang, Refeng. 2002. "Mou Zongsan on Intellectual Intuition." In *Contemporary Chinese Philosophy*, edited by Cheng Chung-Ying and Nicholas Bunnin, 235–46. Oxford: Blackwell Publishers.

Tang, Yijie. 1991a. *Confucianism, Buddhism, Daoism, Christianity and Chinese Culture*. Beijing: Peking University, Council for Research in Values.

Tang, Yijie. 1991b. "Transcendence and Immanence in Confucian Philosophy." In *Confucian and Christian Encounters in Historical and Contemporary Perspective*, edited by Peter K.H. Lewiston Lee, 171–81. New York: Edwin Mellen.

Tang Yijie 湯一介. 1996. *Tang Yijie xueshu wenhua suibi* 湯一介學術文化隨筆 (*Tang Yijie's Academic Essays on Culture*). Beijing: Zhongguo qingnian chuban she.

Taylor, Charles. 1985. "What's Wrong with Negative Liberty? Philosophy and the Human Sciences." *Philosophical Papers* 2: 211–29.

Thompson, Mark R. 2001. "Whatever Happened to 'Asian Values'?" *Journal of Democracy* 12(4): 154–65.

Tu Weiming, ed. 1993. *China in Transformation*. Cambridge: Harvard University.

———, ed. 1996. "Introduction." In *Confucian Traditions in East Asian Modernity—Moral Education and Economic Culture in Japan and the Four Mini-Dragons*, 1–10. Cambridge and London: Harvard University Press.

———. 2000. "Implications of the Rise of 'Confucian' East Asia." *Daedalus* 129(1): 195–219.

———. 2014. "Confucianism." In Encyclopaedia Britannica. Accessed March 13, 2014. http://global.britannica.com/EBchecked/topic/132104/Confucianism/ 25455/The-historical-context#ref1008344.

Vogel, Ezra F. 1979. *Japan as Number One*. Cambridge, MA: Harvard University Press.

Wang Hui 汪暉. 2000. "Dangdai Zhongguode sixiang zhuangkuang yu xiandaixing wenti 當代中國的思想狀況與現代性問題 (Contemporary Chinese Thought and the Question of Modernity)." *Taiwan shehui yanjiu* 37(1): 1–43.

Wang Shouren 王守仁. 1929. *Yangming xiansheng jiyao* 陽明先生集要 (*Essential Works of Sir Yangming*), Vol. 12. Shanghai: Shangwu yinshuguan.

———. 1933. *Wang Wencheng gong quanshu* 王文成公全書 (*A Complete Collection of Wang Wencheng*). Shanghai: Shangwu Yinshuguan.

Wang Ye 王燁. 2012. "Rujia hexie sixiang ji qi xiandaihua sikao 儒家和諧思想及其現代化思考 (The Confucian Thought on Harmony and its Modern Reflection)." In *Zhongguo Kongzi wang* 中國孔子網 (*The Chinese Kongzi Website*). Accessed July 18, 2012. http://www.chinakongzi.org/rjwh/guoxue/lzxd/201207/t20120704_7236633.htm.

Weber, Max. 1951. *The Religion of China: Confucianism and Taoism*. New York: Free Press.

———. 1989. *Die Wirtschaftsethik der Weltreligionen—Konfuzianismus und Taoismus* (*The Economic Ethics of the World Religions—Confucianism and Daoism*). Tübingen: J.C.B. Mohr (Paul Siebek).

Wheeler, Norton. 2005. "Modernization Discourse with Chinese Characteristics." *East Asia* 22(3): 23–24.

Woods, Alan T. 2010. "Fire, Water, Earth and Sky: Global Systems History and the Human Prospect." *The Journal of the Historical Society* 10(3), September: 287–318.

Xia Zhentao. 1996b. *Zhongguo renshilun sixiang shigao, xia* 中國認識論思想史稿, 下 (*A History of Chinese Epistemology, Part 2*). Beijing: Zhongguo renmin daxue chuban she.

Xiao, Zhuoji 蕭灼基. 2007. "Harmonious Society." *China Daily* 29 September: 15.

Xiong Shili 熊十力. 1956. *Yuan ru* 原儒 (*Original Confucianism*), 2 Vol., Shanghai: Shanghai Longmen lianhe shuju.

———. 1959. *Ming xin pian* 明心篇 (*The Clear Mind*). Shanghai: Longmen lianhe shuju.

———. 1999a. "Ti yong lun 體用論 (The Theory of Substance and Function)." In *Ershi shiji zhexue jingdian wenben* 二十世紀哲學經典文本 (*The Philosophical Classics of the 20th Century*), edited by Yu Wujin and Wu Shaoming, 265–77. Shanghai: Fudan daxue chuban she.

———. 1999b. "Xin weishi lun 新唯識論 (A New Treatise on Consciousness-only)." In *Ershi shiji zhexue jingdian wenben* 二十世紀哲學經典文本 (*The Philosophical Classics of the 20th Century*), edited by Yu Wujin and Wu Shaoming, 236–64. Shanghai: Fudan daxue chuban she.

Xu Fuguan 徐復觀. 1951. "Gongchandangde renxing 共產黨的人性 (The Human Nature of the Chinese Communist Party)." *Minzhu pinglun* 2(23): 12–16.

———. 1957a. "Rujia dui Zhongguo lishi yunming zhengzhazhi yili 儒家對中國歷史運命掙扎之一例 (An Example of the Confucian Struggles for the Chinese Historical Destiny)." *Minzhu pinglun* 民主評論 6(20): 3–7.

———. 1957b. "Rujia jingshenzhi jiben xingge ji qi xianding yu xinsheng 儒家精神之基本性格及其限定與新生 (The Basic Character of the Confucian Spirit, its Limitations and its Revival)." *Minzhu pinglun* 民主評論 3(10): 15–38.

———. 1960. "Bu si bu xiangde shidai 不思不想的時代 (A Period without Thought)." *Huaqiao ribao* April 12: 4.

———. 1976. "Yantie lun zhongde zhengzhi shehui wenhua wenti 鹽鐵論中的政治社會文化問題 (The Problems of Politics, Society and Culture in the Debate on Salt and Iron)." *Xinya xuebao* 11: 337–418.

———. 1979a. *Rujia zhengzhi sixiang yu minzhu ziyou renquan* 儒家政治思想與民主自由人權 (*Confucian Political Thought and Democracy, Freedom and Human Rights*). Beijing: Bashi niandai chuban she.

———. 1979b. "Xiang Kongzide sixiang xingge huigui 向孔子的思想性格回歸 (A Return to the Characteristics of Confucian Thought)." *Zhongguo ren yuekan* 1(8): 9–28.

———. 1980a. *Xueshu yu zhengzhi zhijian* 學術與政治之間 (*Between Academic Research and Politics*). Taibei: Taiwan xuesheng shuju.

———. 1980b. *Xu Fuguan wenlu xuancui* 徐復觀文錄選粹 (*A Selection of Xu Fuguan's Essays*). Taibei: Taiwan xuesheng shuju.

———. 1981. *Xu Fuguan zawen ji* 徐復觀雜文集 (*A Collection* of *Xu Fuguan's Essays*). Taibei: Shibao wenhua chuban gongsi.

———. 1982. *Zhongguo sixiangshi lunji xubian* 中國思想史論集續編 (*More Essays on the History of Chinese Thought*). Taibei: Shibao wenhua chuban she.

———. 1987. "Zhongguo renxing lun shi—Xian Qin pian 中國人性論史——先秦篇 (The History of Human Nature—Chapters on the pre-Chin Period)." In *Xiandai xin rujia xue'an* 現代新儒家學案 (*Records of Modern Confucians*), Vol. 3, edited by Fang Keli 方克立 and Li Jinquan 李錦全, 647–62. Beijing: Zhongguo shehui kexue chuban she.

———. 1988. *Rujia zhengzhi sixiang yu minzhu ziyou renquan* 儒家政治思想與民主自由人權 (*Confucian Political Thought and Democracy, Freedom and Human Rights*). Taibei: Xuesheng shuju.

———. 1991. *Zhongguo renzhi siwei fangfa* 中國人之思維方法 (*The Methods of Chinese Thought*). Taibei: Xuesheng shuju.

———. 1995a. "Zhou chu zongjiao zhong renwen jingshende yuedong 周初宗教中人文精神的躍動 (The Awakening of the Spirit of Humanities in the Early Zhou Religion)." In *Xiandai xin rujia xue'an* 現代新儒家學案 (*Records of Modern Confucians*), Vol.3, edited by Fang Keli 方克立 and Li Jinquan李錦全, 647–60. Peking: Zhongguo shehui kexue chuban she.

———. 1995b. "Rujia jingshende xiandai shushi 儒家精神的現代疏釋." In *Xiandai xin ruxue xue'an* 現代新儒家學案, Vol.3, edited by Fang Keli 方克立 and Li Jinquan 李錦全, 667–724. Peking: Zhongguo shehui kexue chuban she.

———. 2000. *Zhongguo sixiang shi lunji* 中國思想史論集 (*A Collection of Essays on Chinese Thought*). Shanghai: Shanghai shudian chuban she.

———. 2001a. *Zhongguo yishu jingshen* 中國藝術精神 (*The Chinese Artistic Spirit*). Beijing: Huadong shifan daxue chuban she.

———. 2001b. *Liang Han sixiang shi* 兩漢思想史 (*The Intellectual History of the Two Han Dynasties*). Shanghai: Huadong shifan daxue.

———. 2005. *Zhongguo renxing lun shi* 中國人性論史 (*The History of Human Nature in China*). Beijing: Huadong shifan daxue chuban she.

Xu, Quanxing, and Huang, Deyuan. 2008. "Theory on the Cultivation of Cognitive Subjects in Chinese Philosophy." *Frontiers of Philosophy in China* 3(1): 39–54. *Xunzi* 荀子. 2011. Available at Chinese Text Project. Pre-Qin and Han. Accessed September 2, 2011. http://chinese.dsturgeon.net/text.pl?node=3925&if=en.

Yang Zebo 楊澤波. 2007. "Mou Zongsan chaoyue cunyou lun boyi—cong xian Qin tianlunde fazhan guiji kan Mou Zongsan chaoyue cunyou lunde quexian 牟宗三超越存有論駁議——從先秦天論的發展軌跡看牟宗三超越存有論的缺陷 (A Refutation of Mou Zongsan's Transcendental Ontology—the Flaws of Mou Zongsan's Transcendental Ontology through the Lens of the Theory of Heaven from the pre-Qin Period)." *Zhongguo lunwen xiazai zhongxin* (www.studa.net). Accessed July 15, 2012. http://www.studa.net/guoxue/060407/11563323.html.

Yang Zuhan 楊祖漢. 1994. *Ruxue yu dangjin shijie* 儒學與當今世界 (*Confucianism and the Present World*). Taibei: Wenjin.

Yao, Xinzhong. 2001. "Who is a Confucian today? A Critical Reflection on the Issues Concerning Confucian Identity in Modern Times." *Journal of Contemporary Religion* 16(3): 313–28.

You Huizhen 尤惠貞. 1997. "Yi 'yi xin kai er men' zhi sixiang jiagou kan Tiantaizong 'yi nian wu ming faxing xin' zhi teshu hanyi 依「一心開二門」之思想架構看天台宗「一念無明法性心」之特殊涵義 (The Significances of the 'One Single Mind Embracing Ignorance and Dharma-nature Simultaneously' in Tiantai Buddhism Examined from the Expositional

Framework of 'Two-Gates-in-One-Mind'). Zhonghua foxue xuebao 中華佛學學報 (*The Journal of Chinese Buddhist Studies*) 11(7).

Yu, Anthony C. 2000. "Which Values? Whose Perspective?" *The Journal of Religion* 80(2): 299–304.

Yu, Jiuyuan. 2002. "Xiong Shili's Metaphyscs of Virtue." In *Contemporary Chinese Philosophy*, edited by Cheng Chung-Ying and Nicholas Bunnin, 127–46. Oxford: Blackwell Publishers.

Yu Yingshi 余英時. 1988. *Xiandai ruxuede kunjing* 現代儒學的困境 (*The Dilemmas of Modern Confucianism*). Available at Mou xue wang. Accessed July 21, 2012. http://www.moophilo.net/viewthread.php?tid=276.

Yu Ying-shih (Yu Yingshi 余英時). 2005. "Confucianism and China's Encounter with the West in Historical Perspective." *Dao: A Journal of Comparative Philosophy* 4(2): 203–16.

Zhang Dainian 張岱年. 2003. *Zhongguo zhexue shi fangfalun fa fan* 中國哲學史方法論發凡 (*A General Introduction to the Methodology of the History of Chinese Philosophy*). Beijing: Zhonghua shuju.

Zhang Liwen 張立文. 2007. *Ziji jiang—jiang ziji: Zhongguo zhexuede chongjian yu chuantong xiandaide duizhao* 自己講講自己——中國哲學的重建與傳統現代的對照 (*Speaking of Oneself—the Reconstruction of Chinese Philosophy and the Contrast between Tradition and Modernization*). Beijing: Beijing shifan daxue chuban she.

Zhang Wei-Bin. 2003. *Taiwan's Modernization: Americanization and Modernizing Confucian Manifestations*. Singapore: World Scientific Press.

Zhang Yixing 張翼星. 2004. "Zenyang lijie 'dadao Kong jia dian' 怎样理解「打倒孔家店」(How to Understand the Slogan 'Down with Confucianism')." *Guangming wang—Guangming ribao she* March 28. Accessed August 31, 2012. http://www.gmw.cn/01wzb/2004-03/28/ content_84 07.htm.

Zheng Jiadong 鄭家棟. 2001. *Duanlie zhongde chuantong: xinnian yu lixing zhijian* 斷裂中的傳統：信念與理性之間 (*Broken Tradition: Between Faith and Reason*). Beijing: Zhongguo shehui kexueyuan chuban she.

Zheng, Yongnian, and Tok, Sow Keat. 2007. "'Harmonious Society' and 'Harmonious World': China's Policy Discourse under Hu Jintao." *The University of Nottingham, China Policy Institute: Briefing Series* 26: 1–12.

Zhong yong 中庸. 2012. Available at Chinese Text Project. Pre-Qin and Han. Accessed July 7, 2012. http://chinese.dsturgeon.net/text.pl?node=3925&if=en.

Zhou Jiayi 周佳怡. 2010. "Zhongguo gudai hexie fazhiguande dangdai quanshi 中國古代和諧法制觀的當代詮釋 (A Contemporary Interpretation of Ancient Chinese Harmonious Legislation)." *Fazhi yu shehui* 法治與社會 February, Part 1: 285.

Zhou Lisheng 周立升, and Yan Binggang 顏炳罡. 1995. "Mou Zongsan xue'an 牟宗三學案 (The Record of Mou Zongsan)." In *Xiandai xin rujia xue'an* 現代新儒家學案 (*Records of Modern Confucians*), Vol. 3., edited by Fang Keli 方克立 and Li Jinquan 李錦全, 371–578. Peking: Zhongguo shehui kexue chuban she.

Zhuangzi 莊子. 2012. Available at Chinese Text Project. Pre-Qin and Han. Accessed July 7, 2012. http://chinese.dsturgeon.net/text.pl?node=3925&if=en.

Zi Zhongyun. 1987. "The Relationship of Chinese Traditional Culture to the Modernization of China: An Introduction to the Current Discussion." *Asian Survey* 27(4): 442–58.

Zou Liufang 鄒劉芳. 2012. "Lun xiandai xin ruxue yu Zhongguo xiandaihuade guanxi 論現代新儒學與中國現代化的關係 (On the Relation between Modern Confucianism and Modernization)." *Jiannan wenxue* 劍南文學 (*The Jiannan Literature*) 2011 (12): 101–2.

Index

Ai Siqi 艾思起, 129n6

bang ben 邦本 (the foundation of the state), 104
ben xin 本心 (original heart-mind), 72, 147, 153, 156, 236n15
ben 本 (foundation, roots), 59, 104, 147
benti quanshi xue 本體詮釋學 (onto-hermeneutic), 149, 235n12
bu rongyi 不容已 (the limitation of the self-capacity), 123

Cai Yuanpei 蔡元培, 66
Caixing yu xuanli 才性與玄理 (*Physical Nature and Metaphysical Reason*), 69
chaojue 超絕 (superb, unique, absolute), 79
chaoyue ziwo 超越自我 (transcendental self), 142, 148
chaoyue 超越 (transcendent), 79, 132–134, 142, 143, 155, 166–168, 172, 184, 187

chaoyuede lixing ziwo 超越的理性自我 (transcendental moral self), 93, 131, 144, 145, 147, 148, 170, 171
Chen Guying 陳鼓應, 46–48, 74, 233n15
Chen Lai 陳來, 187, 194, 252n59
Cheng Chung-Ying (Cheng Zhongying) 成中英, 31, 232n12
Cheng Hao 程顥, 60
Cheng Yi 程頤, 60
chengxian 呈現 (appearance, phenomenon), 63, 90, 123, 167, 177, 251n49
Chun qiu lu 春秋錄 (*Confucius' Spring and Autumn Annals*), 199
Cong Lu Xiangshan dao Liu Jishan 從陸象山到劉蕺山 (*From Lu Xiangshan to Liu Jishan*), 69

dangdai ruxue 當代儒學 (Contemporary Confucianism), 1
dangdai xin ruxue 當代新儒學 (Contemporary Modern Confucianism), 1

288   Index

dao xin 道心 (Way of the heart-mind), 17, 236n15
daode benxin 道德本心 (moral self, the foundation of a moral heart-mind), 8, 100, 176
daode lixing 道德理性 (moral reason), 105, 121–123, 147, 167
daode shijiande zhuti 道德實踐的主體 (subject of moral practice), 142
daode ziwo 道德自我 (moral self), 8, 44, 45, 94, 96–98, 137, 142–158
daode ziwode kanxian 道德自我的坎陷 (self-negation of the moral self), 44, 144, 145, 148, 149
daodede xing er shang xue 道德的形而上學 (moral metaphysics), 64, 65, 69–74, 156–158, 178
daodedi xing er shang xue 道德底形而上學 (metaphysics of morals), 72, 156, 157
de zhi 德治 (moral rule), 37, 42, 43, 105–107, 113
Deng Xiaoping 鄧小平, 22, 85, 227n12
di 狄 (nomadic tribe), 252n54
Dong xi fang wenhua ji qi zhexue 東西方文化及其哲學 (*The Cultures of East and West and Their Philosophies*), 62, 164
Dong Zhongshu 董仲舒, 198, 199, 233n20, 237n23, 239n32
Donghai daxue 東海大學 (Donghai University), 84, 85, 238n28
Donglin shuyuan 東林書院 (Academy of Eastern Forest), 248n34
Du Weiming 杜維明, 31, 232n12

duan 端 (beginning, embryonic stage, tendency), 81
duili fanchou 對立範疇 (binary categories), 16, 134, 135, 148, 231n6, 246n15

er zhongde zhutixing 二重的主體性 (double political subjectivity), 107

Fang Dongmei (Thomé Fang) 方東美, 81, 82, 92, 101–103, 142, 145, 146, 150–153, 167, 169, 170, 179, 187, 203, 208, 226n3, 233n15, 246n18
fei zheng 非正 (not correct, unproper), 31
Feng Qi 馮契, 244n6
Feng Yaoming 馮耀明, 42, 43, 46, 48, 49, 64, 233n17
Feng Youlan 馮友蘭, 30, 60, 237n20
Foxing yu bore 佛性與般若 (*Buddha Nature and Prajñā*), 69
Fu gu pai 復古派 (School of the revival of the past), 227n9

Gaozi 告子 (Chapter in the book *Mengzi*), 157
gewu 格物 (exploring things), 235n9
gong 公 (public), 89
gongfu 功夫 (ability, effort, work, training, technique), 158, 168
Gu Mu 谷牧, 195
guo xue 國學 (national studies), 195
Guoli Taiwan daxue 國立台灣大學 (National Taiwan University), 77
Guomin dang 國民黨 (National Party, Kou-min tang), 25

Han (dynasty) 漢, 25, 26, 28, 52, 55, 75, 85, 87, 88, 92, 198, 202, 215, 219, 227n11, 233n20, 237n22, 237n23, 239n32
Han Feizi 韓非子, 1256n12
Han Qiang 韓強, 215, 216
he (harmony) 和, 4, 44, 52–54, 78–80, 82, 170, 194, 196–208, 226n2, 255n4
He Lin 賀麟, 30, 40, 62, 63, 77, 244n6
hexie shehui jianshe 和諧社會建設 (construction of a harmonious society), 196
hexie shehui 和諧社會 (harmonious society), 202, 208, 209, 216
Hu Jintao 胡錦濤, 197, 202
Hu Shi 胡適, 20, 60, 84, 91, 110, 116, 237n20
Huayanzong 華嚴宗 (Buddhist school), 69, 97

Jiang Qing 蔣慶 (Contemporary Confucian scholar), 2, 11, 74, 227n9
jiao 教 (teaching), 116, 242n9
jiazhi helixing 價值合理性 (rationality of values), 145, 247n22
jimode xin rujia 寂寞的新儒家 (lonesome modern Confucians), 215
Jin Yuelin 金岳霖, 244n6
jing 境 (horizon, sphere, state of mind), 138, 155, 156, 171, 182, 183, 240n41
jing 敬 (reverence), 189, 241n1, 253n61
jingshen ziwo 精神自我 (spiritual self), 94, 131, 232n11
jingshen 精神 (spirit), 35, 36, 80, 94–96, 101, 111–115, 120, 127, 144, 152–155, 159, 161, 167, 182–184, 188–190, 213
jinhua 進化 (evolution), 226n6, 234n7, 240n41
junzi 君子 (Confucian ideal of personality, nobleman), 40, 42, 130, 253n65

Kang Youwei 康有為, 18
keguan shijie 客觀世界 (objective world), 95, 109, 152, 167, 190
kexue fazhan 科學發展 (development of science), 90, 102, 104, 108, 120, 121, 142, 195
kexue yu xuanxue lunzhan 科學與玄學論戰 (*controversy on science and metaphysics*), 41
Kexue, zhexue yu rensheng 科學, 哲學與人生 (*Science, Philosophy and Human Life*), 78
Kong fuzi, Kongzi (Confucius) 孔夫子, 孔子, 32, 55, 61, 76, 82, 83, 87, 89, 105, 106, 131, 137, 180–203, 230n1, 237n23, 239n34, 250n43, 252n56, 253n62–68
kong xin 空心 (empty heart-mind), 236n15

Lee Ming-huei 李明輝, 28, 44, 52, 53, 66, 90, 91, 97, 132, 133, 137, 142, 145, 154, 155, 156, 175, 176, 229n22, 235n13, 240n40, 245n11
Li ji 禮記 (*The Book of Rituals*), 89
li qi 理氣 (structure and creativity), 124

Li Si 李斯, 256n12
Li xue 理學 *(The School of Structure)*, 1, 66, 162, 231n2, 248n34
Li Zehou 李澤厚, 16, 19, 129, 194, 244n1
li 利 (benefit, usefulness, profit), 11, 28, 29, 37, 178, 248n29
li 理 (structure, principle, rationality, pattern), 43, 44, 75, 76, 81, 83, 95, 106, 123, 124, 127–130, 139, 145, 146, 159, 162–169, 171–173, 176, 178, 192, 205, 214, 248n34, 249n37, 250n47
li 禮 (ritual, ceremony, rituality), 97, 98, 112–115, 134, 157, 160, 185, 189, 198
Liang Han sixiang shi 兩漢思想史 *(The Intellectual History of the Two Han Dynasties)*, 85
Liang Qichao 梁啟超, 18
Liang Shuming 梁漱溟, 30, 61, 62, 92, 162–165, 226n7, 231n4, 234n5
liangzhi 良知 (innate knowledge, transcendental foundation of the moral self, which is absolutely and endlessly universal in itself, 48, 68, 108, 143, 156–158, 163, 175, 206
Lin Anwu 林安梧, 257n5
Liu Shuxian 劉述先 (Shu-hsien Liu), 31, 206, 232n12
lixing 理性 (reason), 163, 171
lixingzhi jiagou biaoxian 理性之架構表現 (constructive or extensive representation of reason), 173
lixingzhi yunyong biaoxian 理性之運用表現 (functional or intensive representation of reason), 173

lizhi 理智 (reason), 1, 4–7, 15–17, 20, 21, 47, 66, 67, 72, 94, 100, 105, 112, 116, 117, 119–121, 124–129, 143, 145, 147, 158, 162–181, 191, 203–207, 214, 217, 243n21, 249n36, 249n39
Lunyu 論語 (Confucius' *Annalects*), 53
Luo Rongqu 羅榮渠, 17
Luoji dianfan 邏輯典範 (*Logical Paradigms*), 67

Mao Zedong 毛澤東, 21, 22, 238n31, 244n2
Meng Peiyuan 蒙培元, 194
Mengzi (Mencius) 孟子, 53, 5, 73, 76, 81, 89, 101, 105, 107, 122, 131, 147, 154, 157, 165, 166, 181, 199, 200, 202, 203, 237n23
ming 命 (decree, destiny, fate), 31, 89, 116, 130, 195, 244n7
Ming 明 (dynasty), 1, 31, 33, 48, 62, 69, 75, 81, 111, 157, 162, 163, 191, 221
ming-shi 名實 (name/concept and actuality), 231n6
Minjin dang 民進黨 (National Democratic Party), 26
Minzhu pinglun 民主評論 (*Democratic Critique*), 84, 90
Mou Zhongjian 牟鐘鑑, 194
Mou Zongsan 牟宗三, 2, 30, 33, 44, 59, 65–67, 71–75, 115–123, 132, 143–145, 148, 150, 156–159, 173–182, 184, 203, 204, 206, 231n4, 233n16, 236n15, 238n30, 243n12–15, 250n48, 251n52
mudi helixing 目的合理性

(instrumental rationality), 36, 38, 46, 145, 192, 247n22

Nanjing Dongnan daxue 南京東南大學 (Southeast University in Nanjing), 77
Nanjing 南京, 64, 68, 77, 92, 240n39
neibude zhijue 內部的直覺 (inner intuition, intuitively knowing one's true self), 73
neirongde zhenli 內容的真理 (intentional truth), 117
neisheng waiwang 內聖外王 (inner sage and external ruler, transcendent subject and the empirical self), 42, 68, 106, 115, 138, 143, 232n11
neizai chaoyue 內在超越 (immanent transcendence), 79, 82, 130, 131–134, 170, 187, 190, 191, 212, 231n6, 245n11
neng-suo 能－所 (cognitive potential and the object of recognition, 147, 230n2

panjiao 叛教 ("the systematically sorting of Buddha's teachings" in the Buddhist schools Tiantai and Huayan), 97
Peking daxue 北京大學 (Peking University), 60, 62–65, 77, 197
Pi Lin pi Kong 批林批孔 (The campaign against Lin Biao and Confucius), 195

qi 器 (vessel, physical form), 95, 188
Qin 秦 (dynasty, 221–206 B.C.), 52, 86, 88, 140, 185, 203, 219, 223, 233n20, 238n32, 239n33, 252n55, 256n12
qing 情 (feelings, situation, emotions), 55, 78, 80, 81, 122, 155, 156, 159, 162, 166, 169, 170, 176, 181, 247n25, 248n32
Qing 清 (dynasty, 1644–1911), 18, 34, 111, 221
qingli tuan 情理團 (circles of rational principles and feelings), 78
qingli 情理 (sensuous reason, unity of emotions and reason), 169
quntizhuyi 群體主義 (communitarism), 50, 106

ren xing 人性 (human nature, inborn qualities), 81, 82, 86, 96, 106, 114, 132, 145, 146, 154, 159, 166, 180, 183, 202, 247n24
ren 仁 (co-humanness), 11, 96, 98, 105, 113–115, 131, 134, 144, 149, 152, 159, 160, 170, 178, 186, 187, 189, 191, 213, 216
Renshi xinzhi pipan 認識心之批判 (Criticism of Cognitive Heart-Mind), 70
renshi zhuti 認識主體 (subject of comprehension), 120, 147, 159
renwen shijie 人文世界 (world of human culture), 155
renyi neizai 仁義內在 (inherent morality, autonomy in Kantian sense), 73, 157, 251n52
rong 戎 (nomadic tribe), 254n54
rongyi 容已 (apportioning, capacity), 123, 243n15

San min zhuyi 三民主義 (Three Principles of the People by Sun

Yat-sen), 238n16

shan 善 (good, goodness), 71, 72, 80, 81, 94, 106, 121, 122, 136, 137, 145–147, 149, 154, 157, 167, 168, 170, 179, 180, 201–203, 205, 213, 242n5, 243n14

Shang 商 — 殷 (or Yin dynasty, 1600–1066 B.C.), 181, 185, 186, 219, 230n1, 252n54

shehuizhuyi shichang jingji 社會主義市場經濟 (socialist market economy), 21

shende zhixing 神的知性 (divine consciousness, divine recognition), 74, 156

sheng ren 聖人 (saint), 120, 144, 236n15

sheng 生 (life), 42, 68, 78–80, 101–103, 108, 116, 142, 145–147, 150, 152, 153, 155, 162, 169, 170, 171, 179, 181, 182, 185, 188, 208, 213, 253n66

shengming bentilun 生命本體論 (life-ontology, ontology of life), 79

Shengming cunzai yu xinling jingjie 生命存在與心靈境界 (*The Existence of Life and the Horizon of the Soul*), 95, 155

shengming shengshengbuxide chuangzaoli 生命生生不息的創造力 (continuous organic creativity of the clear spirit), 152

shengmingde huanjing 生命的環境 (living environment), 78

shengmingde xuewen 生命的學問 (teachings of life), 67

shengmingde yuantai 生命的原態 (primary source of life), 78, 79

shenmiaode chuangzaoxing 神妙的創造性 (miraculous creativity), 172

shequnzhuyi 社群主義 (communitarism), 38, 106

Shi ji 史記 (*Historical Notes*), 185, 252n55

Shu jing 書經 (*Book of Documents*), 104

si wen 斯文 (Confucian behavioral codex), 40

Song 宋 (dynasty 960–1127), 1, 31, 33, 48, 69, 75, 76, 81, 157, 162, 186, 191, 223

taiji 太極 (ultimate pole), 81, 169, 231n2

Taizhong 台中 (city in Taiwan), 84, 85, 238n28

Tang Junyi 唐君毅, 2, 30, 33, 59, 68, 69, 77, 92, 94–98, 110–115, 143, 147, 150, 153–156, 170, 171, 172, 182, 184, 203, 206, 207, 213, 226n3, 238n30, 251n53

Tang Yijie 湯一介, 194

tian dao 天道 (Way of Heaven), 132, 181, 190

tian ming 天命 (heavenly mandate, decree of heaven), 55, 113, 167, 181, 186, 189–191, 244n7

tian ren heyi 天人合一 (unity of men and nature), 131, 183, 245n7, 245n13

tian 天 (heaven), 72, 81, 96, 104, 113, 131–133, 136, 146, 155, 159, 160, 161, 167, 168, 181, 183, 186–188, 190, 191, 200, 201, 204

tiande renwenhua 天的人文化

(humanization of heaven), 189, 240n38
Tiantai 天台 (school of Chinese Buddhism), 69, 97
tiren 體認 (bodily recognition), 168, 169, 172, 250n44
ti-yong 體用 (substance and function), 151, 176–178, 246n15
tizhi 體知 (knowledge obtained through the body), 168
tong 同 (sameness, similarity), 198

waiyande zhenli 外延的真理 (extensional truth), 117–119, 148
Wang Fuwu 王撫五, 20
Wang Fuzhi 王夫之, 248n34
Wang Yangming (Wang Shouren) 王陽明（王守仁）, 33, 48, 62, 68, 71, 143, 157, 163, 202, 236n14, 249n37, 250n44, 250n46
Wei Zhongguo wenhua jinggao shijie renshi xuanyan 為中國文化敬告世界人士宣言 (*Declaration of Chinese Culture to the Scholars of the World*), 33, 61, 93
wei 為 (artificial, posterior, gained through education or culture), 179–180, 247n24
Weishi jia yu Bogesen 唯識家與柏格森 (*The Theoreticians of Pure Consciousness and Bergson*), 249n40
weishi lun 唯識論 (theory of Pure Consciousness), 64, 92, 164
wenhua da taolun 文化大討論 (*great debate on culture*), 228n12
wenhua re 文化熱 (*cultural fever*), 228n12

Wu si yundong 五四運動 (May Fourth Movement), 19–22, 30, 32, 73, 77, 87, 97, 11, 119, 126, 194, 251n52
Wu xu bianfa 戊戌變法 (Wuxu reform, 100 Days reform), 18
wu zhi cunyou lun 無執存有論 (detached ontology), 70, 71, 145, 158
Wuchang daxue 武昌大學 (Wuchang University), 77
wuwei 無為 (non-action), 106, 107, 231n2
wuxiande zhixin 無限的智心 (infinite heart-mind, infinite cognitive subject), 8, 72, 73, 15, 173, 178, 180, 211, 212

xia xue er shang da 下學而上達 (studies lie on the physical level, and the penetration rises to a metaphysical one), 190, 253n64
Xia 夏 (Mythological/ dynasty, 2100–1600 B.C.), 185, 219, 248n34
xiandai ruxue 現代儒學 (Modern Confucianism), 1–9, 24–42, 45, 46, 49, 59, 76, 82, 83, 91, 92, 99, 100, 101, 110, 112, 116, 121, 123, 126, 129-131, 133, 137, 138, 141-142, 145, 148, 150, 161-165, 170, 178, 180, 182, 184, 187, 191–193, 195, 197, 199–203, 205, 208, 209, 211–216, 223, 228n14, 232n8, 246n18, 246n19
xiandai xin ruxue 現代新儒學 (Modern New Confucianism), 1, 24

xiandai yishi 現代意識 (modern consciousness, awareness of modernity), 44

xiang 象 (attribute), 95, 155

Xianggang Zhongwen daxue 香港中文大學 (The Chinese University of Hong Kong), 69

xianshi ziwo 現實自我 (real self, phenomenal self), 94, 143, 154

Xianxiang yu wu zishen 現象與物自身 (*Appearance and the Thing-in-itself*), 70, 176

Xiao Zhuoji 蕭灼基, 197

xin benti 心本體 (substance of heart-mind), 94, 154, 157, 172, 176

xin ji li 心即理 (unity of subject and the structural principle), 157

Xin lixue 新理學 (The New School of Principles), 60

xin ruxue 新儒學 (*Modern Confucianism, lit. New Confucianism*), 1, 61–62, 228n14, 254n1, 257n5

xin wenhua yundong 新文化運動 (New Culture Movement), 19

Xin xue 心學 (School of Heart-Mind), 163, 231n3, 234n7

Xin Ya shuyuan 新亞學院 (New Asia Academy), 85, 93

xin zhuti 心主體 (subject of heart-mind), 94

xin 心 (heart-mind, consciousness), 8, 67, 69, 70–73, 87, 89, 94, 95, 120, 122, 147, 148, 153, 154, 156, 157, 159, 163, 165, 167, 170–173, 176–180, 191, 211, 212, 236n15, 239n36, 242n5, 243n13, 248n33, 249n37, 249n37, 249n41, 250n46, 251n51

xinde benti 心的本體 (substance of the heart-mind), 154, 157, 172, 176

xing shan lun 性善論 (theory on the inborn goodness of human inborn qualities, or of human nature), 106

xing 性 (human/ nature or inborn qualities), 68, 96, 131, 143, 166

Xingli xue 性理學 (*Neo-Confucian school of thought*), 1, 162

xingli 性理 (Neo-Confucian concept of reason, the basis of the moral self or the inborn /spiritual/ structure of mind or reason), 48, 156, 163, 171, 249n38

xingti 性體 (inborn moral substance, an elaboration of Kant's, 72, 73, 122, 156, 158, 179

xinling 心靈 (soul), 49, 72, 94, 95, 136, 154–156, 179, 182, 183, 186, 198, 212, 251n49, 256n3

Xinti yu xingti 心體與性體 (*The Substance of Heart-Mind and the Innate Moral Substance*), 69

xinti 心體 (substance of heart-mind), 155, 157, 170, 176

Xiong Shili 熊十力, 30, 59, 61, 63–65, 67, 83, 92, 150, 151, 162, 183, 202, 203, 231n4, 235n9, 250n44

xiu ji 修己 (self-cultivation), 37, 68, 147, 152, 158, 159, 160, 211

Xu Fuguan 徐复觀, 2, 30, 33, 59, 82–90, 92, 99, 103–109, 113, 115, 146–148, 150, 158–160, 167–169, 184–191, 203–206, 238n30, 242n5, 252n55, 253n61

Xunzi 荀子, 2, 11, 52, 53, 56, 76, 81,

88, 100, 199–203, 208, 223, 232n9, 233n20, 237n23, 237n24, 241n3, 256n12

ya yue 雅樂 (Confucian), 199
Yi jing 易經 (*Book of Changes*), 65, 66, 78, 81, 87, 133, 157, 203
yi tian 疑天 (doubting Heaven), 186
yi 義 (righteousness, justice), 55, 88, 103, 105, 106, 122, 134, 165, 196, 242n5, 243n13
yin yang 陰陽, 213n6
yiyi 意義 (meaning, significance, sense), 124, 163, 174, 243n17
yong 庸 (common, familiar or domestic way), 63, 151, 176, 225n8
yong 用 (function) and *ti* 體 (substance), 16, 63, 95, 151, 155, 176
you hun 遊魂 (lost soul, wandering ghost), 215
youhuan yishi 憂患意識 ("concerned" consciousness), 87, 108, 253n61
youhuan 憂患 (concern), 89, 90 113, 208
you-wu 有無 (presence and absence), 231n6
Yu Yingshi 余英時, 31, 215, 217
yuan shan 圓善 (harmonization /or unification/ of happiness and goodness, *summum bonum*), 71, 72, 178, 179, 235n11
Yuanshan lun 圓善論 (*On Summum Bonum*), 70, 71, 178, 203

Zhan guo 戰國 (The Warring States period 475–221 B.C.), 140

Zhang Dainian 張岱年, 7, 129
Zhang Dongsun 張東蓀, 67
Zhang Junmai (Carsun Chang) 張君勱, 30, 33, 61, 164, 232n7
Zhang Liwen 張立文, 194
Zhang Zhidong 張之洞, 16, 110,119, 251n50
Zhao Guanghui 趙光輝, 173, 215, 216
zhen ren 真人 (Daoist truly perfected person), 67, 236n15
Zheng Jiadong 鄭家棟, 194, 257n5
zheng 正 (real, true, correct, proper —the Confucian normative criterion), 198
zhengchan xin 真常心 (true eternal heart-mind), 176
Zhengzhi daxue 政治大學 (Political University), 77
zhengzhi ruxue 政治儒學 (political Confucianism), 2
zhengzhi zhuti 政治主體 (political subject), 107, 142
Zhexue san hui 哲學三慧 (*Three Types of Philosophical Wisdom*), 78, 81, 169, 237n21
zhi ren 治人 (regulation of fellow human beings), 147
zhi xing heyi 知行合一 (unity of knowledge and action), 61, 157, 248n33
zhi xing 知行 (knowledge and action), 63, 168, 248n33
Zhide zhijue yu Zhongguo zhexue 智的直覺與中國哲學 (*Intellectual Intuition and Chinese Philosophy*), 69, 250n48
zhide zhijue 智的直覺 (intellectual

intuition), 8, 69, 71, 148, 150, 158, 174, 176–178, 180, 212, 250n48, 251n49

zhihui zhongzi 智慧種子 (seed of wisdom), 169

zhihuide chuangzaoxing 智慧的創造性 (creativity of wisdom), 172

zhijue (intuition) 直覺, 66, 73, 116, 119, 144, 148, 162–166, 168, 169, 172–174, 240n37, 243n13, 249n37, 251n49

zhishi (knowledge) 知識, 172

zhiti mingjue 知體明覺 (clear understanding of the substance of knowledge), 236n14

zhong he 中和 (harmony of balance), 203, 204

Zhong yong 中庸 (*The Doctrine of the Mean*), 203, 204, 255n8

zhong 中 (mean, middle, balance, equilibrium), 60, 198, 202-204, 255n8

zhong 忠 (loyalty), 36, 53, 60, 134

Zhongguo renxing lun shi 中國人性論史 (*The History of Human Nature Theories in China*), 159, 252n55

Zhongguo zhexue shijiu jiang 中國哲學十九講 (*Nineteen Lectures in Chinese Philosophy*), 72

zhongxue wei ti, xixue wei yong (zhong ti xi yong) 中學為體，西學為用 (中體西用) (*Preserve the substance of Chinese teachings, while applying Western teachings*), 18, 110, 251n50

Zhongyang daxue 中央大學 (Zhongyang University), 68

Zhou 周 (Dynasty, 1066–256 B.C.), 87, 159, 184–189, 219, 251n54, 251n55, 253n59

Zhu Xi 朱熹, 33, 48, 60, 66, 75, 76, 163, 231n2, 236n17, 249n37

zhuguanxing 主觀性 (subjectivity), 7, 44, 86, 103, 107, 108, 118, 126–129, 137, 151, 155, 159, 161, 168, 169, 172, 187, 244n1, 247n25

zhuti jingshen 主體精神 (subjective spirit), 152

zhutide renlei jingshen 主體的人類精神 (subjective spirit of humanity), 152

zhutixing 主體性 (subjectivity), 244n1

zibenzhuyi mengya 資本主義萌芽 (germs of capitalism), 227n8, 242n6

zijuexing 自覺性 (self-awareness), 188

ziwo kanxian 自我坎陷 (self-negation of the self), 120, 144

Ziyou yu renquan 自由與人權 (*Freedom and Human Rights*), 28

Ziyou Zhongguo 自由中國 (*Free China*), 90

ziyoude wuxian xin 自由的無限心 (free and unlimited heart-mind), 71

zongjiao 宗教 (faith, religion), 37, 44, 87, 89, 101, 111, 128, 132, 140, 146, 155, 158, 159, 161, 181–189, 207, 233n19, 242n9, 253n59

Zou Liufang 鄒劉芳, 46